State Subsidies
in the Global Economy

Previously published by Nikolaos Zahariadis:

Essence of Political Manipulation: Emotion, Institutions, and Greek Foreign Policy

Ambiguity and Choice in Public Policy: Political Decision-Making in Modern Democracies

Contending Perspectives in International Political Economy (editor)

Theory, Case, and Method in Comparative Politics (editor)

Markets, States, and Public Policy: Privatization in Britain and France

State Subsidies in the Global Economy

Nikolaos Zahariadis

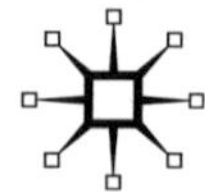

First published in 2008 by
PALGRAVE MACMILLAN™
175 Fifth Avenue, New York, N.Y. 10010 and
Houndmills, Basingstoke, Hampshire, England RG21 6XS.
Companies and representatives throughout the world.

PALGRAVE MACMILLAN is the global academic imprint of the Palgrave Macmillan division of St. Martin's Press, LLC and of Palgrave Macmillan Ltd. Macmillan® is a registered trademark in the United States, United Kingdom and other countries. Palgrave is a registered trademark in the European Union and other countries.

ISBN-13: 978-0-230-60379-0
ISBN-10: 0-230-60379-3

Library of Congress Cataloging-in-Publication Data

Zahariadis, Nikolaos, 1961–
    State subsidies in the global economy/Nikolaos Zahariadis.
       p. cm.
    Includes bibliographical references and index.
    ISBN 0-230-60379-3
   1. Protectionism—21st century. 2. Subsidies—21st century.
3. International economic relations—21st century. 4. Globalization—Economic aspects—History—21st century. I. Title.
HF1711.Z34 2008
338.9'22—dc22
                                                                    2007035426

A catalogue record of the book is available from the British Library.

Design by Macmillan India Ltd.

First edition: March 2008

10 9 8 7 6 5 4 3 2 1

Printed in the United States of America.

To Lucy and Zena

So much fun, so little time

Contents

LIST OF TABLES

List of Figures

Acknowledgments

This book has been a long time in the making. When I began writing about the state's participation in the market in the early 1990s, the themes of subsidies and globalization were already major issues. The old debate on industrial policy was beginning to take a different form away from heavy state intervention and its assumed "beneficial" impact. Although market reforms were still a hot topic of debate, political discourse was markedly shifting in favor of market solutions. The question was no longer whether to reduce subsidies, but how much. Part of this shifting involvement went hand in hand with growing interdependence and global economic integration. Political arguments were made in terms of efficiency and adjustment in the face of global competition rather than development and fairness in the light of income distribution. They still are.

It *is not* surprising to see a downward trend in subsidies around the world, particularly in view of the various international commitments and treaties to which governments are loyal. What *is* surprising is that so many subsidies still exist. Governments continue to subsidize their industries albeit with less zeal than before. Given the free market rhetoric, the key question is: why do they still do it? The answer is, of course, politics. This book is about disentangling this simple answer into various components. Governments, especially democratic ones, dole out subsidies because some organized constituents demand them and because politicians need the votes and money these constituents offer. Under what conditions does this arrangement materialize and are there any exceptions to the rule?

It is often said that behind every author there are many unsung heroes who have read the manuscript, argued and disagreed with the findings, and generally made the author miserable by poking holes into what he erroneously perceived to be the "perfect" argument. This is the case with the present book. Several of my colleagues at the University of Alabama at Birmingham have read and commented on parts of the manuscript. Special thanks go to Holly Brasher who thoughtfully read the first chapter and to Renato Corbetta and

Michael Howell-Moroney for patience and superb help with the statistical aspects of the study. My students also unwittingly heard the arguments at some point in my classes. Little did they know they were actually helping me sort through the material even as I was teaching it to them. Mitchell Smith and Kenny Thomas also heard part of the story at some point, patiently discussing revisions and amendments to it.

A generous sabbatical leave enabled me to put the final touches to the manuscript. Several colleagues overseas also heard the argument in various forms. I want to thank Kevin Featherstone, Spyros Economides, and Vassilis Monastiriotis at the Hellenic Observatory, London School of Economics, for providing space and resources and taking the time to listen to a much narrower aspect of this material. Special thanks also go to Claudio Radaelli, Steven Wilks, Yannis Karagiannis, Oliver Fueg, Hussein Kassim, and the rest of the participants at the very interesting workshop on competition policy at the University of Exeter. They epitomize the argument that rigorous debate and good food always go together. Ioannis Papadopoulos and his wonderful colleagues and thoughtful students at the University of Lausanne had many critical amendments and suggestions. They were absolutely on the money. Finally, I want to thank Friedbert Rüb and his colleagues and students at the University of Hamburg for more thoughtful comments. While many came to listen to a lecture on ambiguity, they patiently, politely, and still inquisitively got lessons on statistical analysis instead.

Finally, my family deserves special acknowledgment for being so understanding. Watching me sit in front of the computer for several years with my mind focused on my work must not be the best sight in their world. Now that it is over, I sincerely hope I can make it up to them.

List of Abbreviations

ACM	after capital mobility
BCM	before capital mobility
CAP	Common Agricultural Policy
CVDs	countervailing duties
DUP	directly-unproductive, profit-seeking activities
EU	European Union
G-H	Grossman and Helpman's political contribution model
GATT	General Agreement on Tariffs and Trade
FDI	foreign direct investment
M&As	mergers and acquisitions
MNC	multinational corporation
NTBs	non-tariff barriers
OECD	Organisation for Economic Co-operation and Development
PR	proportional representation
R&D	research and development
SMEs	small and medium enterprises
VERs	voluntary export restrictions
WTO	World Trade Organization

Chapter 1

Protection for Rent

Globalization frequently imposes asymmetrical sacrifices—benefits and costs affect different elements of society differently. The losers in that process will seek redress through their political system, which is national.

—Henry A. Kissinger[1]

Every nation tries to protect industries it considers strategic.

—José Montilla, Spanish industry minister[2]

It has been almost two centuries since David Ricardo first clearly articulated the benefits of free trade and nearly 160 years since the British first implemented such a policy. In the light of the gains vigorously stressed by economists, entrepreneurs, and politicians ever since, one would expect free trade to be the prevailing international rule and impediments to trade the exception. Yet, protectionism, particularly in the form of subsidies, remains strong even as trade barriers are being dismantled. As Irwin (2005, p. 27) puts it regarding market integration and trade, "If we focus not on how far global integration has progressed in the past few decades but on how far it has to go to achieve full integration, we're impressed by how *little* integration there is" (emphasis in the original). The situation is similar concerning capital flows: "Globalization remains far from complete and in fact is only in its infancy as a process" (Sobel, 1999, p. 6).

The volume of international trade and foreign investment has increased substantially since the end of World War II, but so has protection. Currently, the volume of world exports is twice that of world production (Irwin, 2005, p. 20). In 2006, merchandise exports rose by 15 percent to a record $11,760 billion. In terms of rate of increase, trade growth in 2006 was roughly double the rate of output growth (Williams, 2007). Manufacturing exports outpaced manufacturing production in 2004 by a rate of 6 percent! Foreign direct investment (FDI) relative to world output has grown from 5.3 percent in 1980 to 21.9 percent in 2004 (Wolf, 2006, p. 1). At the same time, virtually all countries practice some type of protectionism in the form of tariffs—although rates have gone down dramatically—subsidies, and more generally nontariff barriers (NTBs). More to the point, governments worldwide have in the last 20 years signaled their support for free trade. However, bickering and the failure so far to agree at the World Trade Organization (WTO) meetings (widely referred to as the current Doha Round) offer testament to the resilience of protectionism and the ability of special interests to get what they want out of their governments.

Understanding the politics of protectionism is clearly an important policy priority in the global political economy. As Faryar Shirzad, U.S. deputy national security adviser for international economics, made abundantly clear recently, "We always have to worry about protectionism because politically it is an easy course for people to take. Trade legislation is hard and politically difficult" (Daniel, 2006, p. 4). He should know, being a close adviser to President George W. Bush and intimately involved in world trade negotiations at the Doha Round. If gains from trade are so large and self-evident, why is protectionism easy and free trade difficult to pursue? Put differently, why do governments offer the levels of subsidies that they do and why and how do they choose among different subsidy instruments? Why do governments subsidize some sectors of their economies and not others?

Vilfredo Pareto (1927, p. 377) summarizes the puzzle and presciently provides a clue to the answer:

> Even if it were very clearly demonstrated that protectionism always entails the destruction of wealth, . . . protection would lose so small a number of partisans and free trade would gain so few of them that the effect can be almost, or even completely, disregarded. The motives which lead men to act are quite different.

Pareto clearly alludes to the politics of trade policy, differentiating sharply between the benefits accrued to some groups as opposed to the benefits accrued to society as a whole. "A protectionist measure,"

Pareto continues, "provides large benefits to a small number of people, and causes a very great number of consumers a small loss" (p. 379). Mapping the circumstances under which some groups support or oppose protection and the conditions under which governments are likely to grant it greatly improves our understanding of political economy and the redistributive consequences of government policy. Most importantly, an explanation of protectionism is a vital first step in public policy. The Nobel Prize winner George Stigler (1975, p. xi) puts it most eloquently: "Until we understand *why* our society adopts its policies, we will be poorly equipped to give useful advice on how to change them" (emphasis in the original). Given current worldwide squabbling over subsidies and talk of reform to reap the benefits of free trade, illuminating the politics of protectionism is a worthwhile academic and policy relevant endeavor.

In this book, I build an asset influence model of trade policy that highlights the motives and ability of social actors to demand and get subsidies from government. I use the terms "protection" and "subsidies" interchangeably because subsidies are a form of protectionism although protection may also take other forms, such as tariffs, quotas, and so on. While there is no universally accepted definition (OECD, 2005a, p. 16), subsidies generally refer to government support to production, which aims to reduce the cost of input factors and consequently to increase the quantity of output produced. I do not deal with consumption (e.g., welfare) subsidies. I offer a political explanation that puts forth the argument that under threat of international competition disbursement of producer subsidies varies systematically with the degree of asset specificity in particular institutional contexts. Asset (factor) specificity refers to the cost incurred from moving factors (assets) across industries. When faced with a decline in prices owing to foreign trade, owners of more specific assets seek to influence policy by making larger political contributions to keep the rate of return, and consequently quasi-rents, high. Quasi-rent is the difference in the rate of asset return between current use and opportunity cost. The rent-seeking capacity of groups affected by free trade and politicians' penchant for campaign contributions make protection "for rent."

WHY ARE SUBSIDIES IMPORTANT?

While the literature on trade and tariff protection is vast, the narrower, more recent, and frequently used instrument of subsidies has not received adequate attention. Most trade analysts conceptualize protectionism largely as support for tariffs, which are duties imposed on merchandise imports, even though this particular instrument has lost its potency by successive General Agreement on Tariffs and Trade (GATT) rounds. Member governments of the original GATT mandate in 1947 clearly recognized "that customs duties often constitute serious obstacles to trade" and committed to "sponsor[ing] negotiations from time to time directed to the substantial reduction of the general level of tariffs and other charges on imports and exports" (WTO, 2007b). Because of these negotiations, national governments now have restricted capabilities to impose tariffs at will. Hence the empirical relevance of that literature on protectionism may be limited. However, examining subsidies poses significant challenges. The main reason for the lack of attention is the paucity of cross-nationally reliable data. We just do not have a clear and accurate picture of the extent of subsidization around the world. The situation, however, has changed in recent years, and this study represents a first step in building a theoretically specified and empirically tested explanation of the important problem of subsidies.

The dismantling of trade barriers at the border, such as tariffs, quotas, and the like, has led to a rise in NTBs (Grimwade, 1989; Bhagwati, 1988). As countries become more exposed to the global economy, they seek to protect national cultures and identities with trade barriers that often take the form of NTBs. For example, Europe has recently passed legislation limiting, and in some cases eliminating, the importation of genetically modified foods or protection of geographic labels as product trademarks on the basis of preserving cultural identity or societal norms. Although the rationale may differ, the net effect is clearly protectionism of home markets against undesired imports without erecting tariff walls (Goff, 2005). Examining evidence from members of the Organisation for Economic Co-operation and Development (OECD), Blais (1986) finds that the illegality of protection at the border has given rise to the legality of protection in the domestic economy. He argues that as the rates of tariffs have decreased in the industrialized world, governments have found it necessary to increase disbursement of production subsidies. The pressures for protection have not waned; they have simply changed form. Bhagwati (1988, p. 53) calls this possibility the Law of Constant Protection: when one form of protection is eliminated, another form pops up somewhere else to take its place.

Governments have proved extremely creative in the protection they grant to their domestic industries. Once some of the more overt forms become illegal by treaty, several others are devised to get around the legal obstacles. Protection in the form of NTBs, which constitutes the bulk of harmful distortions to trade, takes many forms. Consider the differences between quotas and voluntary export restrictions (VERs). While quantitative restrictions in the form of quotas are illegal, the same restrictions in the form of VERs were not illegal until the Uruguay Round concluded in 1994. The reason is because quotas are imposed by the recipient government whereas in the latter case, the exporting nation chooses to "voluntarily" restrict shipments. This is one of the ways Washington sought to stem the flood of Japanese automobile imports in the early 1980s, to no avail of course. There is little doubt that the restrictions were not voluntary, but the point is that tariffs were by then an infeasible and illegal instrument of protection. The imposition of numerical restrictions has been shown to be highly ineffective because they tend to be highly commodity specific. Baldwin (1985) provides many examples. If restrictions in coat exports from certain countries exist, importers can easily import sleeveless coats, which are not subject to those restrictions, in addition to separate sleeves, and then assemble everything in the recipient country. Bhagwati (1988, pp. 57–58) adds industry characteristics as a major source of porousness. Some industries, such as garments or footwear, which produce undifferentiated products or have low start-up costs, are more prone to creative bypassing of VERs.

Producer subsidies are a form of NTBs.[3] The effects of subsidies are different from those of tariffs, and so are to an extent the politics of disbursement. Relative to tariffs, subsidies are less transparent, are revenue expending, support home production *and* export, and generate differences between producer and consumer prices (Horvat, 1999, pp. 132–133). In fact, welfare economists prefer direct subsidies over tariffs under certain conditions because they prevent losses to consumer surplus (Corden, 1997, p. 7). It is important to understand the differences if we are to get a better grasp of the allure of subsidies as a "new" form of protection.

Subsidies are less transparent to outsiders than tariffs or most NTBs. Consider the issue of tariffs or VERs. Barriers are erected at the border to prevent or restrict imports from reaching domestic consumers. The transaction involves both exporter and importer, which makes it very likely that exporters from the sender nation will catch a whiff of the barrier. In contrast, subsidies involve only the Treasury and domestic producers, who obviously have incentives not to advertise the transaction. Subsidies are, therefore, more difficult for outsiders to detect and more visible to domestic stakeholders (Hoekman and Kostecki, 2001, p. 170). Moreover, subsidies can be disguised as aid to underdeveloped regions, which are widespread and considered appropriate. For example, governments grant aid to specific national regions to boost employment and economic growth. Some of the funding may find its way into the hands of companies as distortionary assistance against rising imports.

On the one hand, subsidies are revenue expending. Whereas tariffs involve imposing duties on imports, and thereby raise revenue for the Treasury, subsidies in many instances include payments to firms. Because subsidies in this case involve a net loss for the treasury, officials are more hesitant to use them unless they can offset the loss with revenue in some other way. Moreover, international agreements to limit tariffs increase trade whereas agreements to eliminate subsidies restrict the volume of trade (Bagwell and Staiger, 2002, p. 179). In short, subsidies are disbursed taking into account economic and revenue trade-offs, e.g., political and distributional trade-offs, in ways that tariffs do not.

On the other hand, subsidies are politically very attractive because they directly affect domestic production and export. Tariffs aim to punish importers by making imported goods more expensive. The assumption is that domestic firms can compete on their own without any help if only the government can buy them some time or temporarily raise the prices a bit. Subsidies do not discriminate against imports but rather directly help domestic producers to expand production. Cheaper credit, land grants, or tax incentives reduce production costs, helping to raise output to levels not justified on the basis of free markets alone. In the light of lower costs and higher output, producers may find it profitable to export the excess supply.

Subsidies have different effects on prices than tariffs do. Barriers at the border in general increase the price of imports, making world prices different from domestic prices. Subsidies lower domestic prices to equal world prices. They also generate differences between producer and consumer prices because the treasury now pays part of the production costs (Horvat, 1999, p. 132). In cases where subsidies are granted to producers of intermediary goods, the beneficial effects to domestic producers can multiply. Cheaper inputs, such as steel, may cause the price of a variety of final products to fall, thereby creating an opportunity for previously imported goods to be produced at home and possibly exported.

Finally, under certain conditions subsidies are preferred to tariffs from an economic point of view. The reason is because tariffs introduce distortionary consumption effects when there is a marginal divergence between private and social costs (Corden, 1997, pp. 7–11). In cases where the marginal private cost is higher than the social cost because societies for political, security, or emotional reasons derive social benefits, the disbursement of subsidies is likely to result in gains that are not available through tariffs. The production gains and losses would be the same, but the consumption losses would increase relative to the gains because of the social cost of forgoing some consumption as a result of the tariff.

All in all, subsidies are a politically appealing and rewarding form of protection. Many are legal, to an extent, and less transparent than tariffs, making them a preferred instrument of protection. They directly help local firms, may promote exports, and lower prices in the domestic economy. One negative characteristic that tempers political enthusiasm is the fact that subsidies consume rather than enhance public revenues. The picture that emerges is therefore somewhat complicated. Subsidies are a politically appealing and frequently used instrument of protection. In periods of budgetary constraints, however, governments may be less generous or at least more mindful of the revenue implications. The question of subsidies is clearly a politically important and interesting puzzle to solve.

It should be emphatically noted, however, that subsidies are a harmful practice in general, with some exceptions (OECD, 2005a; Lavdas and Mendrinou, 1999, p. 139). They "are often ineffective (i.e., they fail to benefit their intended target groups) and costly (they have adverse real welfare and distributional implications)" (Schwartz and Clements, 1999, p. 129). According to an estimate by H. Ekdahl (2006), director of trade policy at the Confederation of Swedish Enterprises, the cost of tariff barriers on nonagricultural goods in the majority of countries is less than 5 percent, but the cost of NTBs averages between 2 and 10 percent of the total value of traded goods. Government must pay for the subsidy by raising the revenue from alternative sources (Weimer and Vining, 2005, p. 226).

Subsidies distort competition among firms, biasing the survival of some firms but not others. Apart from the political implications of this choice for survival, subsidies endanger the welfare of the employees of unsubsidized firms. Quite often, even the favored firms may not survive because all subsidies do is perpetuate the inefficient allocation of resources and delay and increase the cost of restructuring. "Ultimately, then," the European Commission (2006a) boldly asserts, "the entire market will suffer from state aid [subsidies], and the general competitiveness of the European economy is imperiled." For this reason, subsidies that distort trade are banned by the European Union (EU) and the WTO, with special rules applying to agriculture. In its

Agreement on Subsidies and Countervailing Measures, the WTO (2007a) defines prohibited subsidies as those "that require recipients to meet certain export targets, or to use domestic goods instead of imported goods." Moreover, there exists the category of actionable subsidies under WTO rules that gives the right to a WTO member to contest to a special tribunal their disbursement by another member if the affected country can demonstrate harm inflicted on its industry or national interests (Hoekman and Kostecki, 2001, p. 173).

WHAT ARE THE STAKES INVOLVED?

How big is the problem? There are no reliable worldwide figures, but even partial evidence is very illuminating. One study by Standard & Poor's, the credit rating agency, reveals that Asian governments have spent $500 billion since the currency crisis of 1997–1998 just to rescue ailing banks—(Guerrera and Yeh, 2005)! China alone spent $45 billion to bail out its two largest banks in 2004. Total aid to industry in the OECD area was estimated to have increased in real terms to $40.1 billion in 1993 from $39 billion in 1989 after peaking at $48.4 billion in 1991 (Nezu, 1998, p. 16). A comprehensive, OECD-wide survey of 1,500 industrial subsidy programs puts the figure in the late 1990s at $50 billion annually from government to the enterprise sector (Pretschker, 1998b, p. 9). Unfortunately, the OECD survey has since been discontinued; so there are no reliable estimates for later years. A more recent OECD (2005a, p. 7) study raised the figure to $400 billion annually to a variety of economic sectors. Nevertheless by way of comparison to industry, U.S. farmers in 2002 were able to extract $180 billion in federal support over ten years (Grant, 2006). Similarly, Europe's farmers received roughly $50 billion from the EU's Common Agricultural Policy (CAP) coffers in 2004, one-fifth of which went to France (Arnold, 2005). On a broader scale, OECD farmers received $235 billion in 2002 (OECD, 2005a, p. 8). No wonder farmers in the developed world are resolutely opposed to negotiating reductions in agricultural subsidies despite their governments' proclamations to the contrary.

Subsidies in Europe—an area that keeps the most detailed, up-to-date, comparable, and reliable data—have been falling in the last 15 years or so.[4] However, the numbers mask considerable differences across European countries (European Commission, 2006c). The Commission's recent figures indicate that the estimated amount of state aid in 2004, that is, subsidies from the national treasuries, stood at €56.2 billion (in constant 1995 terms) or 0.6 percent of GDP for the 15 EU members (which excludes the most recent postcommunist and other entrants; €61.4 billion for the EU's 25 members) (figure 1.1). The numbers represent a decline in real terms from €74.5 billion or 1.1 percent of GDP in 1992 after a peak of €95.5 billion (EU-15) in 1997, although the figure was still 1.1 percent of GDP. Most aid in 2004 went to manufacturing (59 percent) and agriculture (23 percent) (European Commission, 2006b). During that year, Germany gave the highest amount (€17 billion), followed by France (€9 billion) and Italy (€7 billion). In some countries, such as Finland and Austria, most subsidies went to agriculture (70 percent and 63 percent, respectively). In France only 26 percent went to agriculture in 2004. The exact opposite is the case with Italy, Sweden, and Denmark. More than 60 percent of disbursed subsidies went to manufacturing in the same year.

The Commission also provides aid figures by objective (European Commission, 2006a).[5] In 2004, 76 percent of disbursed subsidies (EU-25) went to meet horizontal objectives. They include aid that applies to many firms across the economy, such as aid to small and medium-sized enterprises, training aid, environment and energy-saving aid, research and development (R&D) assistance, employment aid, and regional assistance. The largest share of horizontal aid (25 percent) went to environmental and energy-saving assistance. Some members, such as Belgium and Sweden, spent 100 percent of their total aid budget on horizontal subsidies. In the same year, 24 percent of all aid went to aid

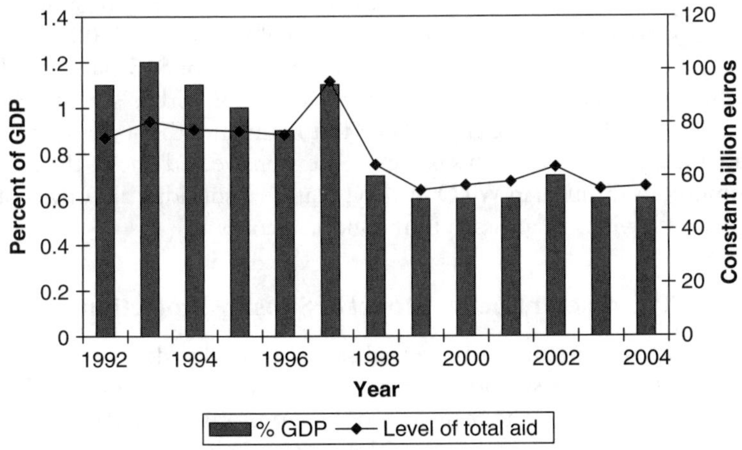

Figure 1.1   Subsidy flows in the European Union.
Source: European Commission (2006b).

with sectoral primary objectives, such as aid to help specific sectors or individual firm bailouts. Some members, such as Portugal and France, spent 78 and 41 percent on sectoral aid respectively.

The absolute amounts may not be particularly high, but they have significant political and economic repercussions that extend beyond the actual figures. Take the example of subsidies to aircraft makers Boeing and Airbus. In its complaint to the WTO, Boeing protests that Airbus, its rival, unfairly and illegally received $17 billion in product launch loans alone since the company's inception in 1970 (*Economist*, 2005, p. 67). For its part, Airbus counters that Boeing has enjoyed R&D subsidies, disguised as defense contracts from the Pentagon, to the tune of $23 billion in just the last 13 years. Whether each company has its own reasons to inflate the figures of its rival is beside the point. Both companies employ thousands of workers, record annual revenues of tens of billions of dollars, and log annual orders of more than 1,000 aircraft each! There is real money at stake in addition to questions about jobs, prestige, and national security.

The actual subsidy figures mask the huge economic stakes. For example, let us assume that Airbus anticipates an order of say, 100 aircraft, from a foreign company to be delivered over the next ten years. At an average price of $150 million apiece (*Economist*, 2005, p. 67), the total dollar amount of the order is $15 billion. For the sake of argument, I hypothesize that Airbus cannot deliver the planes at that price unless it receives $100 million in subsidies (in the form of launch aid, R&D support, and so on). Airbus knows that if it does not get this order, Boeing will. Unwillingness by national governments to subsidize Airbus by $100 million does not simply entail the cost of $100 million but also the loss for Airbus (and gain for Boeing) of $15 billion! Add to this figure the fact that development costs for Airbus's new A350 aircraft are $12 billion before the first test flight, and the stakes increase dramatically. No wonder this is the most expensive and one of the most acrimonious disputes in WTO history! National subsidies are obviously an extremely important issue in the global economy.

The Asset Influence Model of Subsidy Protection

Why do governments disburse subsidies and why do they protect some industries or sectors of their economies but not others? The answer lies in the cost that owners of economic assets face in moving assets across industries, gains and losses from globalization, and the political and institutional incentives that governments have in disbursing subsidies.

The point of departure is Grossman and Helpman's (G-H, 1994) political contribution model. Looking at the domestic policy process, the authors theorize that groups vie for protection from adverse external economic conditions by making political campaign contributions. Policymakers choose to grant protection based on an objective function that takes into account both their own chances for reelection and the voters' welfare. G-H is used here as a platform that enables me to disentangle the politics of subsidy protection. I follow their model's logic but I also add several structural features of my own. Most significantly, although the authors examine protection at the sectoral level within a single national economy, I analyze the implications of the model at the national level across several economies.

The political contribution model is important because it takes into account both the demand for and supply of protection. However, it is also limited by three assumptions. First, the authors assume constant world prices so they may concentrate on the domestic policy process. Second, they explicitly posit a specific-factors framework, that is, they assume it is very costly to move assets across industries. Third, the model assumes an undifferentiated, pluralist, national institutional framework, where groups compete for influence. I relax those assumptions and explore the implications of a revised model of subsidy protection that more accurately reflects cross-national differences.

The argument may be summarized as follows. I begin by viewing subsidies as an insurance element in the sense that government compensates actors in specific circumstances against adversity. I conceptualize a model of political economy in a democracy that operates on two levels. Each is nested within the other and both have a significant impact on policy outputs (Hall, 1999, pp. 148–150). First-order relationships analyze actor behavior. For example, globalization affects returns on assets and actor preferences regarding protection. Second-order relationships deal with institutionalized interactions that affect the stability of first-order relationships. For example, pressure for protection goes through specific institutional channels that mediate, refract, and shape access to policymakers. The willingness of policymakers to act partly depends on the intensity of actor demands and the specific ways that demands are filtered through institutions. The following three propositions describe the core of the model.

1. *The domestic policy process crucially affects the dynamics of protection.* Social actors form lobby groups and confront incumbent policymakers with contributions that affect the latter's chances for reelection. They seek subsidy protection against the adverse

effects created by increasing exposure to global economic forces. The willingness of politicians to listen to affected groups critically depends upon the political power that groups wield. Governments never have enough resources to address all the issues before them. They have to choose what issues to attend and what resources to expend to address the constituents' concerns (Zahariadis, 2003a). In this context, more powerful groups will obviously be more likely to be successful at getting what they want than others. The ability to be heard increases with political power. There are of course other ways to do so, but power is conceptualized here as a function of size. Keeping the costs of collective action constant for the moment, the bigger the group, the larger the membership will be. In that case, disaffected groups may deliver more negative votes. So politicians have to listen to constituents who will play a crucial role in their reelection.

Incentives to supply rewards are carefully circumscribed by the political institutional system within which groups and governments operate. Two types of institutions regulate access and shape rent-seeking and rent-supplying behavior. The first type, corporatism, operates outside the formal public political sphere. The encompassing coalitions implied by corporatist arrangements lead to compensatory deals. Groups negotiate and finalize agreements on more subsidies on a continuous basis in exchange for industrial peace and policy stability. The high level of organization and the structured access to power necessitated by corporatism render policymakers more susceptible to rent-seeking than similar demands placed within the context of pluralist systems. Demands for subsidies, and by consequence the level of subsidies, are likely to be more successful in more corporatist systems.

Formal political institutions also affect the propensity to disburse subsidies because they regulate access and control of the process. In cases where there are more veto points, that is, as the number of partisan coalition members goes up, the level of subsidies increases. Because groups know their agreement is needed to make decisions, they will press hard in favor of their interests, however parochial they may be. In the aggregate, the decisions will tend to satisfy as many coalition partners as possible, which imply more subsidies to more groups. In addition, in electoral systems where preferences are aggregated on the basis of small districts, that is, in more majoritarian systems with single-member districts, policymakers tend to disburse, on average, fewer subsidies. Because the size of the groups and, consequently, their political power are severely circumscribed by the size of the electoral districts, the propensity of individual policymakers to supply rents diminishes. Conversely, in systems with more proportional representation (PR), politicians need to build large coalitions to make policy and increase their chances for reelection. They have more incentives, therefore, to be more attentive to rent-seeking actors.

2. *The ability (or cost) of asset owners to move their assets to more-profitable uses motivates domestic groups to demand subsidies.* Economic exchange is driven primarily by return on assets. The greater the returns on assets in a given activity, the more likely actors are to favor continuing the activity. Specific assets tend to have high rates of return; otherwise, their owners would redeploy them in a different activity. The greater the ability to move assets, the lower the incentive will be to ask for more subsidies. Losses do not loom as large, because actors have options for a more-profitable allocation of assets. Conversely, actors who face significant domestic barriers to entry in and exit out of profitable activities will experience heavier losses. Facing fewer options for exit, they will seek more voice (Hirschman, 1970). Consequently, incentives for more subsidies are determined partly by the degree of asset specificity.

   Protectionist coalitions tend to inflate prices and profits. Subsidies raise final product prices, causing shifts upward along the supply curve. This argument points to two implications. First, incentives for higher returns increase the likelihood that economic actors will use more resources to capture higher rents, generating waste for society as a whole (Tullock, 2005). Second, protection fosters redistributional inefficiencies. Higher returns encourage the entry of producers in areas of comparative disadvantage, taking resources out of productive uses and allocating them to unproductive ones. Rent seeking, in short, has costs that go beyond the actual amount of subsidies.

   There are two aspects of specificity: labor and capital. Although both have implications for protection, specificity among workers affects subsidies more than specificity among capital asset owners. Higher levels of specificity among workers have consistently positive effects on subsidy disbursement. Capital specificity has a positive impact on subsidy disbursement but only at different levels of exposure to global economic forces. The rallying cry is true: subsidies are mostly about "jobs, jobs, jobs."

3. *Increasing exposure to global economic forces affects subsidization efforts.* To understand what motivates actors to act, analysts must specify the type and level of exposure to global markets. Not

only does globalization provide powerful incentives for domestic groups to act, but it also affects the ability of governments to respond favorably to these demands. Not all globalization is created equal. The dimensions of globalization have contradictory effects. While trade and FDI positively affect the propensity of policymakers to disburse more subsidies, portfolio investment has an inverse impact. The difference is attributed to barriers to entry and exit. Because short-term investment, such as portfolio investment, involves fewer sunk costs and can move more easily in and out of national borders, it has a negative effect on protection. In this case, governments in more heavily exposed economies disburse on average fewer subsidies.

However, the answer to the subsidization puzzle is not that simple. The effects of globalization are both independent and conditional. Their direction and strength vary considerably on the basis of asset specificity and institutional configurations. For example, while groups adversely affected by trade appear on average to be less successful in more pluralist institutional environments, their ability to extract additional rents increases sharply with the level of exposure to international trade. At higher levels of exposure, losses generally loom large. Because the system favors adjustment assistance on an episodic, noncontinuous basis, the level of protection is likely to be high. In contrast, because compensatory deals tend to be on a continuous basis to take the edge off the extreme social dislocations produced by wild market fluctuations, the level of subsidies is more likely to be, on the one hand, higher than in pluralist systems at low levels of trade but on the other hand, lower at higher levels of trade.

The argument reinforces the point made by Odell (1990) and others that our understanding of trade policy is not aided by sweeping generalizations about the impact of variables but by exploring the effects of explanatory factors under different conditions. Only then may we begin to acquire a more complete and properly specified picture of the dynamics of protection across different national contexts. The stakes are high as analysts take sides and make impassioned pleas for or against globalization (e.g., Bhagwati, 2004; Rodrik, 1997). The analysis here provides valuable insight that is a necessary first step before voters and politicians lay blame for any failures and act only to make matters worse.

I test the argument using data from 14 EU member states during the period 1992–2004.[6] My choice of countries and time period is guided by three factors. First, the sample of countries contains considerable variation in the factors of interest to provide a complete picture of the dynamics of subsidization. Second, the EU maintains the most complete, transparent, and up-to-date data set on producer subsidies. Although the figures do not go back in time prior to 1992, they are broken down by objective, instrument, and so on. They permit the most complete battery of tests and consequently yield the most comprehensive and accurate answer to the subsidy puzzle. Besides, lack of comparable data precludes extending the analysis to other countries.

Finally, the EU case adds greater weight to the findings. The hypothesized relationships should theoretically be weakest among EU members. EU treaties explicitly prohibit the disbursement of distortionary producer subsidies, except for special cases such as conditions of high unemployment or persistently low economic growth. The founding treaties gave the European Commission strong formal administrative powers to limit the ability of member states to protect domestic industry through state aids (Smith, 1996; Neyer and Wolf, 2003, p. 210). These powers have been amplified since the advent of the single European market. Commissioner Neelie Kroes aptly summarizes the Commission's attitude. In a statement to members of the European Parliament in Brussels, she warned that the notion of national champions was "outdated. I am in favor of global champions located in Europe" (Minder, 2006). Yet, "subsidisation [*sic*] is the only remaining important form of state intervention, because in the integrated European market state aid . . . becomes the only possible national instrument which can be used to favor and protect national industries" (Lavdas and Mendrinou, 1999, pp. 1–2). The findings, therefore, acquire considerably more weight if it can be shown that domestic political considerations affect the disbursement of protection in the face of strong external political, economic, and legal pressure to the contrary. The Commission may have an overall dampening effect on subsidies, as the EU figures above demonstrate, but the point remains: while external economic forces provide powerful incentives, the choice to act still depends on domestic institutional and other considerations. Far from being impotent, democratic states continue to shield social actors from the vagaries of the global market.

Contributions to Theory and Policy

Apart from being one of the very few to quantitatively examine the issue of subsidization, the study contributes to a better understanding of the theory and practice of protectionism. First, the literature on asset specificity remains mostly formal theoretical (but see Hiscox, 2002; Ladewig, 2006). Analysts do not agree on whether asset specificity increases or decreases the amount of subsidies (e.g., Acemoglu and Robinson, 2001; Alt et al., 1996). Compounding this problem is the lack of empirical studies that can settle the question. The "most recent and complete empirical analysis," according to Echenique and Eguia (2005), is by Zahariadis (2001), which was limited in time and scope. The present study addresses those debates by providing statistical evidence from industrialized democracies over a fairly long time period (1992–2004). The time period is long enough to facilitate examination of the determinants of policy choice in the short- and long-term, which permits examination of the predictions of both the specific- and mobile-factors models. Moreover, my study looks at actual levels of protection and the calculus of choosing from among several policy instruments, which is theoretically and methodologically more satisfying than recent work in political science (Hiscox, 2002; McGillivray, 2004), in which protection is conceptualized as legislator vote in favor of specific bills.

Second, the puzzle of subsidization is conceptualized as an income redistribution problem. The present work thus informs arguments about economic policy in the tradition of political economics (Persson and Tabellini, 2000; Rowley, Thorbecke, and Wagner, 1995), which combine insight from economic theory, public choice, and, more broadly, rational choice. The main contention—that the effects of globalization are likely to be keenly felt in certain economic sectors under specific institutional circumstances, which in turn interact with the policy preferences of owners of specific factors to produce protection—operates at the international-domestic nexus (Keohane and Milner, 1996). The study complements macroeconomic studies that link globalization to government spending (e.g., Garrett, 1998; Adserà and Boix, 2002) and micropolicy studies that find a connection between societal demands and state supplies (e.g., Mansfield and Busch, 1995). But it also goes beyond them by specifying the conditions under which the policy preferences of certain economic actors interact with the state to produce redistributive outcomes across different policy domains *and* policy instruments.

Third, globalization, not just trade, affects the formation of political coalitions. Political scientists have recently begun developing propositions about how exposure to trade affects political cleavages and coalition formation. Rogowski (1989), for example, argues that coalitions are more likely to form conditional on the effects of factor price equalization. Under certain conditions, he expects broad factor-based coalitions to form in favor (or not) of protection. Hiscox (2001) refines this claim to suggest that coalitions form along industry lines as well under conditions of low factor mobility. My argument enriches both claims, first, by exploring the effects of various dimensions of globalization and not just trade; second, by developing a model that explains how asset specificity works in the policy process; and third, by examining the way in which societal demands affect government policy through institutional channels. Asset specificity is not likely to have the same effects under all institutional configurations.

The findings have particular political significance in today's era of intense global competition. Many analysts claim that globalization has made it nearly impossible for governments to protect their industries. National governments have simply lost the authority or capability to be masters of their own destiny. Successive GATT rounds reduced the ability of governments, and some argue the demand by industry, to seek tariff protection (Hathaway, 1998). The creation of the WTO and the many free trade areas around the world are testaments to this national aspiration to free trade. The recent removal of capital controls has further eroded states' policymaking power. The more integrated a country becomes in the global economy, so the argument goes, the fewer its options will be to respond to political and social dislocations. Governments have no other option but to foster competitiveness by embracing economic liberalism. The former British prime minister Tony Blair put it most eloquently to delegates at Labour's 2005 annual national convention: "The dam holding back the global economy burst years ago." What works is "an open, liberal economy prepared to constantly change to remain competitive" (Stephens, 2005, p. 17). Alan Johnson, British secretary of trade and industry, was blunter. Speaking in opposition to French attempts to block corporate acquisitions by foreign conglomerates, he said: attempts to "repel the surge of globalization . . . are futile and self-defeating. The paradox of protectionism is that it destroys what it seeks to protect" (Hollinger et al., 2006b, p. 15). Practitioners and academics have similarly noted the removal of capital controls and the creation of a globalized financial system that differs both in kind and degree from the past (Greenspan, 1998; Wriston, 1998; Cerny, 1994). As a result, "the authority, legitimacy, policymaking capacity, and policy-implementing effectiveness of the state" have been irreparably eroded (Cerny, 1995, p. 621). Strange (1996, p. 4) boldly captures the so-called globalist view: "Where states were once the masters of markets, it is now the markets which, on many crucial issues, are the masters over the governments of states." Bhagwati

(1988, p. xii) puts it more modestly: "The deck is not stacked in favor of protectionism . . . there are major new interests and forces, prompted particularly by the growing globalization and interdependence in the world economy, that offer grounds for guarded optimism."

However, I argue the opposite may be true. As Thomas Östros, the Swedish trade and industry minister, aptly says, the "fear of globalisation [*sic*] is undermining most decisions in Europe" (Parker and Smyth, 2006). Conditional on the interaction between asset specificity and certain institutional configurations, a neoliberal convergence on free markets is not inevitable. Because domestic firms are increasingly more exposed to foreign competition (Irwin, 2005), they face higher adjustment costs. They will fight harder for more subsidies from the public purse to provide at least temporary relief. But given the fact that these subsidies are coming under increasing scrutiny from multilateral institutions, national governments will find it harder to provide them.

This relationship reveals a troubling paradox: democratic politics, and globalization in the form of increasing economic integration across national borders may be on a collision course. While markets seem to be gaining at the expense of politics on a global level, there is pressure for the reverse on a domestic level. On the one hand, national governments have recently undertaken commitments to reduce and eliminate, in some instances, harmful protectionist subsidies. This represents the triumph of markets over politics. On the other hand, governments are coming under increasing pressure from their constituents (owners of the factors of production) to alleviate the adverse effects of international economic forces. A good example is the political response over the hostile bid against Arcelor, a Luxembourg-based steel maker, by a Netherlands-based Indian group. Indirectly antagonizing the Indian government, Jean-Claude Juncker, the prime minister of Luxembourg, aptly described his displeasure: "This hostile bid by Mittal Steel calls for a reaction that is at least as hostile" (Hollinger et al., 2006b, p. 15).[7] Democratically elected politicians know they have to respond in order to increase their chances of reelection. Politics prevails over economics. Capturing this sentiment, the former French president Valèry Giscard d'Estaing, once remarked: "The laws of a modern, liberal economy are not those of the jungle" (Thornhill, 2006, p. 13). Politics is called upon to tame the market. As O'Brien (1997, p. 19) puts it, "There is pressure for protection at home, and [liberalization] attack abroad." It appears that many policymakers subscribe to the view that "it is one thing to globalize [*sic*] . . . ; it is quite another to be globalised [*sic*] against" (Thornhill, 2006, p. 13). Efforts to resolve the dilemma lead to uncomfortable conclusions. The relationship between democratic politics and perfect international asset mobility, or, to use Rodrik's (2005) term, "full integration," is problematic and the two may indeed be incompatible.

PLAN OF THE BOOK

Why are there still so many subsidies disbursed by national governments in the face of increasing pressure and political rhetoric to abandon the practice? Why do governments offer protection to some industries or economic sectors but not to others? Why are subsidies voluminous, and how do governments choose between subsidy instruments?

In chapter 1 I sketched out the answer. Arguing against the globalist expectation of a neoliberal consensus, I locate the answer to the subsidization question in the domestic political economy. More specifically, the argument centers on the interaction between societal demands for subsidies and the institutional ability of politicians to supply protection of the sort demanded by pressure groups. Trade, and more generally pressure from global competition, does not affect all countries in the same way. Different factors of production are affected differently. By implication societal demands for subsidy protection are likely to differ across countries, regions, firms, and sectors. Add to this the complication of domestic institutions that constrain the role of the state and society, limiting the ability to pursue certain options while making others more likely. What emerges is a complex web of subsidy tools and a variable logic for deploying them.

In chapter 2 I review previous attempts to explain protection and find them wanting. The main problem is that they focus either on the demand or the supply side of the equation. Analysts generally examine which groups will make more demands and which politicians are likely to respond. The problem is that they are both different sides of the same coin. Despite many benefits, painting an accurate picture of one does not necessarily help us see the entire coin. A good explanation of protection necessitates an accurate picture of both sides. The key, I argue, is in modeling the policy process.

In the remainder of the book I build the asset influence model, carefully deriving and testing hypotheses about relationships between key variables and policy outputs. In chapter 3 I pose the question: does increasing economic integration affect the disbursement of subsidies? The answer depends on how globalization is conceptualized. Conventional wisdom sees globalization as irreversibly tying the hands of governments, reducing their ability to protect industries despite domestic demands to the contrary. In this chapter I look at how exogenous shocks in the areas of trade, FDI, and portfolio investment affect the policy preferences of economic actors. If it can be empirically shown that not all countries are tied to the global economy at the same level, then the strength of the globalist argument is considerably weakened. Different countries are affected differently, which translates into variable pressure for protection. The answer to the globalization challenge depends on the domestic political economy.

Chapter 4 evaluates the impact of asset specificity on subsidies. How are variable preferences for subsidy protection translated into government action? I first hypothesize the independent impact of the cost of moving assets across industries on subsidy disbursements, and then I explore the interactive effects of asset specificity depending on the level of globalization. In continuation of the argument made in the previous chapter, the main point here is that asset specificity is likely to also have a variable impact depending on the level of a country's exposure to international economic forces.

Chapter 5 addresses the issue of political power and institutions. Political power is conceptualized as stemming from the size of a group. Larger groups are likely to be more successful, implying they are likely to be more heavily subsidized than others. Following Garrett and Lange (1996), institutions are divided into two types: socioeconomic and formal political. I first look at how the degree of interest group mediation, that is, pluralism (or corporatism), affects the disbursement of subsidies. Then I elaborate on the impact of two types of formal national institutions: the fragmentation of state power and the disproportionality of the electoral system. While asset specificity provides a glimpse of the desire of societal groups to pressure for more subsidies, the institutional configurations shape the ability and need of governments to respond. Just as in the previous chapter, I analyze the independent effects of institutions and their impact conditional on different levels of globalization.

In chapter 6 I pull the strands of the argument together and put everything to the test, drawing on evidence from European democracies since 1992. The chapter is divided into three sections. The first section tests the hypotheses in terms of total subsidy disbursements. The analysis is then broken down in the second section into two components: sectoral subsidies, which apply to particular sectors, and horizontal subsidies, which apply to the entire economy. If the logic of globalization, institutions, and asset specificity is correct, then governments should be keener to subsidize specific sectors as opposed to using horizontal subsidies. The third section brings the subsidy focus down one level to regions. Does regional aid follow the same pattern tracked in the previous chapters? How do globalization, asset specificity, and national institutions affect the disbursement of regionally focused subsidies?

Chapter 7 shifts the level of analysis and narrows the field of inquiry to different sectors. It is not enough just to look at how governments offer national protection. A complete answer to the question of producer subsidy allocation requires careful analytical scrutiny at several levels. In the first section, I explore the differences between subsidies to manufacturing and to agriculture. Is agriculture a special case or is the argument applicable in this case as well? In the second section I specify the various instruments of subsidization that governments have at their disposal. It is quite obvious that given the existence of a wide variety of tools, for example, grants, tax incentives, loans, or equity infusions, governments will seek to deploy them in different situations. Analysts have long struggled with the question of choice, but the literature remains primarily theoretical and limited (see Zahariadis, 1997). Does the logic outlined in this model guide the choice of tools as well?

In chapter 8 I wrap things up by summarizing the argument and by teasing out the theoretical implications in three areas. First, the model enriches and amends theories of trade and protectionism. Second, it addresses arguments regarding the redistributive implications of government policy and political coalition formation. Third, the analysis addresses the impact of globalization, democracy, and the hypothesized economic policy convergence. Depending on the interaction between asset specificity and certain institutional configurations, a neoliberal convergence on free markets is possible but not inevitable. The findings have policy implications for the current development round under the WTO's guidance. Casting the problem as a dispute mainly between developed and developing countries is grossly inaccurate. Not only are developed countries affected in different ways, but even EU states, which supposedly speak with one voice, are also plagued by different subsidization demands. Subsidies are very difficult to root out in the light of different institutional environments. To break the current impasse, lasting reforms are needed that not only take into account the willingness of governments to break down barriers to trade, but also promote domestic institutional changes to sustain and amplify the desired policies. In this way changes in the global political economy are linked to modifications in domestic politics. In the absence of such explicit linkages, global agreements will only be temporary.

Chapter 2

Perspectives on Subsidies and Trade Protection

That [the theorem of comparative advantage] is not trivial is attested by the thousands of important and intelligent men who have never been able to grasp the doctrine for themselves or believe it after it was explained to them.

—*Paul Samuelson, Nobel Prize winner in economics*[1]

A good way to understand subsidization efforts is to survey the explanations advanced by other analysts. Such review exposes deficiencies in current thinking about trade protection and helps place the contributions made by the present study in a broader context. I review two approaches to trade protection: society-centered and state-centered perspectives. While each illuminates different aspects of the subsidization puzzle, both suffer from serious analytical gaps. I then explore the merit of yet another theoretical attempt that takes elements of the two approaches and blends them in a theoretically concise and meaningful way. I flesh out this synthetic model and identify its limitations, which I overcome in subsequent chapters. Although the overwhelming majority of studies on protection refer to instruments such as tariffs or quotas, the logic applies to protection in the form of subsidies as well.

Demanding Trade Protection

Analysts examining the politics of trade policy generally follow one of two approaches: society-centered and state-centered approaches.

Those following society-centered approaches generally model the demand side of the protection puzzle. Various societal groups or individuals compete with one another to access politicians in support of or in opposition to protectionist policies. Analysts usually model the incentives or preferences actors have in demanding protection. State-centered approaches model the supply side of the equation, specifying politician willingness or ability to disburse subsidies. Whether by examining the power of ideas or institutions, these types of approaches place emphasis squarely on institutional rules or voter norms as the determining variables of trade protection.

In the following paragraphs I survey each approach, identifying its benefits and drawbacks. The main contention is that viewed in isolation, each approach is incomplete. A full model must specify not only both the demand and the supply sides of the equation, but it must also state how and under what conditions they interact to determine policy outputs.

Society-centered arguments follow the pioneering logic of Schattschneider (1935) by considering protection as the result of demands by affected interest groups, labor unions, and political action committees (Destler, 1992). Society-centered approaches implicitly or explicitly assume that politicians have no preferences of their own. While governments may not be forced to accept any societal demands, they do so at their peril in democratic societies. As McKeown maintains, "Governments may choose to ignore these demands in formulating policy, but such behavior normally has high political costs for a governing coalition, particularly in a competitive political system" (1984, p. 216). The key to explaining protectionism, therefore, is to identify which group (coalition) makes the best case or applies the most pressure.

Armed with this insight, analysts have developed models that capture different aspects of the demand for protection. The general line of reasoning is that "losers" from global trade seek to compensate their losses by demanding protection from government. The argument contains two related points. The first aims to identify which groups (or firms) are most likely to lose. The second point refers to the identification of conditions that activate lobbying efforts.

One way to look at the demand side of protection is to conceive of it as a political struggle between producer groups that support protection and the government that looks after consumer welfare. Hillman (1982) offers such a model. The model postulates a government facing a trade-off between political support offered by industry interests and the dissatisfaction of consumers. Industry offers more political support when its profits rise, and consumers are more dissatisfied when product prices rise. Both sides are therefore motivated by price rises. Protection increases prices (and profits) for producers and consumers alike although the former gain and the latter lose. In the light of the fact that government chooses a tariff level that maximizes support, it follows that it will seek a balance between the two. However, consumers always find it more difficult to organize given substantial numbers and wide dispersion in the economy, while producers have an easier time because there are fewer of them. The benefits of protection are likely to be more concentrated and the costs more diffuse. In this case, governments usually find it easier to grant limited protection to small groups of producer interests provided that the costs, and, by extension, consumer dissatisfaction, are neither high nor easily detectable.

Is the assumption of the government's pursuit of consumer welfare plausible? Does government only (or primarily) use this principle as its guiding motivation? The idea seems empirically unrealistic. Even if one were to simplify the government's motives to just one aspect, it is highly unlikely that it would be consumer welfare. The most important reason is because price hikes as a result of tariffs are usually small and diffused. Consumers are unlikely to feel enough "pain" to motivate them into political action. Moreover, the notion outlined above assumes that consumers are aware of the consequences and are able to calculate the effects if tariffs were not in place. The assumption necessarily implies more information than is often available.

A variation to this theme sees the contest as one between supporting and opposing societal groups rather than as one between producers and the government. Analysts have found that groups, particularly in declining industries involved in import competition, lobby parties and politicians in specific districts for protection. Although the argument most often heard rationalizes government support in favor of saving jobs, the rhetoric of protection involves many claims including national security, infant industry, fair trade, strategic trade, retaliation against dumping, and social justice (Rowley et al., 1995, chapter 3). Findlay and Wellisz (1982) propose a tariff-formation function that views protection as a contest between opposing forces. They hypothesize that tariffs are supported by groups in import-competing sectors and are opposed by those in export-producing sectors. The equilibrium level of protection is determined by the incentives that supporters have in lobbying for protection, measured by their losses and the costs of lobbying, and the losses that exporters would suffer if protection were put in place, measured by their lobbying costs and the losses from protection.

Are import-competing industries always the losers? The problem with this kind of theorizing is that it does not take into account the multinational structure of production in some industries or economies of scale (Milner, 1988; Frieden and Rogowski, 1996, pp. 39–41). Some industries may resist advocacy of protectionism if they have the ability to move production offshore. Others may be involved in both exports and imports, for example, automobiles. Still others may find it easier to redeploy resources and compete when domestic markets are exposed to the world economy. Under these circumstances, the assumption of specific industries facing a single set of constraints just breaks down.

When will groups begin lobbying? Protection, according to this line of reasoning, is the equilibrium point of the contest between opposing sides of the issue. In other words, not only does the analyst have to identify winners and losers, but he/she must also specify when lobbying will take place. McKeown (1984) argues that even if firms (groups affected by trade) lose from increasing exposure to world markets, lobbying in support of protection is not automatic. "An organization must decide to commit resources to political activity; whatever latent political strength it possesses must be *activated*" (emphasis in the original; McKeown, 1984, p. 218). When is this strength most likely to be activated? The author hypothesizes that the best time is during the trough of the business cycle. Macroeconomic conditions, such as low demand growth or high unemployment reduce the likelihood that firms will enter new lines of business in search of higher profits. Under these conditions profitability is expected to be low. The implication is that lower factor returns provide incentives for less "exit" from current activities, to use Hirschman's (1970) terms, and more "voice" to increase profits. The end result is increasing demands for protection both in the form of trade barriers and in the form of government assistance to ease the cost of adjustment (Neary, 1982).

There is one more complication to this picture. Optimal levels of lobbying are determined not only by groups in relation to their well-being, but also by government. What if government uses revenues obtained by tariffs (or some other way) to bribe the affected groups? Losers from globalization need compensation support (Leipziger and Spence, 2007). In debating the repeal of the Corn Laws in nineteenth-century England, John Stuart Mill formulated the so-called "compensation principle." If free trade compensates groups for their loss of income, then no one would be worse off (Irwin, 1996). Suppose labor supports protectionism. Government may decide to take the "edge off" protectionist demands by providing assistance to labor to lessen the blow. Labor would lobby less and get less protection through tariffs than would otherwise be the case. Under these conditions and in light of reduced tariff protection, government reduces the cost to labor through direct assistance—but does not eliminate it entirely—alters the cost of lobbying, and increases the rent on capital by improving the terms of trade to levels that exceed those that would occur in the absence of aid to labor. "So long as tariff revenues exceed lobbying costs in the final equilibrium the improved terms of trade improve social welfare" (Feenstra and Bhagwati, 1982, p. 257).

Tullock (2005, p. 103) disapproves of such logic, claiming that government transfers of this type constitute negative sum games. They obfuscate the real cost to the taxpayer and generate more deadweight losses; they are, therefore, inefficient. As Jacobson (quoted in Kapstein, 2000, p. 373) categorically asserts, "A key impediment to implementing compensation programs is that the transaction costs associated with doing so are likely to be many times larger than the costs imposed on those adversely affected by change." The empirical reality is that adjustment assistance schemes may bring about inefficiencies for the economy as a whole, regardless of the nobility of intentions.

There are two main problems with society-centered approaches. The first relates to the ability of groups to get what they want out of government. Government is more or less "black-boxed" and assumed to not only listen but also to respond to group demands. This is empirically unrealistic. Not only do groups not have the same level of access, but access also differs significantly across countries. For example, it is unrealistic to assume that labor groups have the same access to the U.S. Congress as employer groups do during the reign of the Republican Party. In an era when anecdotal evidence suggests that industry groups write their own legislation (Hrebenar, 1997, p. 154), this statement does not mean that access is denied, but it does mean that Republicans are biased against paying attention to union demands. Moreover, institutions (not just ideology) mitigate access. Some institutions encourage groups to collude with one another while others promote an open contest for influence. In addition, a large number of veto points complicate the picture by increasing lobbying costs and limiting the effectiveness of any one group to dominate the process and get what it wants.

The second problem is that demand models do not take into account the preferences or activities of trading partners. Protection is assumed to be endogenous to the political system and rests on the equilibrium point of opposing forces in pursuit of deployment of different policy instruments (Rodrik, 1986). It is very plausible that some protection may be triggered by actions of trading partners, for example, countervailing duties (CVDs), or not granted because of fear of retaliation. Trade wars, in the form of higher protection, result from changes in the political environment of some countries that are then exported to others (Grossman and Helpman, 1995). In many instances, CVDs are not only plausible and their use widespread, but also legal. Demand models must account for the international influence on domestic politics as well as the calculus of choice between instruments.

SUPPLYING TRADE PROTECTION

In contrast, state-centered approaches examine the institutional and electoral determinants of protection. The main argument of these approaches is that emphasis on the demand side of the equation misses out on a fundamental problem of politics, namely, elections and institutions. State-oriented approaches examine the supply side of the equation, claiming that policy outcomes are not simply the result of competition by societal groups but the outcome of state preferences and institutional rules. Democratic politics, in the form of elections and other institutional channels of access, bias the results and make a big difference as to the final policy output.

The approach rests on the fundamental assumption that state officials have preferences of their own and may or may not choose to adhere to societal demands. Krasner (1978), for example, argues that U.S. foreign economic policy is driven largely by the state's conception of the national interest. Busch (1999) explicitly "black-boxes" the state in order to focus more squarely on the linkages between state officials, externalities, and strategic trade policy. Unlike demand models, state-oriented approaches hypothesize the reverse direction of influence. Under conditions of crisis, politicians may seek to proactively alter the incentives of lobbies and impose trade liberalization (Lusztig, 2004). Moreover, because of the United States' rising hegemony, policymakers have been able to overcome industry objections and impose their own preferences on trade policy (Lake, 1988). Protection is not the result of societal demands but the ability of national politicians, in democratic societies and elsewhere, to impose their own preferences on society.

Other analysts have sought to place electoral dimensions at center stage. Mayer (1984) models protection as the outcome of majority voting over tariff levels. He argues that preferences for tariffs depend on factor ownership. Assuming a two-sector, two-factor (capital and labor) economy and a wide distribution of factor ownership, Mayer posits that the level of tariffs will be determined by the income generated by the tariff. Income is strongly connected to the utility function of individual voters and reflects several properties of the economy's structure and voter characteristics, the most important of which is factor endowments—for example, the skills that the voter possesses, the company shares he/she owns, and so on. It follows that voters heavily endowed with specific factors will prefer tariffs that maximize income in sectors that heavily utilize these factors. Viewed from an economy-wide perspective, the model implies that tariff levels will be chosen according to the preferences of the median voter.

The model is a laudatory attempt to analyze the politics of trade protection. By injecting democratic elections at the center of analysis, Mayer explicitly models the political/institutional rules that enable politicians to grant protection. But the rules that he posits are unrealistic for two reasons. First, it is quite a stretch to view trade protection as the outcome of direct democracy. Given the paucity of countries utilizing this form of governance over trade issues, except possibly for Switzerland, it is unreasonable to expect majority voting to reveal the dynamics of trade protection. Besides, direct democracy assumes perfect (or at least adequate) information among voters, a rather dubious assumption at best. Second, trade issues, such as tariffs and more generally protection, are multidimensional, involving complex trade-offs. Mayer's model assumes that tariffs have been chosen and what remains is to set the level of protection. There is no indication of the complex calculus that usually goes into the benefits or costs of choosing among several instruments of protection, in addition to deciding whether protection (tariffs in this case) is even desirable or feasible. In most instances, the use of high-level tariffs is banned under GATT, and now WTO, rules, making the model unable to paint the policymaking process with any sense of realism.

Magee, Brock, and Young (1989) shift emphasis away from the median voter toward electoral competition. Parties compete in elections and lobbies contribute to candidates who commit to policies prior to group contributions. Trade protection is the outcome of electoral competition between candidates and of lobby efforts to sway those elections. Although the authors model to an extent the demand side of protection *via* the analysis of lobbies, the main contribution is the emphasis on electoral competition. Lobbies aim to sway policies by swaying elections.

Two parties compete in an election. Each party puts forth a candidate who commits to implementing a certain policy, if elected. Because elections are expensive, political parties commit to policies they believe will maximize their future income. Organized producer groups evaluate alternative party proposals against their members' preferences and decide to contribute resources to the candidate who promises to their membership the highest level of welfare. Parties now use these additional resources to sway voters, who are assumed to be imperfectly informed about the candidate's positions. The calculus of the politicians is to correctly anticipate increased revenue streams from lobbies in order to win the elections, while the calculus of the producer groups pits the probability of the supported party being elected against the direct cost of the donation and the uncertainty of the election. Set out as a game, the Nash equilibrium identifies the equilibrium levels of protection.

The simplicity of the model is important and so are some of the implications. Placing the electoral motive at center stage, the authors correctly complicate and reverse the direction of influence. While lobbies seek to maximize the welfare of their members, the politicians' penchant for gifts and their need to seek out resources to maximize electoral success imply that contributions are frequently used to sway elections. Protection (or not) is offered as a consequence of the need to win elections and not as a result of satisfying voters or producer groups.

While simplicity is a virtue, it is also a vice. For example, lobbies are assumed to specialize in campaign giving, that is, they contribute to only one political party. Empirical reality, however, demonstrates that parties often receive contributions from more than one lobby. In fact, lobbies often feel obliged to hedge their bets by contributing to both parties simultaneously, assuming only two parties. Moreover, committing to a policy prior to the election in search of future streams of revenue presupposes sudden and frequent reversals over time, a fact that does not fit comfortably with the remarkable stability of preferences political parties seem to exhibit in regard to trade protection (Milner and Judkins, 2004). While the electoral motive is important in illuminating the supply of protection, more realistic assumptions are needed.

Verdier (1994) aims to do just that. He argues that voters indirectly control policymaking and policy outcomes. He maintains that voters control the policymaking process by signaling to producer groups and politicians what is (or not) politically feasible. Under institutions of policymaking specific to individual countries, groups adjust their preferences accordingly. Verdier identifies two sets of variables as important determinants of trade policymaking. The first is issue characteristics—salience and divisiveness. Voter awareness and preferences depend on these two properties. The second variable is institutional rules. Rules create dynamics that determine political preferences and shape policy outcomes (O'Reilly, 2005). If there is a high quorum, that is, voters are included in the policy process, and the voting rule is majority or unanimity, then policies are likely to reflect the preferences either of the governing party or the nation, that is, be deferred to executive decisions. Interestingly, Verdier does not assume preferences are exogenously determined by economic interests—that is, costs or benefits resulting from exposure to international trade—but rather he determines them endogenously by institutional rules and issue characteristics among voters. In other words, under certain conditions producer groups or politicians will not seek to press their specific sectoral preferences onto the process, but rather they will coalesce in groups that cut across economic sectors in support of particular parties. The outcome, trade protection (or not), depends on combinations of these variables.

The model is interesting because the author explores the importance of variable electoral rules and the tool kit of protection. He circumvents the problem of preference formation and places voters squarely in the driver's seat. Trade legislation in democratic societies is the result of voter preferences and decisions under specific institutional rules. It is a satisfying conclusion from a political science point of view. But it is also limiting and overspecified. For one, the question of preference formation is not resolved, but simply bypassed. Do producer groups adjust their preferences or their strategies according to institutional rules? If, for example, some groups, be they labor or employer, face significant adjustment costs due to exposure to international trade, will they demand protection because of those costs, or will they change preferences in support of free trade because they are betting on the winning party? If they support protection, whether *via* pressure group politics or mass parties, the outcome is still the same. The strategy may vary but the preference remains exogenously determined. If so, the model unnecessarily adds yet one more layer of explanation.

Moreover, when do voter characteristics come into play? For a model that touts emphasis on voters, there is surprisingly little said about voters. Where do voter preferences come from? Are they tied to age, gender, or some other variable explicitly linked to individual voters or are preferences tied to issues? Are issue characteristics reflective of voter preferences or of the media's or some other group's manipulation? Clearly, more information is needed to link voters to institutional rules in order to explain policy outcomes.

Do politicians aim to protect just any industry or do they choose industries to support based on their own needs rather than the demands made by actual firms? McGillivray (2004, p. 2) brings to the table the point that "politicians do not want to protect any industry *per se*. They want to assist groups with precisely the right size, spread and location, to target benefits to politically important groups of voters." Armed with this insight, she argues that legislator preferences are canalized by electoral rules and industrial geography. In turn, the strength of parties and the electoral rules, majoritarian versus proportional representation, aggregate preferences into policies. In other words, it is not so much whether groups compete against each other for favors and protection, but whether politicians have an incentive to listen to the winners. McGillivray (2004) as well as Busch and Reinhardt (1999) find that geographically proximate industry appears more likely to get favorable assistance by government.

Looking at protection as a political district–based phenomenon has considerable merit, largely because it is realistic and comparatively tested in various national contexts. However, there are two problems. First, winners and losers from trade are assumed to exist independently of the political process. For example, legislators are conceptualized as efficient political agents. Changes in exposure to trade or some other international factor are likely to change the dynamics of the policymaking process, rendering less costly, under certain conditions, the possibility of legislators granting protection to geographically dispersed producer groups. Protection granted to group A last year may make more palatable protection to group B this year, particularly if the welfare of group A has increased as a result of changes in production technology. Unless we know what groups want, it is unreasonable to assume that politicians will initiate the process of granting protection for their own sake. Second, the author conceptualizes the calculus of protection dichotomously; protection is either granted or not. Rather the puzzle is a choice between levels and instruments of protection. Could the electoral rules and industrial geographic concentration matter less with different policy instruments?

Despite considerable merit, both approaches are conceptually and empirically handicapped. On the one hand, specifying only the demand or supply side of policy yields an incomplete, at best, understanding of the dynamics of subsidy protection (Zahariadis, 2002).

Sacrificing empirical realism for theoretical parsimony is not a virtue; "an adequate theory of trade protection will require a model that successfully marries electoral politics with pressure group politics" (Riezman and Wilson, 1995, p. 112). On the other hand, empirical work on nontariff barriers, an example of which is subsidies, suggests that pressure groups and state interests interact in specific ways to produce levels of protection (Mansfield and Busch, 1995; Henisz and Mansfield, 2006). The question is how to retain theoretical parsimony and still model both sides of the equation.

Synthetic approaches, which blend insights from several perspectives, abound (e.g., Baldwin, 1985). But the point is to construct them in a satisfying way. A synthetic approach is valuable not simply because it is more complete, but also because defending bold theoretical statements about the independent impact of variables may not be empirically plausible. Conditional hypotheses are needed to specify the impact of variables under different circumstances in a variety of national settings (Odell, 1990, pp. 165–166). Majoritarian rules, for example, may not matter by themselves, as in the example of the United Kingdom, but they may actually make a difference in a federal setting, such as that of the United States. Grossman and Helpman (1994) provide such a model.

Common Agency and the Political Contribution Model

Grossman and Helpman (1994) develop a model within a specific-factors framework, that is, assets have no better alternative use, which explains the equilibrium structure of trade protection. The model serves as the point of departure for my own asset influence model, which I elaborate in subsequent chapters.

Protection is conceptualized as a common agency problem where many principals, that is, industry groups, lobby a common agent, that is, government, for support (Dixit, Grossman, and Helpman, 1997). Groups lobby politicians to maximize benefits to their members by providing campaign contributions. Policymakers choose to curry favors, that is, grant trade protection, based on an objective function that takes into account both their own chances for reelection and the voters' welfare. The model's political equilibrium is examined as a two-stage, simultaneous, noncooperative game where lobbies choose their contribution schedules in the first, and the government sets the policy in the second.

The results suggest that government and lobby groups have several options under certain conditions. It makes a difference if the groups compete against each other or if they are able to form coalitions and pass the deadweight loss to the entire economy. Each group's amount of contribution will continue to rise until the marginal benefit derived from contributions equals zero. At this point, the level of benefits depends on the group's political power. In sectors with large domestic output, the owners of those factors stand to gain considerably from a rise in prices while the economy as a whole loses little from protection if imports are low. Heavily organized groups in those sectors have strong incentives to demand protection. Their ability to get it depends on the weight that government places on the country's welfare. The authors assume locally truthful contribution schedules, that is, the shape of the schedule reveals the lobby's true preferences at equilibrium point. Policymakers are also assumed to like increasing contribution schedules because this raises their chances for reelection—the model assumes money is the main vehicle for doing so. Hence they have incentives to "sell" protection to the highest bidder provided the costs of protection do not outweigh the benefits of aggregate welfare. The more policymakers favor campaign contributions over general welfare, the higher the absolute value of protection will be.

At equilibrium, with truthful contribution schedules, the choice depends not on the level of actual contributions but on the extent of organization by affected groups. Because groups do not compete against one another for protection but against the politician's estimate of consumer welfare, that is, the social cost, the level of funding is less important than political power and organization. Besides, groups do not want the contributions to grow too large. As the share of organized voters increases, the rate of protection for the affected industries decreases. They argue that at extreme levels of organization, that is, when all groups are organized as in corporatist systems for instance, free trade prevails. The rivalry between groups is most intense and the government captures all the contribution benefits. When organized groups are few in number, the equilibrium outcome will be sectoral subsidies. All in all, the authors hypothesize that protection is a function of demands by powerful groups most affected by trade, measured by the ratio of domestic output to imports; their ability to pass the cost onto the rest of society, measured by the import demand elasticity; and the organizational characteristics of lobbying, measured by a dummy variable capturing the existence of organization in the particular industry.

Empirical evidence tends to support their overall hypotheses in the United States and in developing countries. Goldberg and Maggi

(1999) test the predictions against evidence in the United States. They collect data from 1983 and proceed to estimate the coverage ratio of nontariff barriers. Politically organized industries are measured as those that spend an amount above a threshold level on campaign contributions. Goldberg and Maggi's findings generally support the model's predictions. The authors also estimate the weight that policymakers place on campaign contributions. They assert that policymakers place up to 70 times as much weight on aggregate welfare as on contributions, levels that are implausibly high as the original modelers conclude (Grossman and Helpman, 2002, p. 18). Other analysts, using again data from the United States, find similar patterns (Gawande and Bandyopadhyay, 2000). They add to the overall predictions of the model that protection of intermediate goods also tends to increase protection in final goods. Shifting focus, Mitra, Thomakos, and Ulubaşoğlu (2002) reach similar conclusions in the case of a developing country, Turkey. They add a temporal dimension by examining the model's predictions against two years, 1983 and 1990. They, too, find that politically organized industries that face higher inverse import penetration ratios are likely to enjoy more protection than others. The authors also add that the finding varies according to political regimes. It is likely to hold better in democracies than in dictatorships because the taste for campaign contributions in the latter case declines (Mitra, 1999). National institutional parameters obviously alter the results of the model, but there is no systematic treatment of this point in the literature.

The G-H model has many beneficial attributes because it is parsimonious yet explanatory of trade protection. It takes into account the policy process as well as the organizational and political characteristics of lobbying. It suffers, however, from three major limitations. First, it assumes constant world prices. Do external economic forces play a role? Do they mitigate or amplify demands for more subsidies? Second, it assumes a framework with only immobile factors. As factors move across industries, however costly or slow the process may be, the amount of harm caused by trade and the intensity of lobbying will wane. Hence the incentives and level of campaign contributions are a direct function of asset specificity. Third, the model looks only at the organizational characteristics of lobbying without taking into account national institutional parameters that greatly affect lobbying. Politicians are not completely free to listen to anyone they choose and neither do all lobbies have equal access to government across countries. For example, governments sanction a specific hierarchy in corporatist settings, forcing a certain level of aggregation that simply does not exist in pluralist institutional arrangements (Katzenstein, 1985). The omission of institutions may be understandable in a single national context, but the argument must hold across different national contexts as well. National institutions cannot be accepted as given or as unimportant if there are clear indications they make a difference (Kapstein, 2000).

Moreover, the political contribution model was empirically tested using U.S. and Turkish data, which are limited. Grossman and Helpman (1994, p. 835) explicitly state that the model applies to a small open (and implicitly developed) economy, which of course rules out the United States as a good case study. In addition, the inclusion of Turkey, while important in its own right, limits the generalizability of the findings to a developing country. My contribution to the literature on asset specificity is the inclusion of a depiction of the policy process, which renders conditional the derived hypotheses. In the light of the fact that subsidies and tariffs are different instruments of protection and empirical tests of the G-H model stop with tariffs, does the logic of their model regarding tariffs also apply to subsidies?

Chapter 3

Globalization and State Aid

Globalisation has so far been a storm. The hurricane is yet to come.

—*Heinrich von Pierer, chairman of Siemens*[1]

Giving away another vital U.S. industry to foreign interests is yet one more example of globalization run amok.

—*Edward Wytkind, president of AFL-CIO Transportation Trades Department*[2]

Globalisation is a positive sum game in the aggregate but one that produces both winners and losers.

—*Danny Leipziger, vice president of the World Bank, and Michael Spence, Nobel laureate in economics*[3]

I build the asset influence model of subsidization by retaining the logic of the G-H model but adding several modifications of my own. In this way, their model works as a platform from which I can build hypotheses that may disentangle the complicated story of protectionism. Any empirical validation does not strictly verify (or not) their findings although specific hypotheses may be confirmed. A major difference refers to the level of analysis. Whereas their model was developed at the industrial sector level within a single country framework, I apply it to the level of the entire manufacturing domain (many industries) within a multiple country framework. Consequently, I drop some of their concerns with differences in contributions among groups to concentrate on other issues of importance at the national level. I also differentiate between objectives, instruments, and sectors—manufacturing and agriculture—to explore variations in model applicability.

To correct for the problems outlined in the previous chapter, I substitute (1) elasticity estimates with asset mobility on the rationale that the degree of harm and the ability to pass on the cost are a function of asset specificity and (2) lobby organization with national institutional configurations on the basis that they determine the levels of lobby organization and access to power. While organizational characteristics at the industry level are important for industry-level questions, their inclusion at the national level is useless. I assume industries are organized, and I conceptualize organizational characteristics as a question of access. Such a shift in focus permits me to look for the answer in national institutional characteristics.

I also take one step back to estimate the winners and losers of globalization. Which group is likely to be the most vocal in favor of protection? Grossman and Helpman (1994) assume all groups value protection because it increases profits, and they model a process that explains which group is most likely to succeed. Following Frieden and Rogowski (1996), I estimate the preferences of groups as a function of external factors, that is, globalization, before modeling the process of domestic political influence.

Consider an economy producing n goods with three factors, each having varying degrees of asset specificity. As the economy becomes more exposed to global economic conditions, some sectors begin to feel the "pain" by witnessing declining prices. Of those, the owners of the more specific factors form lobby groups along industry lines to demand more protection (subsidies). Politicians maximize an objective function with two components: contributions from lobbies and maximum aggregate welfare. The model is conceptualized as taking place in two stages. During the first stage, each lobby presents government with a contribution schedule that incorporates the value of all subsidies to its members minus lobbying costs. Lobbies know the government's calculus and incorporate that information into their contribution schedules. This stage represents the demand side of the puzzle. In the second stage, the government chooses from the menu of schedules and proceeds to collect the contributions. This represents the supply side of protection. Using this framework as a background to my model, I add the effects of globalization, asset specificity, and national institutions, and proceed to explore their implications for the puzzle of subsidization. Figure 3.1 graphs the argument that guides the analysis in this and subsequent chapters.

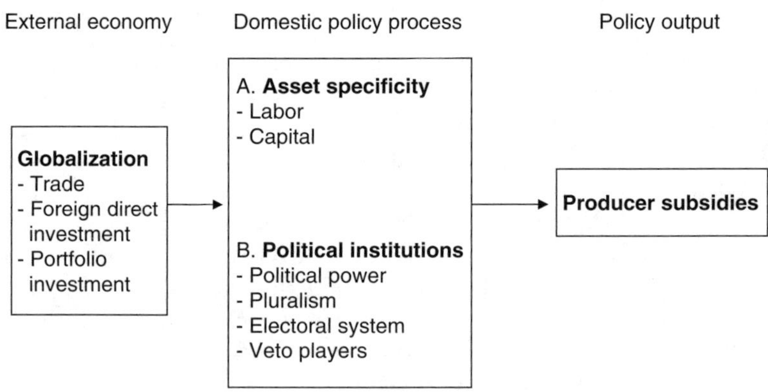

Figure 3.1 The asset influence model of subsidization.

TRENDS IN GLOBALIZATION

Most models of protection begin with a focus on a single country, which faces constant world prices. This simplification permits a sharper focus on domestic politics (Helpman, 2002, p. 191). The intent is to model the interaction between domestic winners, losers, and policymakers under specific conditions. While I, too, focus on domestic politics, I also examine the effects of globalization to estimate, rather than assume, the winners and losers from trade.

Greater exposure to the world economy shapes the preferences of social actors. An exogenous easing of international economic exchange, that is, a decrease in the costs or increase in the rewards of such exchange, increases international, as opposed to domestic, returns of economic activity, creating domestic winners and losers at least in the short run. Some groups will profit from reducing the return differential while others will not. The losers are more likely to demand protection.

In the remainder of the chapter, I investigate the effects of increased exposure to global economic activity on subsidies. I first explore the various aspects of global economic activity to show that it has different components. I then examine the levels of these components—trade, FDI, and portfolio investment—and their differential impact on subsidies. Finally, I close the analysis by discussing issues of measurement to show more clearly and concretely how the levels of exposure to global markets affect the disbursement of subsidies.

WHAT IS GLOBALIZATION?

The globalist view is simplistic. True, the world has become more economically integrated, but integration has proceeded further in some respects but not others. Two points are highlighted in this section. First, globalization has several dimensions. Unless they are disentangled, any estimated effects on the domestic economy will be misleading. Second, countries are exposed to global economic forces at different levels. Such exposure also varies over time. Global economic forces in turn condition the intensity of government response.

Globalization is an issue of major importance in current analytical thinking because significant economic transformations have taken place in the last 20 years in the global economy. Globalists contend that the world has gotten economically much smaller, which is of course an accurate observation. Production has become more internationalized as different countries contribute to various stages of the production process of tradable goods (Berger and associates, 2005). For example, automobile manufacturing is now a truly multinational endeavor as facilities in many countries are employed to build the final product (Thomas, 1997). But what does globalization mean? The term is slippery, leading analysts to use it in ways that suits their needs. Nevertheless, a working definition is an essential first step in analyzing the impact of global economic trends or forces that affect the domestic political economy.

The term "globalization" is used here to refer "to a process—an evolution of closer economic integration by way of increased trade [and] foreign investment" (Weinstein, 2005, p. 2). The definition is purposefully economic in nature to differentiate it from its cultural and other social dimensions, which are important but irrelevant to the study (e.g., Stiglitz, 2003; Eriksen, 2007; Scholte, 2005; Steger, 2003. It also excludes immigration, which, although relevant to the question at hand, presents serious empirical problems owing to the lack of reliable data. I concentrate here only on two dimensions of market integration, trade and capital, which affect the production of goods.

The relative ease with which productive assets can be moved across national boundaries is now an indisputable fact. The increasing ability of owners of these assets to move them at will in search of higher rates of return has tremendous implications for domestic political economies. Protection in the form of subsidies distorts the return rates, causing an exodus to other sectors of the economy. In other cases, asset owners may find it more profitable to move their assets out of the country. Indeed, the whole world presents a delectable menu of options. As the rate of mobility increases, the range of options expands.

The fundamental issue in the global political economy is the presence of national borders. While economic activity, such as the production of automobiles, is becoming more global in nature, political organization is still based on the notion of states. Some analysts even predict the end of the state as a bounded economic entity. Ohmae (1991, p. 18), for example, is very clear: "On a political map, the boundaries between countries are as clear as ever. But on a competitive map, a map showing the real flows of financial and industrial activity, those boundaries have largely disappeared."

Nevertheless, the ideas of life, liberty, and the pursuit of happiness are still best understood, and pursued, within national boundaries. Leaving aside the political goods that states provide, such as security, even economic services, such as trade, are still greatly affected by borders. The presence of a national border appears to inhibit trade. A study by McCallum (1995) found that even in the porous (in the sense of ease of crossing) border between the United States and Canada, trade among Canadian provinces and among U.S. states still outnumbers trade between the two countries by a factor of twenty. Although subsequent studies have substantially reduced this estimate, national borders still remain an impediment to free trade (Helliwell and Schembri, 2005). Borders in the EU, where trade barriers have been officially eliminated, have an estimated penalty of four times the transport costs or an equivalent of a 37 percent tariff (Berger and associates, 2005, p. 111)! Add to this the lack of common currency (in some countries) or language and the amount of trade between countries diminishes even more rapidly in relation to domestic trade.

Moreover, even though governments find it increasingly difficult to control fluctuations in economic well-being, they are still held responsible for any adverse effects. This is particularly true of democratic societies, where accountability of leadership is a crucial and cherished democratic right. As McKeown (1999, p. 27) makes it abundantly clear, in industrialized democracies protection from the adverse consequences of trade is commonplace because "the size of the protected blocs [of voters] is large enough to affect national elections." To understand, therefore, why this happens, one must explore the dynamics of increased exposure to globalization.

EXPOSURE TO INCREASING TRADE

The expansion of trade in goods and services is an important feature of globalization. The volume of world trade has expanded more rapidly since World War II than world production. The gap between the two has widened even further since the mid-1980s. As Irwin (2005, p. 20) points out, world merchandise exports rose by 80 percent in the 1990s while world production in the same goods increased by a mere 27 percent! "Merchandise trade has grown faster than world output in almost every one of the past 55 years" (Wolf, 2006, p. 1).

To be sure, the rise in export numbers is somewhat misleading. Drucker (1997, p. 165) cites a study by the U.S. Department of Commerce that estimates that more than 40 percent of exported goods in the developed world go to company affiliates and subsidiaries. Because of vertical specialization, companies import and export materials in different stages of the production process. They no longer produce many of their material inputs internally, preferring to capture low prices and expertise in different parts of the world. Berger and her colleagues describe this fragmentation of production as taking place in many sectors and making "it possible to break apart research, development, design, manufacturing and marketing and move them to different companies and locations around the world . . . [In fact, the authors recommend that] companies need to keep within their own walls *only* those activities in which they can compete with the best in the world" (2005, p. 51; emphasis in the original). To return to the automobile example above, engines for U.S. automobiles may be assembled in China using Korean steel, Japanese expertise, and Chinese labor. The fact that engines have to cross national borders several times to exploit lower costs is recorded as higher volume of trade even though fairly similar products leave or enter a country. International trade has gone up, but production remains relatively low because the good is still the same. Hummels, Ishii, and Yi (2001) estimate that one-third of the increase in world trade since 1970 can be accounted for by the phenomenon of vertical specialization.

But the fact remains that trade has expanded dramatically. Even in the last 14 years or so, exports and imports in constant year 2000 prices—using consumer price index figures—show an increase of 9.9 percent (OECD, 2006a)! The OECD continues to be the world's importer with the rate of imports outpacing that of exports during this period by 1.8 percent. Trade deficits have widened annually, except for the years 1993 and 1995, from 3.3 percent of total trade in 1990 to 4.1 percent of total trade in 2003.

Not only have absolute numbers risen, but the importance of trade in the domestic economies of OECD countries has become more pronounced. Trade exposure in the entire OECD area, measured by total trade over annual GDP, has risen by 35 percent (OECD, 2006a). Total trade exposure, exports plus imports, went up from 32 percent

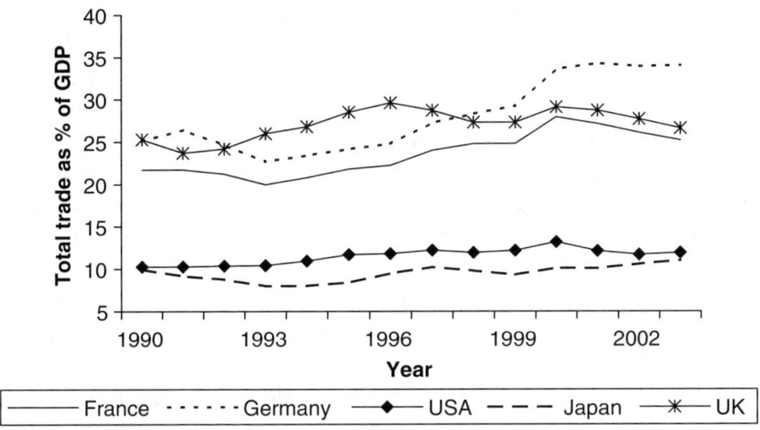

Figure 3.2   Trade flows.
Source: OECD (2006a); IMF (various years).

in 1990 to 43.1 percent of GDP in 2003. The figures for the EU during the same period were a little higher—38.2 percent in 1990 to 48.1 percent in 2003. There are obviously differences between European and other OECD countries. Trade matters more to the Europeans than to the others.

Figure 3.2 provides relevant figures for the world's five biggest economies. The first striking difference is that trade matters less to the U.S. and Japanese economies than it does to the three European economies. The total trade figures for the United States rose a slight 15.5 percent from 10.3 percent of annual GDP to 11.9 percent in 2003. Japan's corresponding figures are less. Despite Japan being hailed as an achiever of export-led growth, total trade matters less for Japan than any other country in this sample. The figures clearly show an increase of only 11 percent from 9.9 percent of total trade exposure to 11 percent during the same period. The three European economies appear to be more in sync with one another rather than with the other two major economies. The most exposed large economy, and the one where trade seems to matter most, is Germany. Total trade exposure grew phenomenally by 35.4 percent from 25.1 percent in 1990 to 34 percent in 2003. France experienced a modest increase of 16.1 percent in the same period, while the exposure in the UK grew by only 5.1 percent.

There are numerous reasons why some countries are more exposed to international trade than others. The most important reason has of course to do with comparative advantage. Countries specialize in producing goods in which they are most efficient and trade for the rest. Neoclassical economic theory supplements this view with one more reason. Smaller countries tend to focus on acquiring economies of scale. Because they cannot produce all the goods that their consumers want, smaller countries tend to specialize in a smaller range of goods and trade for the rest. The implication is that the range of goods they export will be somewhat more limited than the range of goods they import, and that trade matters more to them than to larger countries. The data in figure 3.2 reflect this fact. Trade matters more to the smaller economies, the UK is admittedly an anomaly, than to either the United States or Japan. Garrett (1998, p. 57) adds one more factor. Gravity models in international trade emphasize the role of geographic proximity. The closer economies are to one another, the more they are likely to trade with each other. So European countries are likely to have higher ratios of trade relative to annual economic output than, say, the United States, simply for geographic reasons.

Two points may be gleaned from the discussion above. First, absolute figures of imports and exports have increased since 1990. Trade in 2003 played a bigger role in the OECD than it did in 1990. Second, exposure to international trade varies by country. Consequently, the winners and losers are likely to be different as the intensity of losses varies by country. The implication is that the preferences of social actors are likely to vary across countries.

EXPOSURE TO INTERNATIONAL CAPITAL

The situation is somewhat similar with capital mobility. In 2003, $576.3 billion in FDI left the OECD to the rest of the world, up from $236 billion in 1990. In the same year, roughly $459 billion came in, up from $175.3 in 1990 (OECD, 2005b). The implication is that flows increased dramatically, reaching a peak of $2.5 trillion in 2000. Both inflows and outflows seem to be on a steady decline since 2000 following a steady increase in figures that accelerated since 1997 (figure 3.3). Although the numbers are obviously different, the decline bears similarities to the beginning of the previous decade. The OECD has traditionally played the role of net exporter of capital, and this is borne out by the data, with the exception of flows in 2000. Net outflows in 2003 reached a sizable $134 billion after hitting a high of $152 billion in 1999.

The overall numbers, however, hide substantial variations across countries (OECD, 2005b). Just like in the case of trade, significant variation exists between countries. The United States continues to be

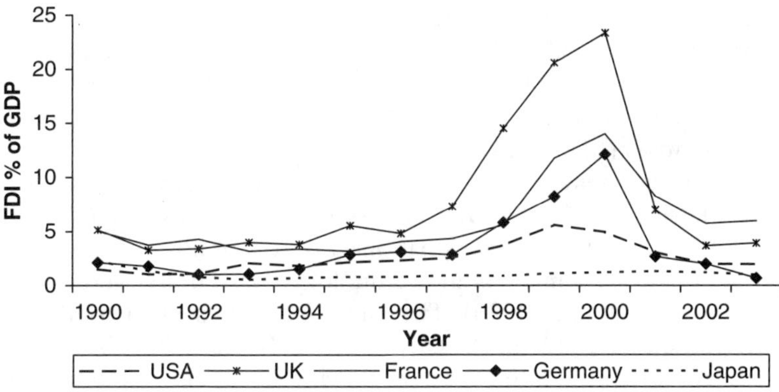

Figure 3.3 Trends in foreign direct investment.
Source: OECD (2006a); IMF (various years).

the main beneficiary of inflows as well as outflows. In absolute numbers it has attracted the majority of funds coming into the OECD among major economies. In 2003, the net FDI outflow was at a sizable $73.5 billion, the highest amount in the OECD. As the authors of the study report, 5 of the 25 biggest cross-border mergers and acquisitions (M&As) in 2004 had a U.S. company as the acquirer (OECD, 2005b, p. 12). On the other side of the spectrum is Japan, which continues to be the least exposed to international capital (in absolute figures) during the period under study. Since 1992, less FDI came out of Japan than any other major economy with the exception of Germany in 2003. In terms of inflows, Japan has consistently followed all the other economies with the exception of Germany in 1992. The reason is the recession and deflation that plagued Japan for most of the past decade.

However, the story is different in relative terms. Figure 3.3 presents relevant FDI data for the three largest European economies. Japan and the United States are included for comparative purposes. Japan, Germany, and the United States have received on average FDI of 2.33 percent of annual GDP from 1990 to 2003. This is low relative to most European countries, which have fared better. In absolute terms, the UK and France follow somewhat similar patterns. They are, respectively, the first and second largest net investors in the world during the period 1995–2004 (OECD, 2005b, p. 23). Somewhat surprisingly in recent years, Germany experienced deterioration in its position as outward investor, rather than inward receiver, of direct investment, partly as a result of repayment of loans by subsidiaries of multinational companies (MNCs) to their parent companies. In relative terms, the British and French average of FDI over GDP is 6.87 percent, attracting almost three times the average of the other three countries (figure 3.3).

Looking at capital mobility from the point of view of individual firms, the situation in the OECD is similar. M&As are becoming an increasingly bigger part of cross-national investment flows as companies seek to tap into new markets and technology more cheaply and quickly (Simmons, 1999, pp. 49–50). The value of M&As in the period since 1995 peaked in 2000 to a total of $2,295 billion (OECD, 2005b, p. 20). Although the numbers went down dramatically in the ensuing years, they rebounded in 2004. By 2005, the total value was estimated to be $1,051.7 billion, a level lower but still close to that of 2001. But this figure masks differences across countries. Although most cross-border M&As proceed without backlash, there are significant impediments at times in many countries. Witness the furor in Congress over the prospect of CNOOC, a Chinese oil company, trying to buy Unocal in 2005; the British retroactive change of the rules in 1988 to prevent a Kuwaiti company from acquiring a big stake in British Petroleum; or the French reaction to the hostile bid against Arcelor, a Luxembourg-based steel company, in early 2006. In all cases politicians vocally and assertively intervened in support of their constituent interests against corporate takeover by foreigners (Thornhill, 2006).

In terms of short-term capital, the situation is somewhat different. This type of investment is naturally more volatile. Just like in the case of FDI, portfolio investment rose dramatically in the late 1990s to 2000, only to fall precipitously since. However, it rebounded in 2003 (figure 3.4). Again, the UK, France, and Germany received the highest amounts as a percent of their respective GDPs. They got a bit more than twice as much on average as did Japan and the United States during 1991–2003. Interestingly, Japan is the only country in this sample whose short-term capital figures in 2003 still lagged behind those of 1991. Even more interestingly, for all the problems with growing economic integration that made France infamous recently—for example, the youth riots, the rejection of the EU constitution in 2005, and the student riots against labor laws enacted to combat unemployment among youths in 2006—France has been the leader in terms of inflows and outflows of both short- and long-term capital since the beginning of 2001.

Why do national governments impose capital controls? Why are we not seeing greater exposure to internationally mobile capital?

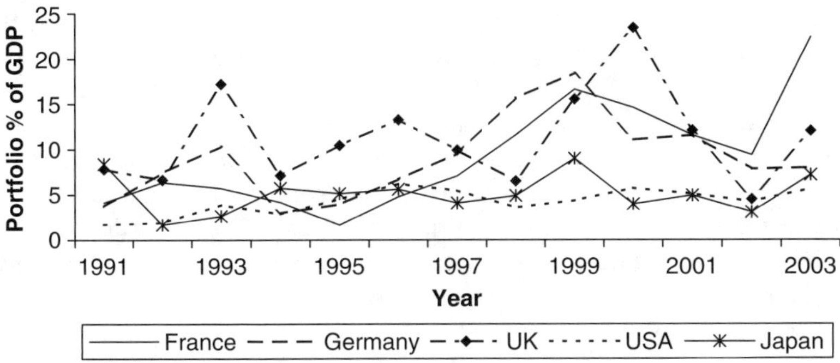

Figure 3.4 Trends in portfolio investment.
Source: OECD (2006a); IMF (various years).

Controls limit the volatility of short-run flows so that currency crises, for example, may be avoided (Bhagwati, 1998). In addition, controls are used to retain domestic savings, that could presumably leave the country in search of more favorable rates of return, and to maintain the domestic tax base (Mathieson and Rojas-Suarez, 1994). Most controls involved some type of exchange restriction on capital account convertibility, limits on capital movements, and taxes on external financial transactions. It all ultimately came down to defending the fixed exchange regime and having enough capital to finance government expenditures (Alesina, Grilli, and Milesi-Ferretti, 1994). However, the collapse of the Bretton Woods system ushered in a new era of volatility that rendered obsolete fixed exchange rates and increased dramatically the cost of monitoring possible violations of controls. The twin objectives of controls weakened substantially, and by the early 1980s, capital mobility predictably began to rise.

There are several reasons why capital mobility has increased in recent years. After taking a nosedive in the period since World War I, international investment as a percent of GDP is now at levels higher than any attained since the 1870s (Obstfeld and Taylor, 2003). By any measure, more countries are now more exposed to international capital than at any other time in postwar history.[4] The main reason for the explosion in cross-border capital flows was the U.S. current account deficit in the 1980s (Simmons, 1999, p. 44). Even after the deficit was reduced, flows continued unabated, exhibiting resilience and inertia. "Once internationalized, firms and investors do not readily retreat from their global vantage." Such flows have created the requisite conditions for the removal of any leftover controls. Responding to the needs of producer firms, institutional lenders, such as banks, demanded reductions in capital controls to service their clients. Bhagwati (1998, p. 11) adds to the mix the ideology of markets. Once markets were considered problematic, rendering state intervention necessary; "the steady move away from central planning . . . toward letting markets function has now reached across many sectors and countries." These reasons, coupled with advances in technology and cuts in transportation costs, have conspired to force governments to drop national capital controls in the industrialized world, albeit at different rates (Goodman and Pauly, 1993).

It is worth pointing out that countries most exposed to trade are not necessarily those most exposed to capital. A brief comparison between the figures showing trade and FDI or trade and portfolio investment reveals the differences. Trade, but not investment, matters most in Germany. In contrast in the United States, investment matters more than trade. Japan seems to be the least exposed country of the five examined in both trade and both types of investment. France and the UK are somewhere in the middle. The differences are of course based on averages. Each country has experienced variations in exposure over time, tempering the strength of the claims made above. For example, Japan had the highest amount of FDI inflows among the five countries in 1990 although it fell to the next to the lowest by 2003 (OECD, 2005b). Similarly, the UK's exposure in terms of total trade as a percent of annual economic output grew to the highest levels of all the countries in the figure during the period 1993–1998. The situation is similar in regard to Germany's trade for the period since 1998. Differences exist across dimensions, countries, and time.

Why do these differences exist? Garrett (1998, p. 58) speculates that smaller economies have a greater need to maintain a stable balance of payments. Huge fluctuations under economically liberal capital regimes may cause major disruptions in trade. There is significant potential for volatility in flows, particularly reversals, at the onset of trouble, what Calomiris (2005, p. 45) calls the "sudden-stop" problem. When capital evaporates, firms are hard pressed to come up with the funds to repay their creditors, leading to significant economic and political unrest. Smaller economies are likely to be hit harder by this problem because of their shallower domestic capital markets, which could serve as alternative financing sources. Consequently, smaller countries tend to impose capital controls to cushion the impact of a potential disruption. Therefore, exposure to international capital is likely to be lower on average in those economies.

The analysis of country exposure to trade and capital has revealed two interesting findings. First, globalization is a multidimensional concept. Understanding its effects necessitates a differentiation between trade and capital. Second, countries differ in their exposure to the global economy. Differences exist not only across countries but also vary over time within the same country. Analysis of the impact of globalization on subsidies requires careful specification of the dimensions of globalization across countries and over time.

GLOBALIZATION AND SUBSIDIES

Globalization affects subsidy disbursement. The impact is not uniform across countries but it varies on the basis of trade or capital. Although greater exposure to global economic forces generally tends to result in positive aggregate economic welfare, the effects are varied and often contradictory.

Which actors are likely to experience gains or losses? To answer this question, I turn to Frieden and Rogowski's (1996) insight on factor returns and actor preferences. They argue that preferences are shaped by returns, which are in turn shaped by exposure to global economic activities. Greater exposure to globalization leads to greater pressures to import global economic trends in the domestic political economy (p. 31). It follows that under easing conditions political ramifications will be even greater for the domestic political economy.

If all else is equal, world prices and domestic prices should be equal. Prices are signals by which information is transmitted. The greater the difference between prices, the stronger the pressure to exit in search of higher returns. For a moment, let us assume constant specificity so that we may focus analytically on the effects of exposure to exogenous economic activities. An exogenous easing of international exchange has predictable effects on domestic factor returns. Easing may take place because of advances in technology, fluctuations in transportation costs, financial crises, and the like. As easing intensifies, domestic producers feel the effects differently. The greater the difference between world and domestic prices, the higher the costs of protection, and consequently the greater the differences in factor returns. The groups that witness lower domestic prices because different sectors experience different exposures at any one time will prefer protection. Domestic prices have to increase or groups will exit. They are the losers. Those groups that experience gains from exposure, that is, high domestic prices, will prefer greater liberalization. They are the winners.

According to Ricardo's theory of comparative advantage, countries will experience welfare benefits when they specialize in the production of goods in which they are the most efficient producers, and trade for the rest. But efficiency is not a given. It varies from country to country and over time within the same country. This implies that even if factor endowments remain the same over time, meaning that a country always has abundant labor or capital, there would still be significant economic and social costs associated with trade. When imports begin to make inroads in the domestic market, firms have to adjust. Those firms closest to a country's comparative advantage will demand more trade openness and consequently fewer subsidies because they stand to gain.

Demands for more subsidies are likely to come first from those firms that compete directly with imports. As imports begin to flood the domestic market, market shares and profitability begin to shrink. Firms will demand relief or at least a temporary respite from foreign competition for two reasons. First, they might argue that foreign competitors are subsidized so they need to receive some aid to "level the playing field" (Snape, 1991). This argument is most often heard in agriculture, textiles, and generally labor-intensive industries in OECD countries. The reason is because technology, rather than low-cost labor, is the main factor of comparative advantage in industrialized democracies. Second, firms may argue that a certain level of temporary subsidies is needed to provide time for those firms to adjust their production costs to new realities. This is particularly true when the prices of basic input factors rise sharply and unexpectedly. For example, the oil price hikes of the 1970s and more recently have generated demands for temporary relief.

Adjustment entails costs, such as social upheaval when laying off workers, or corporate insecurity when designing new and more efficient production processes. In theory these costs have to be borne by the firm, but in practice many firms prefer to seek subsidies. The time horizon of subsidies makes a difference. In the short run, industries hurt by imports are likely to demand subsidies to protect themselves. But in the long run, industries that have been subsidized *and* incurred adjustment costs are more likely to favor fewer trade barriers because they are now more flexible and in a better position to adjust to competing imports (Hathaway, 1998). They may have also dispersed the various stages of production to different countries, making these firms more likely to favor reducing barriers to trade and by implication expanding their own ability to structure their production in ways they see fit (Schwartz, 2000, p. 279).

Losers from import competition are more likely to lobby for subsidies than winners from export subsidies for two reasons (Baldwin, 1994, pp. 71–72). First, gains from subsidized exports increase profits. It in turn attracts entry by new competitors, which depresses profits and lowers the gains from lobbying and subsidies. Firms that stand to lose, however, will fight harder for subsidies to increase their below-market returns. They are not likely to face new competitors until their profit rates return to normal market levels. Second, prospect theory suggests that actors respond to losses differently than to gains. They will fight harder to avoid losses than to enjoy gains (e.g., Levy, 1997). This means that firms that experience a decline in their market shares will fight harder to reverse it than firms who are gaining market share.

However, it should be emphasized that demands are also likely to come from export-oriented firms. Milner and Yoffie (1989) add that import-competing firms with no foreign operations tend to fight for protection, that is, subsidies, while export-dependent firms prefer lower trade barriers. But they also argue that even in the case of export-oriented firms, the rate of erosion of market share affects a firm's preference. When international market shares rapidly decline, exporting firms are likely to prefer protectionism (subsidies). When there is slow erosion in market share, firms are in favor of strategic trade policy, that is, trade barriers for the home market if foreign markets are protected. The main point is that analysis that focuses solely on import competition misses an important piece of the puzzle. Both inflows and outflows should be taken into analytical consideration.

Global economic forces create short-term losses (and gains), providing strong incentives for affected groups to seek protection. Higher rates of exposure to both trade and FDI should increase subsidization and general protection. Witness the rancor in France created by Mittal Steel's hostile bid for Arcelor, which is not even a French company. The same happened in Spain, Poland, Italy, the United States, and elsewhere. As the number of cross-border acquisitions rises, so does the fear of political unpopularity, which raises the specter of interference and protection. For example, the image of private equity investors has been tarnished in Germany "as locusts bent on asset-stripping" (Smith, 2006, p. 13). But one should not take this argument too far. As Hollinger et al. (2006a, p. 13) boldly state, "While the politicians agonize over further [European] integration, some of the corporate titans are disregarding national borders in the battle to unlock investor value." Despite media attention to a few celebrated examples, most foreign acquisitions occur without fanfare. The implication is that voices for protection will grow as trade and FDI go up.

H3.1: Higher levels of trade openness are likely to lead to more subsidies.

H3.2: Higher levels of FDI openness are likely to lead to more subsidies.

However, not all globalization is created equal. There is one exception to the argument made above. Trade in widgets is very different from trade in dollars (Bhagwati, 1998). Short-term investment flows have a different impact on calls for subsidies. Such flows have increased exponentially in recent years largely due to the dismantling of capital controls in the 1980s under pressure by international organizations and the United States (Berger and associates, 2005, p. 14). As capital controls disappear, new risks and opportunities for higher rates of return emerge. Investors now move capital in and out of countries with the push of a button. Greater exposure to global capital may increase the chances of financial crises and recovery costs (Blyth, 2003, p. 242; Bhagwati, 1998). But the rise in capital flows puts a damper on protection.

Setting short-term flows apart from FDI or trade focuses attention on two things: portfolio investment's impersonal nature and subsidization's deadweight costs. Subsidies tend to be targeted responses, that is, they involve protection in reaction to specific threats from foreign companies, whether the threats are perceived as coming in the form of imports (in the case of trade) or locally produced goods (in the form of FDI). Portfolio investment is impersonal in the sense that there is no specified target. The threat comes from foreign equity capital, which involves no sunk costs. Companies are more reluctant now to sink long-term capital into buying brick and mortar facilities, when they have other options at their disposal, such as outsourcing (Berger and associates, 2005, p. 15). Protection punishes host governments and domestic firms by creating a less-attractive investment environment. Subsidies create inefficiencies in resource allocation. This type of inefficiency and the deadweight costs associated with lobbying for subsidies increase the cost of raising capital in the open market. Higher costs lower the rate of asset return. Unlike trade or FDI, the high cost and likelihood of punishment in the case of portfolio investment silences all but the strongest calls for more subsidies. For this reason, portfolio investment is likely to have the inverse effect.

H3.3: Higher levels of openness in portfolio investment are more likely to lead to lower subsidies.

MEASURING GLOBALIZATION

I collected data on all EU members, except Luxembourg, for the period 1991–2003. The paucity of separate national data and its unusually small size are the reasons for omitting that country.

Globalization is measured along the two dimensions postulated above: trade and capital. *Trade openness* is measured as annual percentage of exports plus imports of goods over GDP to get a sense of a country's trade integration in the world economy. Data are expressed in U.S. dollars, using average exchange rates, and are included in the OECD (2006a). Higher degrees of openness indicate higher exposure and greater significance of trade in the domestic economy.

I use similar logic to capture the essence of financial capital mobility. I calculate the percent ratio of total FDI flows over GDP in a given year in a given country to measure *FDI openness*. Higher percentages indicate greater market integration into the global economy. The bigger the portion of the total capital that comes from (or leaves for) abroad, the greater the exposure to the vagaries of the global economy will be. In the case of an increase in FDI, I expect countries to increase their subsidies. To further disentangle the effects of the time horizon of investments, I include one more ratio: *portfolio openness*, which is measured as percent portfolio investment over GDP on a national annual basis. Higher levels of FDI should lead to more subsidies, while higher levels of portfolio openness should lead to fewer subsidies.

Table 3.1 presents data on the three indicators used in this study. Data refer to 14 EU members (excluding Luxembourg). FDI flows are taken from the OECD (2005b) and figures measuring portfolio investment are taken from IMF (various years). What is striking about the indicators is that the means vary wildly. Countries are most exposed on average in terms of trade although FDI and

Table 3.1 Descriptive statistics of globalization variables*

Variable	Minimum	Maximum	Mean	Standard deviation
Trade openness	18.00	91.10	38.77	17.88
FDI openness	.13	163.27	7.62	14.10
Portfolio openness	1.01	201.30	19.51	32.87

* Percent of GDP
Source: OECD (2006a); IMF (various years).

portfolio investment are prone to more extreme fluctuations. Different countries have varying levels of exposure in terms of trade, FDI, and portfolio investment. Ireland in 2000 experienced the most dramatic increases in trade exposure while Spain was the least exposed in 1991. Greece received the least amount of FDI in 1998 while Belgium got the most in 2000. Not surprisingly, in the light of the low cost of moving capital across borders, portfolio investment experiences the wildest fluctuations over time. Ireland was the most exposed to portfolio investment in 2003. Spain received and invested abroad the least amounts in 1996.

Construct validity threats of indicators measuring capital flows are well known. Flows may reflect volatility in market conditions rather than evidence of capital market integration (e.g., Frankel, 1992). However, the use of alternative indicators is equally ridden with problems. Take the example of savings and investment correlations (Feldstein and Horioka, 1980). The reasoning behind the use of this indicator is simple. In a world of integrated financial markets, domestic savings should not greatly affect domestic investment because capital from abroad would be attracted to domestic investment opportunities. In a world, however, of limited international capital mobility, there should be high correlations between the two. Apart from problems with the assumptions upon which this measure is based, the most important issue for my purposes is practical. The indicator only provides estimates for a group of countries as a whole at a given point in time. Given the structure of my approach and the need to provide estimates for capital mobility across countries and over time, I cannot use it.

Other analysts use restrictions on capital flows as an indicator of mobility. Constructed from IMF estimates on restrictions on capital account flows, bilateral payments, and foreign deposits, this indicator is widely thought to be the most appropriate and accurate measure of international capital mobility (e.g., Garrett, 1998; Basinger and Hallerberg, 2004; Simmons, 1999). The problem with this indicator is that its value does not vary significantly over the time period under investigation. Restrictions on capital movements were formally abolished in EU member states and the United States by 1992. By the late 1990s, hardly any OECD country maintained serious restrictions. In other words, the value of the indicator for the period under investigation would be zero in most instances.

Still another widely used measure of capital mobility—covered interest rate parity—contains similar limitations. In a financially integrated world, the cost of capital across countries should converge. Deviations of such costs, captured by interest rates, may be attributed to various barriers, such as expectations of future inflation and exchange rates. Covered interest parity distinguishes among these barriers by using a forward contract to remove exchange rate risk (Popper, 1997). The main problem with this indicator is the introduction of the single currency in 1999, which eliminated currency risks for most EU members.

Finally, some analysts call attention to the *potential* for capital mobility; it is the potential for capital to exit rather than actual flows that has the greatest political consequences. Sinclair (2001, p. 96) argues that capital flows hide "important discontinuities." For example, there is evidence to support the notion that capital has a home bias because of government policies and domestic political institutions (Sobel, 1999). Rather than wandering around the globe in rational pursuit of the greatest return, most savings, in the United States or Japan for instance, are actually invested at home where the returns may not be the highest. Further rationalizing attention to potential for flows rather than actual flows, Thomas (1997, p. 55) claims that actual and potential mobility are complementary in that actual mobility lowers exit costs and makes firms' threats to exit more credible. This fact gives firms a tremendous advantage in negotiating terms of investment, and by extension subsidies, with host governments. Competition between states, whether in Europe or in the United States, has been blamed for an increase in state subsidies to attract individual firms to locate to that state (Thomas, 2000). For example, Alabama's incentive package to steel giant ThyssenKrupp in 2007 was valued at $811 million (roughly one-fourth of the total investment of $3.7 billion). While it was not as high as Louisiana's, which was competing for the same steel mill, the amount clearly shows that the credibility of a company choosing an alternative site surely increases the subsidies states are prepared to dole out to attract large investments. Governor Bob Riley makes the point very clear in his address to the Birmingham Rotary Club: "The day we do not offer an incentive package, then we are out of the running for any kind of economic development project of that magnitude" (Dean, 2007, p. 1B). It is precisely the potential of ThyssenKrupp choosing to locate elsewhere that convinced Alabama to purchase the land for $45 million, prepare the site for $314 million, and construct, among others, a $115 million port that allows the company to unload steel made in Brazil from ships docking in Mobile (Peacock, 2007, p. 3B; Sayre, 2007, p. 2D).

The problems with this argument are not that it does not make sense but the fact that potential is not a substitute for actual capital flows and that it is extremely difficult to measure. It involves engaging in considerable counterfactual and uncertain exercises, trying to disentangle who threatened whom and how the threat (potential) of mobility was used. Thomas (1997, p. 66), for example, posts the declining costs of telephone service and airline travel as giving "us an idea of the potential for moving productive capital internationally." True, but the problem is that it is unclear whether the indicator should measure averages or actual company data, and if so which company. Additionally, why focus just on telephone data and not power-operation costs, which, according to Louisiana governor Kathleen Blanco, were a major stumbling block in attracting a plant that uses a lot of power (Sayre, 2007, p. 2D). In short, although the potential for capital mobility has additional explanatory power in terms of exposure to global economic forces, it is no substitute for measuring the actual capital flows.

In addition to the aforementioned concerns, all alternative indicators show problems with robustness, depending on assumptions employed. For example, the savings-investment correlations assume a separation of savings and investment functions, which may not correspond to empirical reality (Mendoza, 1994, p. 85). Moreover, simulations seeking to approximate empirical conditions in two countries, Canada and Mexico, show that macroeconomic indicators used to measure capital mobility, such as those described above, are either not informative or are sensitive to specific conditions. "The best alternative," as Mendoza (1994, p. 108) appropriately concludes, is "an approach based on direct measurement of international flows of financial capital." For all their problems, direct measurement of capital flows still constitutes the simplest, best, and most informative way of capturing exposure to global financial capital.

CONCLUSION

In this chapter I laid the foundations of the asset influence model by investigating the impact of globalization on the call for more subsidies. As exposure to global economic forces increases, domestic producers experience pressures to adapt to world prices. If domestic prices are higher than world prices, then producers are likely to demand some form of subsidy protection to provide relief from the loss of profits. Other things being equal, higher exposure to trade and FDI will increase calls for more subsidies.

However, short-term capital is likely to have the inverse effect. Higher exposure to portfolio investment will render mute most calls for subsidies. The relatively costless movement of portfolio capital across borders in search of higher rates of return will likely put pressure on domestic producers to adapt to world markets. Any form of subsidization creates inefficiencies and deadweight losses, which in turn scares away potential investors. Given the low cost of cross-national movement, calls for more subsidies in this situation will likely fall on deaf ears.

Once the effects of external forces are specified, it is time to turn analytical attention to the domestic economy. Globalization exercises a strong impact on the decision to protect sectors and firms, but it is hardly the only variable of significance. How do gains and losses as a result of globalization translate into actor preferences and ultimately action?

ASSET SPECIFICITY AND THE DEMAND FOR SUBSIDIES

Even if the result is more profits for multinational corporations, do we truly believe that exporting those jobs will lead to a better life in this country, for our workers?

—Lou Dobbs, CNN business anchor[1]

Having shown the effects of globalization on subsidization efforts, I now turn my focus to the domestic policy process. While exposure to global economic forces has an important independent impact on subsidies, the effects are also filtered through domestic groups. Asset specificity, that is, the relative cost of moving productive assets across industries, has important implications for subsidies. The degree of asset specificity shapes the preferences of social actors for more protection (or not) through political coalitions and lobbying. Asset specificity among producer groups is then linked to their ability to demand more subsidies. Equally importantly, globalization shapes actor investments in more specific (or not) assets. The effects of asset specificity are therefore likely to vary in intensity depending on the level of exposure to global markets. Globalization has important independent and interactive effects.

I first examine the relationship between asset specificity and state subsidies. Groups with more specific assets are more likely to demand higher subsidies. Then I look more closely at the links between globalization and asset specificity. Globalization affects factor returns, which in turn influence asset specificity. If this is so, demands for subsidies by owners of more specific assets are likely to vary in strength depending on the level of exposure to globalization. Finally, I address measurement concerns with the variable of asset specificity to show more clearly where countries stand in terms of owning specific (or not) assets.

ASSET SPECIFICITY AND PROTECTION

Asset specificity raises the adjustment costs confronting firms in the face of foreign competition, altering a firm's or social actor's political behavior (Alt et al., 1999; Alt and Gilligan, 1994; Frieden, 1991). The asset influence model proposed here assumes social actors (be they individuals, firms, or unions) prefer policies that maximize their incomes. Economic characteristics can, therefore, determine the types of government policies actors prefer to see enacted. Preferences are shaped endogenously by the degree of external market liberalization and the ability of owners of factors of production to put these assets to alternative domestic uses (Frieden and Rogowski, 1996). The harder it is to move factors from one domestic activity to the next, the greater the likelihood that factor owners will favor this activity. Under these conditions, it is logical to expect actors to demand policies that privilege this activity, *ceteris paribus*.

Economic exchange is driven primarily by return on assets. The greater the returns on assets in a given activity, the more likely actors are to favor continuing the activity. Quasi-rents constitute the difference between the rate of return in an asset's current use and the opportunity cost, that is, the best alternative use. Specific assets tend to have high rates of return; otherwise, their owners would redeploy them in a different activity. Higher asset specificity also implies larger quasi-rents (Frieden, 1991). For example, a machine that makes only Honda Civic parts is highly valuable to Honda but only as long as Honda makes the Civic. Once Honda abandons the Civic line, the machine's alternative use may be as scrap. Under these conditions, the rate of asset return is high and so are the quasi-rents.

Owners of the factors of production have an incentive to lobby for policies that keep quasi-rents high. Under threat of international competition, revenues are likely to decline, all else being equal. Assuming production stays the same, the rate of asset return declines causing an exit of mobile factors to other parts of the economy. The factors that remain fixed face higher adjustment costs leading to an overall decline in income. But rational actors will go to great lengths to lower costs. Owners of more specific assets have a greater incentive to expend more resources to avert this economic loss.

Demand for more protection (higher subsidies) entails that excess cost is passed on to society. The greater the asset specificity, the greater the likelihood will be that economic actors will invest resources to demand (and sustain) protection. Protectionist coalitions have incentives to inflate prices and profits. Subsidies increase final prices, which cause movements upward along the supply curve. There are two implications flowing from such price and supply movements. First, incentives for higher returns increase the likelihood that groups will expend more resources to capture higher rents. Rent-seeking activities generate more waste for society as a whole because competition for rents often promotes the allocation of resources in excess of the total amount of rent available (Tullock, 2005). For example, one may think of a lottery (Lusztig, 2004, p. 5). More money is spent on tickets than is paid out as a prize. Second, protection promotes redistributional inefficiencies. Higher returns promote the entry (or sustenance) of producers in areas of comparative disadvantage. Resources are taken out of productive uses and allocated to unproductive ones. Rent seeking, in other words, has benefits that go beyond the actual amount of subsidies.

It is fruitful to recall the example of Boeing versus Airbus in chapter 1. The subsidy to one producer entails not only the monetary benefits of subsidizing that company but also the ability to increase total revenues through more sales. The concentrated benefits to the affected producers provide strong rent-seeking incentives. The amount of benefits, and hence the incentive to expend rent-seeking resources, varies according to the degree of asset specificity. The more specific the assets, the greater the incentive is to invest in rent-seeking activities to stem more losses and realize more gains.

Alt et al. (1996) posit asset specificity as a key variable in understanding lobbying activities. If actors stand to lose from economic exchange, they will try to lobby politicians to enact policies that favor current activities that increase quasi-rents. In the case of firms this means they are more likely to lobby for subsidies, which lower costs and increase firm profitability. Losers are more likely to lobby for subsidies than winners (Baldwin, 1989). This is because gaining from subsidized exports increases profits. Higher profits in turn attract entry by new competitors, depressing profits and lowering the gains from lobbying and subsidies. Firms that stand to lose, however, will fight harder for subsidies to increase their below-market returns (Grossman and Helpman, 1994). They are not likely to face new competitors until their profit rates return to normal market levels.

In a more recent paper, Alt *et al.* (1999) test the hypothesis that asset specificity leads to greater demand for subsidies. Providing evidence from a survey of Norwegian firms in 1988, they find that asset specificity increases the likelihood of lobbying activity when other factors, such as firm size and export share, are taken into account. But the generalizability of their findings may be limited due to the single national context at only one point in time.

What effects does the inclusion of asset specificity have on the G-H model? Recall that groups affected by exposure to global economic trends are likely to lobby policymakers to maintain or change policies that privilege profits. The link that ties lobbies to politicians is political contributions. Politicians need to finance their electoral campaigns and groups need to maintain profitable activities. Let us set politician motives aside for a moment to concentrate on the demand for subsidies. Policymaker motives will be examined in more detail in the next chapter. The G-H political contribution model rests on a specific-factors platform. Groups lobby for helpful policies because they feel the pinch and cannot (or find it costly to) redeploy their assets elsewhere.

What happens as the cost of moving assets to more profitable activities decreases? The stakes become lower because asset owners may move assets rather than spend resources to lobby government for subsidies. Their profits will not be squeezed as much and their voices for protection will not be as strong. In the case of perfect mobility, the stakes for protection among, say, owners of capital, are zero, assuming a capital-abundant economy.

H4.1: Higher asset specificity leads to more subsidies.

In national economies with more specific assets, industry is more likely to demand sector-specific subsidies because it incurs higher costs of adjustment. But the types of subsidies industry might want and get will vary considerably. Subsidies that have a narrower focus are likely to be the most attractive. This is because sector- or firm-specific subsidies are likely to be most beneficial to the intended target since they are tailor-made for that industry. For example, rescuing ailing firms involves putting together a package that addresses the needs of that specific firm and not general economic problems that may or may not be relevant to the firm's problems. Asset specificity increases the probability of these types of subsidies being given because industry does not have to build grand coalitions and therefore has no incentive to distribute benefits widely. Besides, sectoral subsidies might be politically easier to pass because they generally involve lesser amounts than horizontal subsidies that apply to the entire economy.

H4.2: Higher asset specificity leads to more sectoral subsidies.

Conversely, higher asset specificity should lead to lower levels of horizontal subsidies. Because such type of protection applies across the entire economy, for example, worker training or environmental assistance, it distributes benefits widely. In fact, the European Commission has made it abundantly clear that it prefers that governments disburse horizontal aid to industry as opposed to sectoral aid because it creates fewer distortions to competition given its breadth. The key issue is the domestic component of competition, and its blunt effect. By implication, companies should not be terribly interested in spending significant resources to get such aid because it does not give them a considerable advantage over their domestic competitors—though it may do so against their international competitors. Industries that confront higher costs of adjustment in the face of foreign competition should be less enthusiastic about these types of subsidies because they do not address their specific problems. Such subsidies are also more difficult to pass because they affect many industries and are therefore likely to bring to the negotiating table more actors with different and potentially conflicting demands. Besides, they tend to be costlier from society's point of view because they entail inefficiencies and waste due to their nonspecific nature.

H4.3: Higher asset specificity leads to fewer horizontal subsidies.

Globalization, Asset Specificity, and National Subsidies

But the effects are not likely to be the same at all levels of asset specificity. There are significant interactive effects that need to be exposed. When specificity is low and under threat of international competition, the costs of adjustment are also low. This implies that firms or other social actors, either in isolation or in groups, are more reluctant to spend the resources necessary to lobby for and win subsidies. At higher levels of specificity, however, and still under competitive pressures from abroad, the adjustment costs are considerable because production now has to change to respond to the threat. Such costs eat into profitability making it difficult for firms to stay in business. In the face of international competition, therefore, firms and other actors are more likely to lobby harder for subsidies when their asset specificity is above a certain level.

To understand more clearly the essence of this argument, I decompose specificity in two elements: factor returns and actor preferences. Globalization affects factor returns, which in turn influence asset specificity. Greater exposure to global economic forces generally creates more pressures for investment in more specialized and consequently more specific assets. Preferences manifest themselves in terms of asset specificity. I then analyze the conditional effects of asset specificity and gains or losses from exposure to global economic forces.

Factor Returns

I begin by conceptualizing preferences as investments. Actors possess productive assets from which they expect a certain rate of return. When rates fall below a certain level, actors are likely to consider the possibility of moving the assets. Movement is costly and it hinges upon the size of the quasi-rent, that is, the difference between the present rate of return and the opportunity cost of deploying the assets somewhere else. The more specific the assets are to a particular function, the costlier it will be to put them to alternative uses.

Consider the following example from the literature on transaction-cost economics. Firms possess assets, such as human capital, physical capital, and the like. Both technology and workers are finely tuned to the demands of a particular firm. They have developed production processes that are specific to the firm and take advantage of the specific machinery that the firm possesses. Let us assume the firm faces the prospect of entering into an agreement with a potential customer downstream for a major sale of the company's products. The problem is that the customer wants a particular variation of the product, which, if implemented, will be costly because it will involve a retooling of production processes—investment in new equipment and worker upgrade of skills to run the new machines. The contract is high volume and potentially profitable. What incentives does the company have to close the deal?

The answer depends on the degree of specificity and the marginal replacement costs relative to the unrealized profits. Asset-specific transactions are investments of considerable duration, which might lose value if the transaction is prematurely terminated (Williamson, 1985). In other words, transactions of this type make firms vulnerable to the high cost of investment, should the process be terminated, because the asset may not be easily redeployed elsewhere. Negotiating such transactions is expensive and the outcome uncertain. Costs need to include not only the actual cost of the investment, but the expenses to negotiate and implement the agreement, the uncertainty of the outcome, and the opportunity cost, or income lost from alternative uses. For this reason, firms seek nonmarket solutions, such as vertical integration of operations, or enter into long-term contractual agreements to lock in customers so that the cost of the investment may be recouped (Murphy, 2004, p. 17).

Labor operates in a similar fashion. When workers possess job-specific skills, they are likely to enjoy a high income that comes from such specialization. These types of workers are far more likely to demand policies that privilege their position. They seek compensation insurance to secure high returns to their investment in skills. Conversely, the more portable the skills, the less likely it will be for workers to demand insurance (Iversen and Soskice, 2001). Workers with portable skills stand a lower risk of losing a good portion of their income if they become unemployed. In addition, they have not invested as much in training for the specific job they are employed, so the rate of expected return is lower. The quasi-rent for generally skilled workers, that is, the difference between current income (above and beyond what would normally be conferred) and alternative uses, is lower.

Globalization and Actor Preferences

How does globalization affect actor preferences? It does so by influencing return on assets. When the income received from assets begins to diminish as a result of greater exposure to global economic forces, actors are hard pressed to upgrade their skills. They are far more likely to upgrade their skills than to redeploy their assets elsewhere due to transaction costs. Quantitative evidence from the United States shows that higher exposure to exports and FDI leads to greater wage dispersion and, by extension, higher labor specificity (Jensen and Troske, 1999; Moran, 1999). The more specific their skills become, the greater the likelihood of higher income. Trade preferences are in turn shaped by the ability to hang on to this income (Scheve and Slaughter, 2001).

But effects are not likely to be felt uniformly across countries or even within the same country. The previous chapter stressed the point that globalization has two analytically useful dimensions: trade and financial capital. Each dimension has different implications for preferences. Actors in countries that are equally exposed to both face conflicting pressures. On the one hand, increased exposure to trade increases pressures for specialization and efficiency, magnifying the importance and effects of asset specificity. On the other hand, increased international capital mobility in the form of short-term investment has a tendency to depress specificity effects. Because increased financial integration makes it easier to gain entry and exit in and out of specific industries, owners of capital assets are more likely to prefer more liquid assets so they can put them to different uses. Countries that are highly exposed to both trade and capital will experience these pressures more intensively. Countries exposed to increasing world trade but not capital will need and use more specific assets, while countries exposed to less trade but more capital will need and use less specific assets. This is not to say that exposure to global trade and capital flows is the only factor affecting preferences and magnifying (or not) the effects of specificity. But for purposes of my argument, the usual assumption will suffice. Other things being equal, globalization affects actor preferences and helps shape the impact of asset specificity.

The effects of trade on preferences and specificity are straightforward. The theorem of comparative advantage suggests that increased trade leads to greater specialization. Asset owners tend to "up-skill" in search of higher rates of return. The more intensified the international competition in the form of trade, the stronger the demand of firms will be for a more highly skilled workforce (Boix, 1997). Workers have an incentive to upgrade their skills, so that they can capture more efficiency gains, and therefore higher rates of return, for example, wages. It may be stating the obvious, but the statement is worth repeating: unskilled or less skilled workers, for example, those who possess the most portable skills and by extension more mobile assets, tend to lose the most from globalization in the developed world. Berger and her associates (2005, p. 291) are very clear: "Unless the skills of the American workforce provide a compelling reason for locating activities at home, the appeal of foreign labor markets with educated workers at lower wages is likely to induce the very race to the bottom that we fear the most under globalization."

Unskilled workers are the first to be laid off because they contribute the least to the production of tradable goods in industrialized economies, which are characterized by labor shortages and capital abundance relative to developing economies. Unskilled workers are also the most mobile because they are the first to get a job in a different sector. Their wage demands are minimal and so is investment in their skills. By contrast, skilled workers are more likely to invest in upgrading their skills because their earning potential increases dramatically. Potential gains may go up, but so does specificity. The more they invest, the less likely they are to move because investment now increases the cost of exit. Highly skilled workers, for example, in the production of automobiles are less likely to move in search of higher wages in other industries largely because it is implausible to assume their skills will apply equally well in another industry.

Owners of capital assets, for example, employers, face similar pressures. Employers in the tradables sector, which faces the stiffest competition, tend to favor substantial reorganization and retooling efforts that foster higher wage differentials (Hall, 1999, p. 156). They are far more willing to tolerate inequalities in wages and profits in collective bargaining arrangements than those conceded in the sheltered sectors (Pontusson and Swenson, 1996; Iversen, 1999). The reason is fairly simple. Sectors more exposed to international trade face greater pressures to yield higher rates of return. Both importers and exporters tend not to favor reduced entry and exit into a specific sector but rather an upgrade of technology, production processes, and the like, in order to increase productivity and consequently profits. It is possible that some owners will seek to redeploy their assets to different sectors, but such a move is likely to be costlier than an upgrade on skills and capital technology, at least in the short run. Upgrades necessarily imply greater tolerance for more inequality or gaps in profits and wages.

The effects of international short-term capital mobility are the opposite of those of trade. Higher exposure to capital creates incentives for less specificity. Developments in global financial markets have given companies more options and greater flexibility (Ohmae, 1991, p. 155). To understand why, let us consider two worlds, one before capital mobility (BCM) and one after capital mobility (ACM) (Frieden, 1991). In BCM, the number of firms in a given sector is a function of several factors, one of them being the availability of capital relative to the rate of return. Given a fixed amount of available capital and a certain rate of return, the number of firms in a given sector is k. Benefits of barriers to entry for each firm are z/k, where z denotes benefits (profits). Assume that more capital is pumped into the economy from abroad in search of higher rates of return. The availability of fresh funds makes it easier to start new competitor firms or for firms in other sectors to now enter the market, $k+1$. In ACM, pressures build to bring down the barriers to entry or exit. For one, undesirable effects cannot be avoided. For example, barriers may exist because of specific government policies aiming to aid particular industries or firms. Potential entry into the sector becomes more realizable because setting up the competitor firm is now less costly. It, therefore, becomes politically less sustainable to maintain legal arrangements to keep firms out. Moreover, the availability of new competitors *via* FDI dissipates the targeted benefits for each firm, $z/k+1$. The maintenance of artificial barriers to entry is less profitable for domestic producers and consequently less sustainable.

But there is more to it than that. Quite often the rate of return and consequently asset specificity are tied to the existence of available technology. To the extent that the ability to enter or exit sectors is linked to technology, the entrance of foreign competitors by way of production, not just exports, makes the same technology more available to local firms. It is easier to study and replicate, for example, in-time production processes or marketing strategies that are implemented by local manufacturers who operate within the same national environment than to adapt techniques that are operative in diverse national environments. The fact that a new manufacturer has set up shop in the country implies that a certain degree of technological adaptation has already taken place. In this sense technology is now easier to replicate and diffuse to other domestic firms. The automobile industry provides good examples. Japanese manufacturing and distribution techniques became far easier to replicate once Japanese automakers set up shop in the United States in the early 1980s, partly in order to bypass protectionist legislation.

However, not all capital integration remains the same. Some aspects of capital are more globally integrated than others. As Frieden (1991) notes, capital integration is multidimensional and it involves bank claims, equities, and FDI. Each asset involves an investment of a specific duration. The shorter the duration, the more mobile the asset is likely to be. There are two dimensions that are of particular importance to this study: equity (portfolio) investment and FDI. Equity assets are more mobile than FDI (Frieden, 1991, p. 429). As Ohmae aptly (1991, p. 167) says: "Money slips across borders in the blink of an electronic eye. Infrastructure cannot." Most capital controls to equity markets have disappeared in the last 20 years, especially among industrialized countries. It is now standard practice for most mutual funds to also include equity options in foreign countries. By way of contrast, FDI involves sunk costs—the building and maintenance of immobiles, such as factories. By definition, FDI is of longer duration because of sunk costs. One cannot just pack up and leave a national boundary at will without incurring substantial cost. Equity flight involves quite literally the push of a button. I anticipate the effects of globalization on asset specificity to be more pronounced in the case of portfolio investment than in FDI.

To be sure, globalization is not the only factor shaping the effects of asset specificity. Alt and Gilligan (1994, pp. 174–175) argue that several variables affect a country's level of specific assets and their intensity. The first and most important is the level of economic development. It could be argued that higher levels of development increase the propensity to exploit gains due to specialization and differentiation. Hence specific assets are more likely to be encountered in developed economies. In addition, increases in transaction costs—such as monitoring of economic activity or broader regulatory measures that address health, safety, or quality standards—increase specificity. Moreover, incentives to invest in more specific assets depend on the historical evolution of domestic institutions (Thelen, 2004). Institutions focusing on skill acquisition and training and legislation of employment protection in different countries provide variable incentives to upgrade skills because they may shield workers from exposure to global economic forces or make it costlier to upgrade (Hall and Soskice, 2001). For example, labor laws governing worker training and licensing in Germany, which date in some instances back to medieval times, coupled with relatively high unionization rates, have resulted in a highly skilled and expensive labor force. Attention to quality competitiveness in the form of skilled human and physical capital is one of the defining features of the German postwar economic model (Schmidt, 2002, p. 169).

Trade and National Subsidies

The ground has been set for a clearer exposition of the interactive effects of globalization and asset specificity on national subsidies. I have shown that globalization affects specificity through factor returns and actor preferences. What remains to be done is to demonstrate how increasing exposure to global markets depresses (or not) gains and losses to owners of specific assets. Losers are likely to demand more subsidies.

Losses by domestic producers stem largely from exposure to international economic forces. I now turn to the factor proportions theory of international trade to shed light on who loses and why. While it was originally formulated in reference only to trade, its logic can be applied to international capital movements as well. The theory maintains that trade is a function of asset (factor) endowments, such as land, capital, and labor. Formulated by Swedish economists E. Heckscher and B. Ohlin, the theory was advanced to explain the pattern of international trade. Although it has had success in illuminating the determinants of trade, it is ironic, as Vousden (1990, p. 3) maintains, that "subsequent developments (most notably by Paul Samuelson) have made it a popular general equilibrium framework for analysis of *impediments* to trade in competitive markets" (emphasis added).

The general gist of it says that countries with relatively abundant factors will specialize in those products that use those factors and trade for the rest. The main difference between this argument and that of Ricardo's comparative advantage is the number of factors of production considered to serve as economic inputs.

Consider two countries producing two products, textiles and wine, using two factors, labor and capital. Employing a voluminous and fairly restrictive set of assumptions, the theory predicts that the composition of trade between the two countries follows their resource endowments. Assuming that the factor use ratio for commodities is different for a given pair of factor prices, one commodity, say, textiles, may be termed as capital intensive because it uses a higher capital/labor ratio than the other, which by definition is labor intensive. Given a certain relative endowment ratio in each country, rather than the absolute factor amount, it can be shown that capital-abundant countries, say, the United States, will specialize in producing and exporting textiles, that is, capital-intensive goods, because relative factor quantities are higher and prices lower. Conversely, the labor-abundant country, say, Portugal, will produce and export wine because it has a relative advantage in producing labor-intensive products, such as wine.

Stolper and Samuelson (1941) supplement this argument with the insight that increases in relative commodity prices lead to fluctuations in real factor returns. Trade increases the rate of return for owners of relatively abundant assets and decreases the return for those who own scarce assets. To understand why, a crucial assumption must be stressed: factors are free to move across sectors. In other words, there is perfect intra-national factor mobility. Following specialization, resources are released in search of more productive uses, for example, more capital has shifted toward textiles in the United States and more labor has moved toward the production of wine in Portugal. Assuming full employment, the capital-labor ratio has increased in the United States and decreased in Portugal. The process implies that the price of capital has increased while the price of labor has decreased. The distribution of income in each country has changed since the introduction of trade with the relatively abundant factor gaining, capital in the United States and labor in Portugal, and the scarce factor losing.

In an insightful study, Rogowski (1989) explores the political implications of this argument. Coalitions are likely to be formed around factors of production seeking specific benefits from government. Because international trade benefits labor and harms capital in labor-abundant economies, labor is likely to prefer free trade and capital is likely to oppose it. Protection in such circumstances tends to favor capital and to harm labor while liberalization of trade benefits labor and impairs capital. Depending on factor endowments, Rogowski predicts factor-based political coalitions forming to demand or oppose protection.

The argument is elegant, logical, and simple. It strips trade to bare essentials and despite limitations posed by its numerous assumptions, it does have an empirical basis. For example, trade between countries with very different resource endowments follows the general pattern predicted by the theory. Capital-abundant countries, such as the United States, tend to produce and export generally capital-intensive products while labor-abundant countries, such as many developing countries, tend to produce and export mainly labor-intensive products. Moreover, the theory predicts class conflict under conditions of expanding trade in, say, nineteenth-century Germany. Labor is the free trading element and land and capital coalesce in support of protection (Rogowski, 1989, chapter 2). More generally, coalitions and pressures for protection in different national settings vary, according to Rogowski, relative to factor endowments and exposure to international trade.

Empirical reality, however, shows that quite often capital and labor coalesce along industry lines to demand protection. Political coalitions, and therefore incentives to form such coalitions, seem to follow sectoral rather than factoral bases. Labor and capital employed in the same industry often find themselves on the same side of the fence. For example, an analysis of the position of labor and capital groups in testimony for and against the U.S. Trade Reform Act of 1974 found in most instances both types of groups demanding similar responses, either protection or free trade (Magee, Brock, and Young, 1989). The reason for this empirical anomaly to the so-called mobile factors model is because assets are not free to move across industries in search of higher returns, as Stolper and Samuelson assume.

The alternative model, called the Ricardo-Viner model, views rates of return, and hence demands for protection, as confined to the fortunes of industries that face lower prices and cannot redeploy assets elsewhere (Jones, 1971). The model typically assumes a two-sector, say, agriculture and manufacturing, three-factor—land, capital, and labor—economy. Land is specific to wheat and capital is specific to textiles. Labor is assumed to be mobile and a necessary input in both sectors. Each sector produces goods according to a fixed quantity of the specific factor, land or capital, and a certain portion of labor. Labor mobility ensures that the wage rate is equalized across sectors; otherwise labor would move in search of higher returns to the other sector.

Let us suppose that Portugal is land abundant so that it has a comparative advantage in wheat production. When free trade is introduced, the domestic price of wheat rises. Labor is drawn from textiles to wheat in search of higher wages. The marginal rate of return to land has risen, and consequently the endowment ratio has changed in land's favor; so has the real rate of return. The opposite has happened to capital. Landowners gain under these conditions while capital owners lose. There is a conflict of interest between owners of factors specific to importing versus exporting sectors. Labor as a whole may gain or lose from this situation depending on the share of goods consumed by that factor. Because the wage rate rises relative to the price of textiles but falls relative to the price of food, if workers consume mostly food, they are likely to lose. If they consume mostly textiles, they are likely to gain. Under these conditions, coalitions demanding protection will form along industrial rather than factor lines (Hiscox, 2001).

Both alternative explanations deal with ideal cases where assets (factors) are either mobile or immobile. Many analysts have sought to synthesize the two models by arguing that intra-national factor specificity is a temporary phenomenon. Hence asset owners may find it is in their short-run interests to collude along sectoral lines in favor of protection even though it may be detrimental to the long-run interests of at least one of them (Vousden, 1990, p. 18). Some authors argue that economic adjustment introduces factoral mobility in the long run (Mussa, 1974; Neary, 1978). This implies that the predictions of the Ricardo-Viner model hold only for the short-term and are wrong in the long run. Others disagree with this interpretation, questioning the rationale behind gradual mobility (Alt and Gilligan, 1994). Once protection is introduced and given inertia in government programs (Rose and Davies, 1994), it is highly unlikely that there will be factoral movement in search of higher rates of return in the absence of exogenous shocks, such as changes in technology or costs of transport. Once introduced, in other words, protection is unlikely to be abandoned because of shifts in preferences of the owners of factors of production and their political ability to hold on to benefits (subsidies) disbursed by government. By implication, subsidies are expected to be "sticky," in the sense that they may still be allocated long after they have fulfilled their aims. Agricultural subsidies in the United States and Europe are good examples of aid being given long after meeting the original objective of securing a nation's food supply.

Nevertheless, under conditions of increasing exposure to global markets the reality of partial mobility yields the expectation that demands for protection depend on the degree of factor mobility (Hill and Mendez, 1983; Brawley, 1997; Hiscox, 2002; Ladewig, 2006). Grossman (1983) investigates the effects of inter-sectoral capital mobility even in the short run. He finds that its magnitude determines the effects of tariffs on asset owner incomes.

Taking this argument one step further, Frieden and Rogowski (1996, p. 33) categorically assert that increasing exposure to global forces raises the opportunity cost of closure. As it becomes easier to trade or borrow internationally, the cost of keeping the economy closed increases because society now foregoes more to keep the economy closed. Gaps between world and domestic prices widen and more investment flows to inefficient, sheltered industries. Assuming there are readily available gains to be had from international trade or capital mobility (such as in the case of high levels of total factor productivity), pressures to liberalize increase exponentially. Total factor productivity refers to a residual that captures knowledge, technology, organization, and the like after capital and labor productivity are taken into account.[2] The implication is that because the cost of closure accelerates with increasing international exposure, the pressures to specialize and create more specific assets will fluctuate proportionately. Really low levels of exposure may lead to fewer subsidies regardless of the degree of specificity. The incentives of groups to put pressure on government for more subsidies are not high when the stakes are low. But the pace of creating more specific assets will accelerate as exposure increases. In that case, demands for more subsidies will increase dramatically. In the light of the hypotheses advanced in the previous chapter about the effects of globalization, I add:

H4.4: In countries not heavily exposed to the global market, the effects of asset specificity will be minimal; subsidies are expected to be generally lower.

H4.5: In countries heavily exposed to the global market, the effects of asset specificity will be magnified; subsidies are expected to be generally higher.

Table 4.1 summarizes the expected relationships derived above. It contains hypotheses for both independent and interactive effects across total subsidies as well as horizontal and sectoral aid.

Table 4.1 Hypothesized effects of globalization and asset specificity

	Total subsidies	Horizontal	Sectoral
Independent effects			
Trade	+	+	+
FDI	+	+	+
Portfolio investment (PI)	−	−	−
Labor specificity (LS)	+	−	+
Capital specificity (CS)	+	−	+
Interactive effects			
Trade*LS	+	−	+
Trade*CS	+	−	+
FDI*LS	+	−	+
FDI*CS	+	−	+
PI*LS	−	+	−
PI*CS	−	+	−

ESTIMATION CONCERNS

I use the term "asset specificity," that is, the cost of moving factors of production from one industry to the next, as synonymous to greater specialization. More specialized assets are also less portable. To operationalize the concept, I rely on Williamson's (1985) insight on transaction costs and asset specificity. The value of some assets, such as capital equipment, may be tied to the specific job they are currently performing. Were their use redirected for some reason to serve an alternative function, the return on such capital may not be as high, that is, the move is costly. For example, more trade may lead Honda to purchase machinery that produces specific parts used only in the Honda Civic model. This particular equipment is very costly to purchase but it also creates great efficiency gains because it is perfectly in tune with the current production of Civics. The high return on the equipment is tied to its current use. If, however, production needs to shift to the Honda Accord model, the value of the machinery is reduced dramatically because it was not designed to fit into the new production line. The efficiency gains will be much lower unless extensive modifications are performed. The same goes for the operator of the equipment. Assuming a significant investment of time and money in acquiring and training to run this equipment, the operator's skills have become more specialized but also less portable. Greater specialization is an indicator of asset specificity, and as the example shows, more specialized assets are also less portable or at least more costly to put to equally or more profitable alternative uses.

Asset specificity has several facets. Two are important: physical and human asset specificity (Joskow, 1988).[3] They correspond roughly to the factors of production: capital and labor. *Physical* assets refer to the ability of industry to capture quasi-rents based on physical (design) characteristics. To capture capital asset mobility, I use profit differentials (annual absolute difference between value added minus wage costs per employee as percent of capital per employee invested in industry j). Estimates yield a range of nine numbers, which represent nine industries for which complete figures exist. Data are expressed as coefficients of variation (standard deviation over mean) and multiplied by 100 for ease of interpretation (Hiscox, 2002). Higher differentials indicate higher specificity. If assets are mobile, higher returns should be arbitraged away. Hence the differentials under conditions of perfect mobility should be zero. Anything above zero signals the cost of moving assets across industries.

The essence of *human* specificity is to capture the ability of individuals to move across industries. More specific skills create individual incentives for greater nonmarket protection (Iversen and Soskice, 2001). The more the individuals' skills are tied to a particular firm or industry, the higher the asset specificity will be. The indicator occasionally used is gross job creation plus gross job loss controlling for total jobs (Alt *et al.*, 1999; Davis and Haltiwanger, 1992). Unfortunately, such detailed data do not exist for all countries and years in my study. So I employ a different measure to capture the essence of labor movement across industries. I calculate wage differentials, which are the annual absolute distance of wages from the mean wage in industry j, in nine industries for which complete data exist and conditional on the number of employees. I calculate the standard deviation and mean of the resulting range of nine numbers per year into a coefficient of variation and multiply it by 100 for ease of interpretation.[4] Higher differentials indicate higher specificity. Data for both indicators are computed from the OECD's *National Accounts* (various years), *Labour Force Statistics* (various years), and supplemented by information in the OECD's *Structural Analysis (STAN) Database* (2004), which includes more detailed information for specific industries.

Table 4.2 contains descriptive statistics for the two indicators of asset specificity. Not surprisingly, labor specificity has a higher mean, which indicates that it is costlier or more difficult on average for labor to move than capital. Workers have a more difficult time moving across industries than capital owners. Labor involves retraining and physical

Table 4.2 Descriptive statistics of asset specificity indicators*

Variable	Minimum	Maximum	Mean	Standard deviation
Labor specificity	25.18	109.49	64.47	15.06
Capital specificity	13.85	123.67	42.88	22.86

* Coefficients of variation in percent
Source: OECD, *Labour Force Statistics* (various years), *National Accounts* (various years), and *STAN* database (2004).

movement to often a different location, all of which are costly activities. Capital is more mobile, whether this involves money or actual physical equipment. For this last reason, capital tends to also be subject to wilder fluctuations. Table 4.2 shows that capital specificity is subject to more extreme movements.

Figures 4.1 and 4.2 contain graphic information on trends in five major industrialized economies in the period 1991–2003. What is interesting about labor specificity depicted in figure 4.1 is that wage differentials have increased over time with the more marked fluctuations registered in the three European democracies. All countries found themselves clustered around similarly low levels at the beginning of the decade, with the exception of France. The French experience shows a decline over time, indicating greater movement across industries and less specificity. The UK follows the exact opposite pattern, with specificity increasing dramatically over time. Rising incomes coupled with hefty economic growth in the 1990s have apparently reduced worker appetite for movements across industries in search of better wages and working conditions. The only country that did not witness an increase in the period under investigation is Japan, an expected result in the light of Japanese company policy of "life employment" (Gordon, 1998; Kume, 1998). Even though the policy has been curtailed in the last 20 years or so, the data suggest that worker movement continues to be lower than elsewhere.

Capital specificity, depicted in figure 4.2, is on average less than labor specificity by several percentage points. In three cases, capital specificity declined over time, with the United States registering the steepest decline by almost 50 percent. In contrast, specificity increased in Germany and Japan, with the steepest rise registered in Germany. Not surprisingly, economic growth during this period remained sluggish, providing little incentive to owners of capital to move their assets to more productive areas. In a period of general macroeconomic malaise, there are predictably few such profitable areas.

There are also alternative ways to measure physical asset specificity. Economists working in this field have traditionally understood physical specificity to mean research and development (R&D) intensity (Santarelli, 1991). R&D "creates asset specificity because firms that sell products with close substitutes are likely to do less research and development," claim Acs and Isberg (1991, p. 324). Political science work on lobbying also considers R&D intensity to be the principal

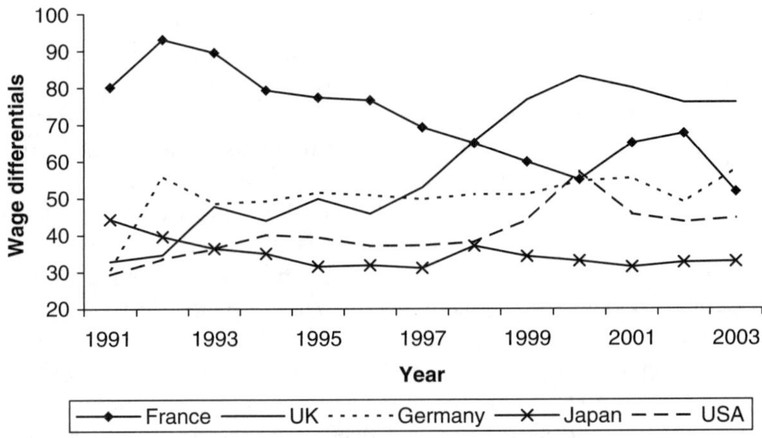

Figure 4.1 Labor specificity.
Source: OECD *Labour Force Statistics* (various years), *National Accounts* (various years), and *STAN Database* (2004).

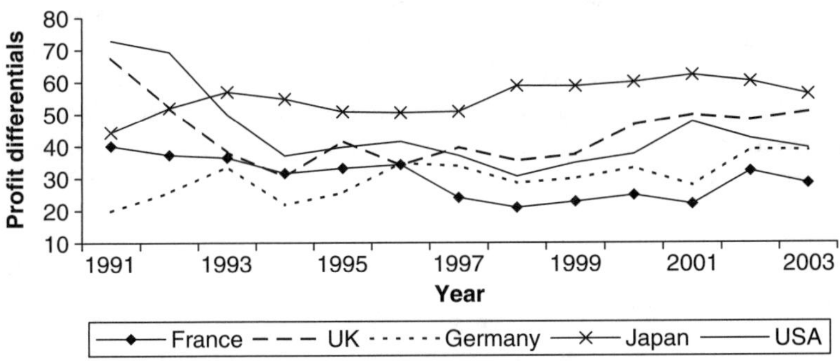

Figure 4.2 Capital specificity.
Source: OECD *Labour Force Statistics* (various years), *National Accounts* (various years), and *STAN Database* (2004).

measure of asset specificity (Alt *et al.*, 1999; Zahariadis, 2001). The problem with this indicator is that it is less appropriate for studies measuring a national specificity rather than a firm-specific specificity. Moreover, a national measure of R&D intensity can hardly capture inter-industry movements. As the two figures above make clear, wage and profit differentials more accurately depict movements of workers and capital across countries and over time within the same country.

CONCLUSION

I have argued that asset specificity, separately and interactively with globalization, affect the propensity of subsidy demand. External economic forces alter the environment within which social actors operate. They create economic risks and opportunities. Actors in turn are also motivated to act by their ability to move assets across industries in search of more profitable uses. The greater the ability to move assets, the lower the incentive will be to call for more subsidies. Conversely, actors who face significant domestic barriers to entry in and exit out of profitable activities will experience heavier losses and will consequently have more incentives to demand protection.

However, the argument needs to be qualified. While asset specificity is expected to have significant independent effects on subsidies, it also has important interactive effects. Conditional on low levels of exposure to global economic forces, asset specificity is less likely to have a dramatic effect on subsidies because the losses to affected groups are fewer. The cost of rent seeking outweighs the benefit of protection from foreign competition. It is only when globalization levels grow higher that the impact of asset specificity is likely to be felt. The reason is that world markets now strongly affect the domestic market, and consequently the profitability of domestic groups, be they workers or capital owners. The losses are likely to be higher and so will the potential gains from protection. Under these conditions it pays to seek protection because the benefits far outweigh the costs of rent seeking.

C H A P T E R 5

DOMESTIC POLITICS AND THE SUPPLY OF SUBSIDIES

Economic freedoms . . . are eternally vulnerable, and never more so than when governments are weak or prone to populism.

—Dan O'Brien, senior Europe economist, Economist Intelligence Unit[1]

We still believe the state has a role to play in the European economy.

—Leke van den Burg, Dutch member of the European Parliament[2]

Having explored the demand side of the subsidy equation, I now turn to the domestic politics of translating demands into more producer subsidies. Producer groups may demand more subsidies, but are policy-makers willing to supply them? I amend and elaborate the institutional aspects of the G-H model, namely the impact of political power and national institutions on the government's ability to provide subsidies. The literature on trade policy is replete with references to the importance of institutions (e.g., Mansfield and Busch, 1995; O'Reilly, 2005; Henisz and Mansfield, 2006). What is missing is a model that incorporates this variable within a broader picture of the policy process.

I argue in this chapter that political power and national institutional configurations shape the ability of social actors to demand subsidies by limiting access and refracting the capacity of national governments to respond to those demands. I first look at the impact of political power. I then divide the analysis into two parts. I first look at the effects of the socioeconomic institution of corporatism, and finally

I examine more closely the effects of two formal public institutions, the fragmentation of state power and the degree of disproportionality of the electoral system.

POLITICAL POWER AND SUBSIDIES

A key concept of the asset influence model is the notion of power. The ability of groups to get more protection is a function of their ability to put pressure on politicians. If groups are politically weak, politicians have few incentives to listen to their demands, let alone comply with them. Conversely, when they are politically strong they may be more capable of imposing their own preferences. So much so, says Cox (2007, p. 63), that when subsidies are given in order to alleviate damage caused by trade or some other factor, "the amount of the policy concession [subsidy] is more a function of the influence of the pressure group than the amount of harm that might be incurred." The argument is not controversial, and the logic is simple and straightforward.

There are usually more problems confronting policymakers and less money to address them than is optimal. Obviously, politicians have to choose which groups to listen to and what problems to attend. The literature on agenda setting is replete with observations about the importance of turning issues into problems and capturing the attention of politicians who can address these problems (e.g., Zahariadis, 2003a; Jones and Baumgartner, 2005). Because campaign contributions are of vital importance to democratically elected policymakers, groups may manipulate power by withholding or redirecting contributions. In the case of weak groups, the contributions to politicians' campaigns are likely to be lower, and their capacity to supply votes will be limited. As such, policymakers are less likely to heed these groups' demands.

Political power is conceptualized as a function of group size. The key point is that larger groups have more members and therefore a greater likelihood to contribute more and deliver more votes. Their credibility in terms of threatening to switch contributions to other policymakers or to withhold them is greater than that of other groups. Larger groups are more politically powerful, so politicians are more likely to adhere to their demands. The argument that growing size at least over a certain range, increases power has empirical plausibility. In his seminal work, Olson (1965) notes the free-rider problem in large groups, suggesting smaller groups may overcome this problem. As a result, some authors have built models that claim smaller groups are likely to overcome collective-action problems and are consequently more powerful (e.g., Lohmann, 1998). While this is an interesting contention, it does not directly flow from Olson's argument. What Olson said was that smaller groups may find it easier to solve collective-action problems. However, "if large groups could solve the problem, by creating private goods or other specific incentives to induce potential members to join, then they may well be more powerful" (Acemoglu and Robinson, 2001, p. 650).

Although the record is somewhat mixed, there is empirical evidence to support the argument that size matters (e.g., Becker, 1986; Sloof, 1998). For example, Cameron (1988, p. 572) clearly supports the notion of size as an important ingredient of political power. Individuals have incentives to form lobbying groups if the potential membership is large enough to allow them "to anticipate greater power and hence greater collective rewards." When it comes to agricultural trade policy, Kindleberger (1951) and Tracy (1989) find that superior numbers of farmers were partly the reason why France and Germany imposed tariff protection in the 1880s but the UK did not. One may add this rationale to explain why protectionist measures in developed economies have declined in the last 30 years or so. As the numbers of those employed in manufacturing has shrunk, both in absolute and relative to the economy terms, the political power of adversely affected groups from international trade has concomitantly declined. If size matters, one would expect politicians to have been more willing to impose subsidies in the 1970s than in the 1990s.

H5.1: Governments are likely to respond with more subsidies to demands from more politically powerful groups.

As part of the supply side of the equation that is tied to political cost and indirectly to power, the penchant for supplying protection grows weaker as the elasticity of import demand increases. This argument by Grossman and Helpman is based on the insight that high import elasticities imply greater deadweight losses from protection. This is because any subsidies given to groups in those markets increase the loss to consumers because the latter are more likely to switch products. Conversely, if import demand is uniformly inelastic, there are no deadweight losses from taxing this good (subsidies may be thought of as a form of taxation). The ability to pass the cost of this product on to consumers as a whole is greater, the optimal rate of taxation is higher, and therefore, governments may subsidize them at higher levels.

The point makes sense when individual industries are the unit of analysis, but the effects are diluted in the particular model advanced here. I am interested in exploring the analytical insights of the model at the national level. Of concern are national measures of subsidy protection rather than the subsidies that particular industries get. Differences in individual import demand elasticities can affect the propensity to subsidize one particular sector rather than another, but have little meaning when explaining subsidization patterns aggregated at the national economic level. If politicians are guided by the ability to pass the cost on to consumers, individual industry differences yield little insight.

One could conceivably generate such estimates for an entire economy and compare values across different countries to estimate the propensity of politicians in different countries to pass the cost on to consumers. The problem with this approach is the severe empirical difficulty of generating import demand elasticities for different countries at different time periods. Hooper, Johnson, and Marquez (2000), for example, find that elasticities for some countries, such as Germany, are unstable even in the short run, while short-run price import elasticities for all but one of the seven countries they examined are not statistically significant in sensitivity tests. The point is "that the price channel is weak, if wholly ineffective, with respect to continental European countries" (Hooper, Johnson, and Marquez, 2000, p. 13). Given that the present model is based on price differentials to identify preferences, such a conclusion renders the empirical inclusion of this variable very problematic.

Besides, the inclusion of asset specificity and institutional dimensions crucially shape the effects of import demand elasticity. Varying degrees of asset specificity reduce overall losses to producers. Such reductions in turn not only affect the intensity of lobbying for protection but also the calculus of politicians to supply it. The fewer the losses, the lower the cost will be that politicians must pass on to the economy as a whole. In this case, subsidies become both easier to allocate and are more likely to be disbursed at lower levels. Institutions also affect the cost to the economy as a whole. Certain institutional characteristics, for example, corporatist arrangements, provide forums of consultation and collusion between labor, capital, and the state to pass these costs on to everyone. In other words, the choice is not for policymakers alone to make. Their ability to pass the cost of protection on to society is dictated and may in fact be encouraged by consultation with societal groups. In those instances, the political cost of doing so decreases dramatically, rendering specification of elasticity an exercise of dubious utility.

The Importance of Institutions

Policymakers do not operate in institutional vacuums. The incentives of politicians to act are partly shaped by national institutions. Institutional factors critically affect the behavior of political actors by shaping access channels to government. They also provide policymakers with incentives that limit courses of action and redistribute costs and benefits in the economy (Garrett and Lange, 1996).

Institutionalism has a long history in political science. There are several approaches that offer no agreement on what institutions are and how they affect policy (Peters, 2005; Hall and Taylor, 1996). Consistent with the logic of the overall argument presented here, I follow rational choice institutionalism. Actors seek to maximize personal utilities, for example, they engage in rent seeking, by operating within institutional environments that constrain action (Eggertsson, 1990; Scharpf, 1997). Institutions regulate access to policymakers, shield some groups from adverse economic conditions, and refract and mediate the effects of globalization by altering actors' gains and losses. In other words, they help shape incentives and options.

Institutions are a multidimensional concept that refers to repetitive situations in which humans find themselves organized by norms, strategies, and rules (Crawford and Ostrom, 1995). I focus on a single dimension, rules. They constitute shared understandings that prescribe action in particular situations by agents responsible for monitoring and sanctioning (Ostrom, 2007, p. 23). All rules are designed to increase regularity and predictability in human affairs. They describe particular contexts and actors, and encourage or constrain particular classes of action. The main point behind the argument is the view that actor "behavior is deeply conditioned by [the] institutional environment" within which actors are embedded (Hall, 1999, p. 148). Once institutionalized relationships are taken into account, it becomes easier to see how the translation of actor preferences into political demands is partly shaped by national political institutions. While there is regional variation, national institutions are important because a national institutional structure frames actor incentives and constrains microeconomic behavior (Soskice, 1999).

There are many different types of rules, but to keep the analysis simple and relevant, I concentrate on the effects of one type. Ostrom (2007) calls it the aggregation rule. It corresponds roughly to Koremenos, Lipson, and Snidal's (2001) control and centralization principles. What is the level of control that individual actors have over the decision-making process? How accurately do individual preferences translate into group preferences? How is the choice made in such institutions, and who gets to make it? Examples of aggregation rules include electoral rules, such as majority, unanimity, and the like.

In the following sections, I investigate the effects of aggregation rules on subsidies, conditional on certain levels of globalization. As can be gleaned from the discussion below, there is overlap between some institutions. However, each of them captures the essence of different institutional aspects, which greatly affect the subsidies puzzle. For this reason, I discuss them and estimate their effects separately. I examine two types of institutions: socioeconomic institutions and formal political institutions (Garrett and Lange, 1996). Corporatist intermediation (its presence and degree) in a given political system is the socioeconomic institution I discuss. I analyze the effects of two formal political institutions: preference aggregation, that is, the degree of electoral disproportionality, and the fragmentation of state power, that is, the number of veto points. They cover roughly the types of formal political institutions analyzed by Garret and Lange (1996). In general, the wider the dispersion of state control, the stronger the effects of globalization are likely to be on subsidies because pressures for protection will more accurately reflect the full range of adversely affected economic interests.

COLLECTIVE ACTION AND SOCIOECONOMIC INSTITUTIONS

While incentives to lobby are important, actors must have the ability to organize in order to exert effective political pressure (Grossman and Helpman, 1994). If groups encounter fewer collective-action problems, actors operating under specific institutional rules are likely to be more successful and vice versa. More severe collective-action problems reduce the likelihood of success. Success is understood here to mean actors get what they want, that is, subsidies.

The ability to organize for the provision of collective goods is greatly affected by the existence of barriers to entry, be they institutional, technological, or financial. When high barriers to entry into a certain activity exist, groups tend to be small. The converse is true with low barriers to entry. Put differently, when factor returns are confined to one or few industries where they are used, as in the case of imperfectly mobile factors, the size of the group affected in terms of number of actors will be relatively small. Hence the coalitions that will be built to demand subsidies will be more heterogeneous than when factors are mobile (Ladewig, 2006; Gilligan, 1997; Alt and Gilligan, 1994, pp. 187–188). When factors are perfectly mobile, the size of the group will be much larger because an entire class is now affected (Rogowski, 1989; Hiscox, 2002). All in all, collective-action problems are fewer when factor returns are confined to the industries where they are employed.

Barriers to entry are to a large extent tied to political institutions. Demands for redistribution of wealth, such as producer subsidies, depend on the responsiveness of governments. Governmental response, in turn, is conditioned by the degree of institutional access actors enjoy and the need (or not) for actors to negotiate or coordinate their demands with other actors, including state agencies. Not only do institutions have a direct impact on governmental behavior, but they also affect the access and intensity of actor demands. As Garrett and Lange (1996, p. 53) put it, "Institutions affect both the macroeconomic constraints under which governments operate and their responsiveness to distributional pressures for policy change."

Corporatism (or conversely pluralism) describes "producer group coalitions which operate, albeit not exclusively, outside electoral politics" (Hall, 1999, p. 150). I anticipate socioeconomic institutions to have a major impact on the disbursement of producer subsidies beyond that of formal political institutions because of the ability of producer and labor groups, indeed the need in corporatist instances, to organize and demand adjustment assistance. Demands for subsidies are likely to be more pronounced in systems where institutions provide forums for the articulation of demands and the making of compensatory deals. Katzenstein (1985) makes the point abundantly clear in his exploration of adjustment schemes in small European economies owing to increased exposure to international markets. Small European states developed corporatist arrangements in order to cope with the pressures of the international economy. Because these states are rule-takers rather than rule-makers, they have developed more coordinated ways to deal with the potential adverse side effects.

An extensive literature has developed around the creation and effects of systems of interest mediation on economic outcomes. Analysts have documented the effects of specific institutional configurations among others on macroeconomic outcomes (e.g., Katzenstein, 1985; Olson, 1982; Lijphart, 1999; Garrett and Lange, 1996), welfare and more generally government expenditures (e.g., Crepaz, 2001; Crepaz and Moser, 2004; Rothstein, 1998; Swank, 2002), and trade protection (e.g., O'Reilly, 2005; Mansfield and Busch, 1995;

Milner and Judkins, 2004; Henisz and Mansfield, 2006). The main thesis of the literature is that political institutions filter or refract the effects of openness to the global economy by reducing the risk associated with increased exposure. The end result is higher levels of compensation as the price for doing so.

The logic of the argument is simple. Increased exposure to world markets enhances external risk. Governments mitigate this risk by providing compensation insurance in the form of welfare spending or protectionism (Zahariadis, 2002). Recall that subsidies involve more than just rescuing ailing firms. They also include labor training, environmental aid, funds for R&D development, aid for energy saving, and aid to small and medium-sized enterprises. Cameron (1978) describes one mechanism that links openness and institutional configurations to public spending. He maintains that more open economies have higher levels of industrial concentration and consequently higher unionization and stronger labor organizations. Both factors facilitate the formation of strong peak associations and centralized bargaining, which in turn lead to higher government spending. Katzenstein (1985) extends this argument to a wider array of incentives in small and more open economies. He includes historical factors and economies of scale. Rodrik (1998) finds empirical support for the argument, using a broader sample of developed and developing countries and broadening the dependent variable to include government consumption and transfers. In corporatist arrangements, highly organized actors are able to demand greater compensation insurance to mitigate the risk of volatility from world markets. In return they promise wage moderation, flexible adaptation to production processes, and policy stability and industrial peace. The end result of these extra-parliamentary negotiations is more state aid, such as job training, aid for failing industries, and the like.

If the compensation principle posited above makes empirical sense, there may be specific interactive effects that have so far been left unexplored. The ability of policymakers to provide protection (subsidies) in the light of increased exposure to world markets hinges upon political considerations, such as the capacity of actors to extract such concessions. In other words, increased exposure does not necessarily imply increased compensation. Protectionism also hinges on the credibility of political commitment, which in turn depends on the incentives and strength of different actors to command compensation (Boix, 2004). Taking a transaction-cost perspective, Dixit and Londregan (1995) argue that redistributive policies, such as subsidies, are likely to be higher than is economically optimal because of the problem of credibility. If one assumes that subsidies are forthcoming owing to import competition, funding levels will be higher over time than is warranted from an economic efficiency point of view because politicians cannot make a credible commitment to workers to compensate them if they relocate to more productive opportunities. So workers are likely to stay and demand higher subsidies to support declining industries. "If the political process could make an initial binding contract that would compensate workers conditional on their moving away from the declining industry, an outcome could be designed to be better for everyone. But such long-term contracts are not feasible . . . because threats to withhold benefits to those who fail to make such choices are not credible" (Dixit, 1996, p. 44). Hence the institutional attributes through which political demands for protection are placed have an effect on the final outcome.

As exposure to globalization increases, subsidies are expected to go down in corporatist systems. Because corporatism is supposed to smooth out adjustment efforts, the amount of subsidies is likely to be higher on average. However, as globalization increases over time, some of the adjustment costs have already been borne, resulting in fewer losses, weaker demands, and less willingness by politicians for protection. For example, Finland, a country with a more corporatist institutional configuration had a relatively closed economy, heavily subsidizing its industry until the late 1980s (Kauppinen, 1998, p. 78). As the economy began to open up to world markets, politicians of various parties in government began to float the idea of reducing subsidies to industry and focusing instead on creating a favorable business climate. Consultations were held with both unions and employers, with most taking a critical stand against subsidies for budgetary reasons (pp. 80–81). As a result, while exposure to global economic forces increased, demands and willingness to subsidize industry in corporatist Finland waned; aid was supposed to be slashed by half. Conversely, in more pluralist systems, losses loom larger because fewer subsidies are disbursed for adjustment purposes. In this case, actors in pluralist countries will find it advantageous to coalesce to demand more subsidies. The absence of institutional channels that may insulate politicians against political pressure from a wide variety of sources implies that they are more likely to succumb to protectionist temptations. For example, Portugal, a country considered to be relatively pluralist (Lijphart, 1999), spent .83 percent of GDP subsidizing industry in 1992. As exposure to trade, FDI, and especially portfolio openness went up every year, compensatory industrial subsidies were increased to 1.1 percent of GDP by 2004 (European Commission, 2006c).

Apart from affecting the disbursement of subsidies, globalization also has an impact on corporatist institutions. The literature is mixed on the effects of increased exposure to global economic forces. Kurzer (1993), for example, claims that increased global capital mobility relative to labor mobility has undermined inclusion of labor in national bargaining over wages and government spending. As a result of the threat of exit, corporatist arrangements have become less effective over time. In contrast, Katzenstein (1985) finds empirical support for the argument that corporatist institutions thrive in the face of heavy exposure to global economic forces because they enable social partners, labor, and capital, to get what each wants with minimal industrial disruption. The short time horizon employed in this study cannot fully address this question. For this reason, institutions are considered to be time invariant and subject to change only over a long period of time. While globalization has had an impact, the literature is replete with empirical cases of significant variation in national capitalist models, predicated largely on institutional differences (e.g., Hall and Soskice, 2001; Schmidt, 2002). In the light of glacial institutional change, I assume that domestic configurations are independent variables, that is, they have remained largely intact, and concentrate instead on examining how variable exposure to global economic forces leads to different levels of subsidies conditional on the presence of corporatist institutional arrangements.

As Olson (1982) has shown, all-encompassing coalitions nationalize certain problems and make it easier to make deals that promote free trade and encourage compensatory side payments. For example, centralization of wage bargaining through corporatist institutions creates higher levels of organizational capacity among capital and labor. If so, the effects of asset specificity will have to be filtered through institutions, making it possible to extract more producer subsidies in corporatist arrangements in the form of compensation schemes. Conversely, in more pluralist regimes, where organizational capacity is weaker and policy fluctuations higher, there is reduced political commitment.

H5.2: In more corporatist political systems, subsidies are expected to be higher.

H5.3: As exposure to world markets increases, policymakers in more corporatist systems may insulate themselves against protectionist political pressure, resulting in fewer subsidies.

Formal Political Institutions and Subsidies

Apart from socioeconomic institutions, formal political institutions make a difference. Political systems are structured in ways that create risks and opportunities for social actors and for policymakers. For example, when actors place demands in the context of institutions where there are multiple veto points, their political power is diluted because their ability to get what they want depends to an extent on the deals they can make with other groups with different objectives and demands. Convincing policymakers in one institution to support one's demands does not necessarily ensure success when there are other groups doing the same in other institutions whose assent is needed to produce the final outcome. As a result, policymakers may feel less pressured to grant subsidies. However, once subsidies are granted, it is more difficult to eliminate them for the same reason. There are now many groups whose support is needed to change policy, which effectively maintains the status quo in most instances, that is, more subsidies. I examine the effects of two dimensions of institutional rules: the fragmentation of state power, that is, the number of veto points, and preference aggregation, that is, the degree of majoritarian or PR in the country's electoral system.

Fragmentation of State Power

Lijphart (1999) makes a fundamental distinction between two types of democracies: consensus and majoritarian. The main division separating the two types is the answer to the question: who governs? Consensus democracy claims the answer is "as many people as possible." Such a system generally entails rules that provide incentives for greater shared responsibility and inclusiveness. Majoritarian democracy's answer is "the majority." Also known as the Westminster model, it includes institutional rules that provide for less inclusion and more concentration of power in the hands of the majority. The differences between the two types of democracy cluster around two main institutional dimensions: the "executive-parties" dimension and the "federal-unitary" dimension. Birchfield and Crepaz (1998) have adapted this logic to describe institutional veto points and term the first "collective veto points" and the second "competitive veto points." They are two, qualitatively different forms of diffusing political power, which have redistributive implications.

Collective veto points refer to consensual institutional incentives that enable access to a broad array of actors and "force" political bargains to be made in the face of conflict and adversity. The best way to conceptualize this dimension is through a continuum of shared responsibility and collective agency on the one hand and divided agency and responsibility on the other (Goodin, 1996). Collective veto points disperse political power within institutions. Different actors "operate within the same body . . . and interact with each other on a face to face basis" (Birchfield and Crepaz, 1998, p. 182). Under these conditions, policies tend to be more responsive to different interest groups because of "logrolling." High degrees of partisanship will likely bring the process to a standstill because groups need to find common ground before they come to a decision (Schmidt, 1996). More inclusive, accommodating, and accessible institutions will likely reflect the wishes of the median voter more accurately, in the sense that more diverse preferences are taken into account (Huber and Powell, 1994).

Collective veto points are a composite measure of several dimensions. Systems with fewer collective veto points include (1) the degree of concentration of executive power in a single party, (2) executive dominance, (3) a more or less two-party system, (4) a majoritarian system with single-member districts and plurality or majority rule, and (5) a pluralist (less coordinated, less organized) system of interest group mediation. Systems with more collective points include characteristics at the opposite end of the continuum. In this case, power is more diffused among parties and branches of government. The system is more representative of diversity; for example, in an electoral system of PR, interest groups are more organized and negotiation more coordinated and institutionalized.

The redistributive capacity of the state increases as the number of collective veto points goes up. Countries with higher scores on the measure are likely to give out more subsidies than others. Institutions, such as multiparty coalition governments, for instance, tend to force bargaining and logrolling among participants. Because the assent of many parties is needed in order to form a government or pass legislation, compromises will include satisfying a higher number of claimants than would otherwise be the case. Groups adversely affected by trade push for these types of bargains on a continuous basis, driving up government expenditures (Crepaz and Moser, 2004). In countries with such "enabling" institutions, protection is more likely to be the outcome as opposed to countries with a single majority party government.

Competitive veto points refer to a situation where political power is diffused among different and separate institutions. In this case, actors hold mutual veto powers, leading occasionally to deadlock and immobilism. Competitive veto points are what most analysts understand veto points to be. For example, Tsebelis (2000; 2002) uses the term "veto player" to denote any actor whose agreement is needed for a political decision. The rules are set up in a way that as the number of veto players increases, the ability to reach consensus decreases because more players now wield veto power. Although Tsebelis focuses more on partisan players and to a lesser extent on institutions, he conceptualizes veto players essentially as competing for influence. To be sure, there are differences in the way veto points are conceived apart from the obvious terminological discrepancy. In essence, Tsebelis's argument implies that control of institutions changes with partisan control; consequently, the number of veto players may change dramatically across elections (O'Reilly, 2005, p. 657). In my conceptualization, institutional veto points, such as federalism, structure interest-group access and diffuse power across levels of government in ways that partisan control cannot change. Competition and conflict are inherent attributes of the system.

The notion of competitive veto points is a composite of five dimensions, the most important of which is federalism. "The most typical and drastic method of dividing power" is federalism. "In fact, as a term in political science, 'division of power' is normally used as a synonym for federalism" (Lijphart, 1999, p. 185). In addition, four other dimensions make a difference: (1) the existence of unicameral legislature, (2) the presence of more rigid constitutions, (3) the degree of judicial review, and (4) the degree of central bank independence. As the number of competitive veto points rises, systems disperse more powers to subnational governments, that is, they become less unitary, develop two legislative chambers, have more easily amended constitutions, have a stronger and independent judiciary, and have a more independent central bank.

The literature generally hypothesizes that as the number of institutions with veto power rises, the ability to change policy diminishes (Tsebelis, 2002; Crepaz and Moser, 2004; O'Reilly, 2005). There is merit to this argument, particularly in regard to subsidies. For example, if more bureaucrats are entrusted with making decisions, governments will be less responsive to societal demands. In countries with more independent central banks, expansionary policies are likely to be counteracted by central bankers raising interest rates. Because the ability of interest groups to access central banks is very limited and the intensity of governmental influence over them is limited by design, it follows that policy change will not necessarily reflect societal (or even governmental) political preferences. Central bankers do not have to run expensive political campaigns, which means that lobbying contributions will have a very limited impact on them (Clark, 2003). By implication, the ability to demand subsidies is likely to be weaker in those states.

But the relationship is not as clear-cut for all institutional dimensions. The existence of a federal system implies the proliferation of subsidy schemes for two reasons. First, it is easier to hide subsidies under complex deals between various levels of government. The argument is similar to the principle of obfuscation (Magee, Brock, and Young, 1989; Ono, 2006). The less transparent the policy instrument, the more likely the government is to use it, and by implication the higher the subsidies will be, because governments can hide the true cost from public view. For example, the U.S. federal government has consistently refused to publicize subsidy figures on the rationale that they are disbursed largely by states over which it does not have jurisdiction. This is despite the fact that many subsidies at the state level also involve more than just advice on how to maximize assistance from the federal government. For example, subsidies to incoming foreign (and domestic) producers to the state of Alabama include a good portion of federal incentives (tax breaks) as part of the overall package (Zahariadis and Morgan, 2005). Second, the higher the number of potential subsidizing agencies, the higher the overall amount of subsidies will be. This is because more agencies are now involved in providing fewer subsidies each, but which if added together would probably equal higher amounts. The implication for owners of specific assets is that losses (or potential gains) need not be as high to trigger subsidy allocation in federal systems. Losses are lower because the amount of compensation is lower and the cost to the smaller economy (for example, Alabama) can be spread over a larger economy (for example, the United States).

In addition, the presence of a bicameral legislature means that more access points are available to ask for subsidies. If the U.S. House of Representatives votes down the request, there is always the Senate. In the light of the fact that powers are effectively equal, that is, each chamber holds veto power, the chances of getting subsidized increase. The literature is replete with such institutional venue shopping in search of the chamber with the most likely favorable response to societal demands (e.g., Jones and Baumgartner, 2005; Sabatier and Weible, 2007). In contrast, the case is more clear-cut in unicameral legislatures. The demand for more subsidies is likely to fall on deaf ears if it does not fit the interests of the majority party in power. There are few other institutional venues to turn to.

Subsidies are expected to be higher in countries with more competitive veto points for the reasons stated above plus one more. Because of the prominence that Lijphart (1999) attaches to the dimension of federalism and to the index of unicameralism, the presence of many veto points implies that policy will be difficult to change. Because governments inherit programs such as subsidies, they are less likely to be able to change them at partisan will (Rose and Davies, 1994). Many opposing forces need to agree to the proposed change, making it less likely. The argument effectively implies that in the case of a downward trend in allocations, changing subsidies in countries with more competitive veto points will face more institutional obstacles, resulting in higher levels of protection than in cases of countries having fewer competitive veto points. In sum, I expect subsidies to be higher as the number of collective and competitive veto points increases but for essentially different reasons. In the case of collective veto points, subsidies will be higher because actors want them for reasons of inclusiveness, and in the case of competitive veto points subsidies will be higher because once inherited actors will find it more difficult to change them.

H5.4: As the number of collective and competitive veto points increases, the likelihood of subsidies also increases.

There are also interactive effects. Competitive and collective veto points have different impact depending on the level of exposure to global economic forces. When more actors are needed to make a subsidization decision, groups need to lobby harder because there are more chances of a negative decision. The implication is that the amount of resources (lobbying costs) goes up, and so does the opportunity cost. Under these conditions, groups must lose more to activate their membership to lobby government. At low levels of losses, lobbies may not have an incentive to act politically because they think of the lobbying costs as too high relative to the benefits. For example, if the chemical industry loses $100 million because of increased exposure to global trends, it may find it beneficial to lobby, provided that the campaign contributions do not go over, say, $50 million and the amount of subsidies exceeds $150 million. In decentralized governments with two or more veto players, such as the U.S. government, the amount of campaign contributions would be higher because there are more veto players to whose campaigns one needs to contribute to achieve the desired end. Assuming the extra amount equals $50 million, the lobby in the U.S. system would not find it beneficial to act even though the lobby in the UK would. The implication for globalization is that incentives to act change as institutions refract the extent of losses and the ability to act. At low levels of globalization, institutions will have a certain effect, which is likely to be magnified as exposure goes up. Losses may be larger but the incentive to lobby for more subsidies increases disproportionately because more institutions need to be accessed and greater resources expended. In other words, the losses need to be substantial and the subsidies even more so to activate lobbying efforts.

H5.5: High levels of exposure to globalization magnify the effects of more veto points, leading to more subsidies.

Preference Aggregation

Preference aggregation refers to the way votes are translated into seats. It is an aspect of the electoral system, and it describes how coalitions affect government response through the ballot box. There are two fundamental ways to structure any electoral system, with several variations within each: PR with multimember districts, where votes translate directly and proportionately into seats; and majoritarian systems with single-member districts, where a plurality or majority of votes wins the sole available seat.

Of course, PR and majoritarian systems are ideal types. Countries have adopted variations of each. Rogowski (1987, p. 209) argues that PR affects the power that producer groups have in influencing policy. "Pressure groups are restrained where campaign resources or the legal control of nominations are centralized in the hands of party leaders." For example, in cases where the electoral system tends to reward more votes with more seats, for example, a PR system, large coalitions are needed to supply subsidies. Assuming there are differences in preferences across groups, several groups need to coalesce in many districts to capture the majority of votes needed to pass a subsidization bill. National representatives who do not have narrow, geographically based constituents have fewer incentives to offer protection (McGillivray, 2004). In contrast, in systems where winner takes all, for example, majoritarian systems, the coalitions need to be large enough to capture single districts. In essence, the opposition in the latter case loses out completely because only one member can be elected.

To understand the mechanism that links a country's level of *electoral disproportionality* to particular levels and types of subsidies, analysis needs to turn to the concept of policy networks (Zahariadis, 2005). Policymakers employ and private actors seek subsidies to build and maintain policy networks. Policy networks are defined as "systems of informal relations between rational individuals that create a stable infrastructure for the exchange of personal favors" (Verdier, 1995, p. 5).

Political transactions are risky. Private actors (individual or corporate) voluntarily join the networks to reduce economic and policy risk while politicians seek to create policy networks to lower political risk. Private actors face market risk. To insure against social and economic dislocations, for example, losing a job or a business, they join networks. Networks provide for easier access and greater likelihood of success in demanding state subsidies. By virtue of being utility maximizers, politicians aim to increase their chances of reelection, and improve their career while in opposition, by placing a premium on constituent loyalty. Loyalty is fostered by generous disbursements of subsidies in times of need.

Networks limit risk and amplify opportunities for special rewards and subsidies. They necessitate commitment, high fixed costs, and a long time horizon. Because networks involve a series of reciprocal favors, they take a long time to build and require considerable energy by politicians. As a result, there is a high fixed cost and returns can be recouped only in the long run.

There are two types of networks: dense and diffuse. Dense networks involve tight relationships between actors with highly specialized, similar interests. These interests may be geographic or industry-based. A network may be local in orientation in that a group of individual workers and employers share a keen interest in the fate of a particular region or electoral district. Local constituents are mobilized to lobby politicians for subsidy relief when the region faces economic recession or high unemployment. Firms and workers in the same sector, say, steel or automobiles, operate in a similar, densely organized fashion. Diffuse networks are thin, loosely linked individuals or firms with general interests. They involve members of several sectors, for example, employers or labor, and may be class- or party-based.

The degree of disproportionality tends to promote the creation of a particular type of network. More diffuse networks are more likely to be found in PR systems. The very fact that large coalitions are needed implies that networks are more likely to be diffuse to accommodate different needs and demands. As a result, more horizontal (economy-wide) subsidies are likely to be disbursed. Alt and Gilligan (1994, pp. 185–197) raise a similar point when they claim that the Stolper-Samuelson model, that is, more widely dispersed coalitions and consequently protection, is more likely in systems where more individuals are involved in the decision-making process, that is,

PR systems. Because majoritarian systems contain smaller, single-member districts, the networks that develop will be dense. The more specific the subsidies, the more lucrative they are likely to be to their intended targets. The interests of such geographically focused regions will likely overlap, creating the requisite conditions for more concerted action on behalf of common interests by affected groups and the politicians who represent them. Because government has disproportionately more power in parliament, the subsidies disbursed will be more narrowly focused, for example, sectoral or regional subsidies.

As a result, disproportionality affects electoral competition and ultimately structures the incentives of politicians to supply subsidies. Because politicians strive to maximize constituent loyalty, which involves campaign contributions, they have an incentive to maximize the benefits distributed to their supporters. The higher the marginal benefits, the greater the likelihood of support and loyalty will be. Policymakers are more likely to offer higher amounts of overall protection in PR systems because more groups with diverse interests coalesce to elect candidates.

Rents generated by horizontal subsidies are less likely to be discarded when politicians move from government to opposition, because the new government would not want to drop policies that benefited its constituents. In contrast, the previous government's regional and sector-specific subsidization policies now benefit the new opposition's constituents, and they are therefore more likely to be dumped. In systems with more PR, coalition governments are likely to include some continuity in the sense that the chances are high that one or more coalition partners have been in power before. Sharp reversals of policy are rarer in this case than in majoritarian systems where different parties move in and out of power. Horizontal subsidies are not needed in that case to ensure continuation of benefits when out of government.

H5.6: As electoral disproportionality grows, that is, as systems become more majoritarian, the overall amount of subsidies will decline.

But the effects of globalization, which determine the losses and gains from international competition, will not be the same at all levels of disproportionality. When exposure to globalization increases, domestic manufacturers turn to politicians for relief. The higher the exposure, the greater the demand for subsidies will be. Politicians, however, are constrained by electoral competition. They are much more likely to be receptive to manufacturers' demands when there is relatively weak electoral competition. This means that the most effective networks under high exposure to global economic forces will be dense. Therefore, more specific subsidies (regional or sectoral) are likely to be disbursed under high trade and FDI openness and majoritarian constraints. When exposure recedes, the need for highly specific subsidies diminishes. This does not mean that companies do not want more subsidies. It simply means that they will change tactics and demand different kinds of subsidies. As the companies with incentives for subsidies change, so will the scope of subsidies. There is no sense of urgency to beat imports in the domestic market, and subsidies do not have to be tailored to specific firms or regions. Consequently, horizontal subsidies will be more likely to be disbursed provided that politicians have the incentive to supply them. The implication is that the relationship holds under conditions of more PR.

H5.7: In the light of high exposure to global economic forces, higher levels of electoral disproportionality encourage the disbursement of more regional and sector-specific subsidies. When exposure recedes, higher levels of electoral disproportionality lead to the disbursement of more horizontal subsidies.

Table 5.1 summarizes the expected effects of domestic political variables and subsidies. For purposes of presentation, it also reiterates the hypotheses regarding globalization in order to clarify the

Table 5.1   Hypothesized effects of globalization and domestic politics

	Total subsidies	Horizontal	Sectoral
Independent effects			
Trade	+	+	+
FDI	+	+	+
Portfolio investment (PI)	−	−	−
Political power	+	+	+
Pluralism (PL)	−	−	−
Disproportionality (DIS)	−	−	−
Cooperative veto (CV)	+	+	+
Competitive veto (COV)	+	+	+
Interactive effects			
Trade*PL	+	+	+
Trade*DIS	−	−	−
Trade*CV	+	+	+
Trade*COV	+	+	+
FDI*PL	+	−	+
FDI*DIS	−	−	−
FDI*CV	+	+	+
FDI*COV	+	+	+
PI*PL	+	+	+
PI*DIS	+	+	+
PI*CV	−	−	−
PI*COV	−	−	−

interactive relationships between globalization and domestic politics on levels and types of subsidies. Regional subsidies are assumed to follow the pattern of sectoral subsidies.

OPERATIONALIZATION AND ESTIMATION CONCERNS

While the impact of institutions on various aspects of policy has been well established in political science, the ability to accurately capture the essence of institutions has not enjoyed equal favor. By definition, institutions change very little over time, a fact that reduces their usefulness in studies utilizing time series analysis. Moreover, it is very difficult to accurately measure institutional variables, such as corporatism/pluralism, in a meaningful way. Corporatist features presuppose higher levels of labor and capital organization *via* peak associations, but measuring the degree of, say, unionization, does not capture the essence of the term.

Political power is a difficult concept to measure. There are many different faces of power and consequently a multitude of ways to conceptualize and measure power (e.g., Boulding, 1989; Wartenberg, 1992). I am interested in capturing the ability of affected groups to influence policy decisions. Because the essence of the asset influence model is political contributions, the logical answer to the problem would be to include political campaign contributions by interest groups. Unfortunately, there exist no such figures for the majority of countries, partly because such numbers are generally not made public and partly because in most countries contributions are given directly to political parties rather than to individual politicians. Therefore, cross-nationally comparable figures simply do not exist.

Grossman and Helpman (1994) propose using the inverse of import penetration ratios as the proxy for power. I follow their lead because higher import penetration ratios signify greater portions of the domestic market being captured by outsiders (importers). Such groups do not enjoy great power because the factories and jobs, that is, potential votes, are not necessarily domestic. In contrast, the inverse of those ratios signifies greater power of domestic producers because local and national groups capture a higher portion of the domestic market. The ability to deliver votes for or against policymakers is greater because the number of affected voters is higher. Group size, in other words, matters. Import ratios are taken from the OECD (2006b). They are expressed in percentages. I use the inverse numbers, expressed as ratios. Table 5.2 contains descriptive statistics about the indicator. Higher numbers indicate more political power.

As stated above, socioeconomic institutions are expected to have an impact on subsidies. There are several studies measuring the *pluralism-corporatism* distinction (e.g., Siaroff, 1999; Lane and Ersson, 1997; Lijphart and Crepaz, 1991). The problem is they emphasize different aspects; therefore, the figures differ across studies (Lijphart, 1999, p. 178). Some, for example, measure countries on the basis of the presence and strength of peak associations while others consider the degree of wage bargaining centralization to be of paramount importance. While both emphases are important components of the institutional environment within which interest groups operate, the end result is that different countries score differently on indicators, making comparisons across studies very problematic.

Lijphart (1999) has addressed this issue by providing a complete measure of interest group influence in national settings for 36 democracies since 1945. His figures are based on and supplement Siaroff's (1999) study of corporatism in 24 industrial democracies in the last 40 years. Siaroff ranks countries from one to five on the basis of eight dimensions, which include indicators of social partnership, degree of industry-level coordination, and national policymaking patterns. He then averages these measures to arrive at a comprehensive indicator, which captures the degree of interest group mediation. Lijphart's (1999) figures, which I use, are based on Siaroff's data. However, Lijphart divides the last 50 years into two time periods. The first encapsulates the period 1945–1996. The second measures the pluralist-corporatist distinction only since 1971. I use the latter data. There is a small difference in some countries, but the more recent figures are more appropriate for my purposes than the numbers of Lijphart's overall time period. Table 5.2 includes figures that range from .5 (Sweden) to 3.5 (Greece and the UK). For ease of interpretation, I label the

Table 5.2   Descriptive statistics of political variables*

Variable	Minimum	Maximum	Mean	Standard deviation
Political power**	.0098	.0625	.0319	.0119
Pluralism	.50	3.50	2.09	1.11
Electoral system	1.29	18.65	5.32	5.16
Collective veto points	−1.39	1.66	.37	.95
Competitive veto points	−1.19	2.53	−.05	.93

* Index numbers
** Inverse of percent domestic market share taken up by imports
Source: OECD (2006a); Lijphart (1999).

indicator as pluralism. Higher scores indicate more pluralist political systems, while lower numbers refer to more corporatist systems.

The distinction and measurement of veto points follows Lijphart's (1999) typology of consensus and majoritarian democracy. Birchfield and Crepaz (1998) adapt this reasoning to the veto point literature by differentiating between two types of veto points: collective and competitive. Collective veto points correspond to what Lijphart terms the "executives-parties" dimension, and competitive veto points correspond to the "federal-unitary" dimension. Each dimension is a standardized score of several indicators of veto points and each indicator captures a different dimension of the concept of veto points. Table 5.2 contains the relevant descriptive statistics. Higher numbers of collective veto points indicate a greater tendency toward shared responsibility and consensus democracy. The scores range between 1.66 (Finland) and −1.39 (UK). Competitive veto points refer to the second dimension, where institutions have equal say, and therefore veto power, in making policy. In general, more federal systems where state power is more widely dispersed score higher on the index. The scores range from 2.53 in federal Germany to −1.19 in unitary Britain.

Preference aggregation is measured as an index number. As Lijphart (1999, p. 143) makes it clear, "The typical electoral system of majoritarian democracy is the single-member district plurality or majority system; consensus democracy typically uses PR." He proceeds to construct an index of *electoral disproportionality*, which takes into account the degree of deviation from the ideal polar opposites that systems may exhibit. In essence the index takes into account the squared differences between the percentage of seats and the percentage of votes parties receive in national legislative and presidential elections. In the latter case, Lijphart takes the geometric mean of the disproportionality of legislative and presidential elections, where appropriate. In the case of more PR, the score tends toward one. The number increases as the system becomes more skewed toward majoritarianism. Table 5.2 includes the relevant figures, representing the period 1971–1996 (Lijphart, 1999). The scores range from 1.29 (Holland) to 18.65 (France).

CONCLUSION

In this chapter, I have examined the effects of national political institutions and power on the likelihood of protection. Attention was paid primarily to the supply side of the equation, focusing squarely on the conditions that make it more likely for politicians to grant subsidies to affected groups. Two factors were examined in greater detail: the political power of affected groups and the institutional constraints that regulate the ability of groups to demand and the willingness of policymakers to supply subsidies.

The willingness of politicians to listen to affected groups is critically dependent upon the political power that groups wield. Governments never have enough resources to address all the issues before them. They have to choose what issues to attend to and what resources to expend in addressing the concerns of the relevant groups. In this context, it is trite to argue that more powerful groups will obviously be more likely to succeed at getting what they want than others. The ability to be heard and the likelihood of delivering rewards or punishments to government increase as a function of power.

Incentives to listen and ability to supply rewards are also carefully circumscribed by the political institutional system within which groups and governments operate. I paid close attention to two types of institutions that regulate access and shape rent-seeking and rent-supplying behavior. The first type operates outside the formal political sphere. It brings together organized groups, coordinating actions and demands. The redistributive capacity of the state is limited by the pluralist-corporatist degree of interest mediation. Demands for subsidies, and consequently the level of subsidies, are likely to be more successful in more corporatist systems. The encompassing coalitions implied by such arrangements leads to compensatory deals. Groups agree to more subsidies on a continuous basis in exchange for industrial peace and policy stability.

Formal political institutions also have an effect on the propensity to disburse subsidies because they regulate access and control of the process. In cases where there are more veto points, that is, as the number of institutional (be they collective or competitive) veto points goes up, the level of subsidies increases. The logic is very simple. Because groups know their agreement is needed to make decisions, they will press hard in favor of their interests, however parochial they may be. In the aggregate, the decisions will tend to satisfy as many coalition partners as possible, which imply more subsidies to more groups.

TESTING THE ARGUMENT

I have built a model that explains subsidization patterns by national governments with reference to four variables. Increasing exposure to global economic forces create domestic economic winners and losers.

Depending on the degree of asset specificity, losers are likely to apply pressure on national governments to grant more subsidies to alleviate the costs. The success of these demands depends on the political power of these actors and the national institutional configurations that compel policymakers to act.

The model's predictions are tested in the following two chapters. In chapter 6, I estimate the effects of globalization on total subsidies. I then break down the dependent variable into two groups—horizontal or economy-wide subsidies and sectoral or sector-pecific subsidies—and repeat the estimation process. Finally, I analyze the issue of regional subsidies, which involve geographically concentrated interests. Does the model explain the disbursement of regional aid as well? In chapter 7, I first break down the dependent variable into manufacturing and agricultural subsidies to explore any differences between different policy sectors. I then look at the calculus of choice between policy tools. Does the model explain equally well the levels of subsidies as well the choice between instruments of subsidization?

Chapter 6

Objectives and Regions

That [the theorem of comparative advantage] is logically true need not be argued before a mathematician.

—Paul Samuelson, Nobel Prize winner in economics[1]

In the previous chapters I built the asset influence model of national subsidization efforts. In this chapter, I put the hypotheses to the test. The chapter is divided into three parts. In the first part, I discuss estimation concerns. In the second part, I break down the dependent variable into three groups—total aid, horizontal or economy-wide subsidies, and sectoral or sector-specific subsidies—and estimate the main and conditional effects of the independent variables on the disbursements of each of them. In the third part, I look at the effects of the variables on regional subsidies. How well does the model explain the choice between the various objectives of subsidies?

Data and Estimation Concerns

The asset influence model is built around the impact of four variables on national subsidies: globalization, asset specificity, group political power, and national institutions. The model includes hypotheses that involve main and interactive effects.

National subsidies are a form of state intervention used to promote certain economic activities. The implication is that certain sectors, firms, or types of activities are treated more favorably than others. It is precisely this distortionary element that makes subsidies incompatible with the free market. The transfer of state resources need not be granted by the state itself; public or semipublic intermediaries may be involved. Moreover, subsidies, as the European Commission's (2006c) *State Aid Scoreboard* makes clear, must be selective, confer an economic advantage, and negatively affect competition and international trade.

Data for all indicators of national subsidies are taken from the European Commission's (2006b; 2006c) *Scoreboard,* supplemented by numbers included in earlier surveys. The Competition Directorate-General provides annual figures of national subsidies (or state aids as it calls them) disbursed by every EU member state. The dataset offers the most complete and detailed picture of state subsidies by any international organization with figures that are cross-nationally and temporally comparable. Although the set has some limitations—essentially it involves recalculating figures collected by national authorities according to a standardized methodology—it is the best and most up-to-date collection of data on national subsidies (Thomas, 2000). Data begin with the year 1992 for all member states and end with the year 2004. The only exceptions are Austria, Sweden, and Finland that did not join EU, and therefore figures are not provided, until 1995.

There are two sets of indicators of the dependent variable. The data on total subsidies are expressed as annual percent of total aid over GDP. This figure includes subsidies to many sectors and some services, for example, financial services, although the actual figures regarding services are in most instances miniscule compared to aid in manufacturing or agriculture. The data do not include assistance to railways.

The figures on sectoral, horizontal, regional, manufacturing, and agricultural subsidies are expressed in million euros in constant 1995 prices (rereferenced to 2004). However, to address issues of extreme variance in the dependent variable, the raw numbers are logarithmically transformed to their natural base. The reason why I do not express them in GDP percentages is because of the low amounts that are disbursed in some cases. As figure 1.1 showed, total subsidies in some cases amounted to less than half percent of GDP. Breaking this amount down to various components yields very small fractions, which may be unable to pick up important variations across countries.

In this case, however, one has to control for economic size. Because the economies of, say, Germany and Greece vary considerably in size, the same amount of subsidies to manufacturing, for instance, may be of different political and economic importance to each. Moreover, large states are vested with disproportionate market power. They have incentives in most instances to subsidize their industries even in the face of possible retaliation by foreign governments because the harmful effects from retaliation will not be as strongly felt when imposed by smaller states (Mansfield and Busch, 1995). The best way to capture this point is to include a term for size of the economy, such as annual GDP at time t. GDP is expressed in constant year 2000 prices dollars and logarithmically transformed to its natural base. Data on economic output were taken from OECD (2006a). Constant prices were calculated using the consumer price index included in the same source.

The independent variables include the following. Globalization is measured by three indicators. As I explained in chapter 3, there are two important dimensions of globalization: trade and capital. Trade openness is measured as annual percent of exports plus imports of goods over GDP. Capital openness is measured in two ways. The first indicator includes FDI (or long-term investment) figures. The second indicator includes portfolio (or short-term) investment numbers. Both figures are expressed in millions of U.S. dollars, converted into percentages of GDP. Higher levels of the indicators signify higher levels of openness. Data on trade and GDP are taken from OECD (2006a). FDI figures are from OECD (2005b) and portfolio investment from IMF (various years).

Asset specificity is measured by two indicators. Following Hiscox (2002), I calculate labor specificity as the coefficient of variation (standard deviation over mean in percentages) in wages across nine industries, and capital specificity as the coefficient of variation in profits across nine industries. Data are taken from the OECD's databases on *National Accounts* (various years), *Labour Force Statistics* (various years), and the *Structural Analysis (STAN) Database* (2004).

The institutions variable looks at three elements: pluralism, veto points, and electoral system. Pluralism is measured as a time-invariant index number. Veto points are similarly time invariant and captured by the use of two indicators. Competitive and collective veto points are expressed as index numbers. The disproportionality of the electoral system is also expressed as a standardized index number. All data are taken from Lijphart (1999).

The variable of a group's political power looks at the ability of groups to extract subsidies from the government. Following Grossman and Helpman (1994) it is expressed as the inverse of import demand. Figures for import demand are percentages of the total domestic market taken up by imports. They are found in the *OECD Trade Statistics Database* (2006b).

I use pooled time series analysis to investigate the question at hand. A brief look at the levels of variance inflation factors suggests that the level of collinearity among the independent variables is significantly below what is considered to be problematic in the literature (Fox, 1991; Chatterjee, Hadi, and Price, 2000).[2] The estimates should, therefore, be unbiased and consistent. Unfortunately, examination of the Durbin-Watson statistic reveals the presence of strong serial correlation within units. For this reason, I transform the data *via* the Prais-Winsten technique, which includes an AR(1) estimation that retains the first observation.

Panel data of this kind also frequently suffer from heteroscedasticity. There are two ways to deal with this concern. Stimson (1985) recommends a fixed-effects model. It involves using dummy variables for all but one country in the sample. The fixed-effects model has the additional benefit of capturing unobserved differences in each country, which could potentially bias the results (Green, Kim, and Yoon, 2001). The problem with this approach is the presence of time-invariant variables in my model (all institutional variables). For this reason, analysts generally opt to calculate either robust standard errors or panel-corrected standard errors. Panel-corrected standard errors are recommended in cases where the temporal intervals are greater than the number of units (Beck and Katz, 1995). In my case, the number of countries, 14, is slightly higher than the number of years, 13. For this reason, I follow the recommendation by Beck et al. (1993) and calculate robust standard errors for every equation that follows.[3]

To capture the budgetary logic of the puzzle of subsidies, I lag the main independent variables by one year so that, say, asset specificity at time *t-1* is used to explain the disbursement of national subsidies at time *t*. The only exceptions are the institutional variables, which are time invariant. The interactive terms are the products of the independent variables at the time of measurement, that is, all of them contain time lags except for institutions.

There exists the possibility that two countries in my sample, Ireland and Spain, are outliers. Ireland traded the most and received significant amounts of portfolio investment throughout the period of study. Spain was on the opposite end of the spectrum. It is possible that including them may bias the estimates. I ran the equations excluding them, but there were no substantive changes in the results.[4] Therefore, I include them in the reported findings.

In formal terms, the equation that guides the model is the following. In the sections of this chapter and the next that measure the dependent variable using absolute numbers I modify the equation by adding absolute constant GDP figures on the right-hand side.

$$SUBSIDY_{i,t} = a + b1ASSET_{i,t-1} + b2GLOBALIZATION_{i,t-1}$$
$$+ b3INSTITUTION_{i,t} + b4POLITICAL\ POWER_{i,t-1}$$
$$+ b5GLOBALIZATION*ASSET$$
$$+ b6GLOBALIZATION*INSTITUTION + u$$

where a is the constant term, i is country, and t is year. SUBSIDY refers to the amount of funds allocated as subsidy. ASSET refers to asset specificity, measured as coefficient of variation in wage costs and profits. GLOBALIZATION contains three indicators: trade openness, measured as percent trade in goods over GDP; FDI openness, measured as percent total FDI (incoming and outgoing) over GDP; and portfolio openness, measured as percent portfolio investment over GDP. INSTITUTION refers to national institutions and includes four indicators: pluralism, measured as an index number; competitive veto points, measured as an index number; consensus veto points, measured as an index number; and electoral system, measured as an index number. POLITICAL POWER refers to the affected group's power to get subsidies and is measured as the inverse of import demand. The remaining two variables are multiplicative terms (Jaccard, Turrisi, and Wan, 1990). GLOBALIZATION*ASSET refers to the interactive term of the three indicators of globalization and the two indicators of asset specificity; GLOBALIZATION*INSTITUTION is the interactive term of the three indicators of globalization and the three indicators of institutions; and u is the disturbance term.

To account for alternative explanations, I estimate the equations with two control variables. The literature makes a strong argument that demands for subsidies are more likely to intensify when the economy is weak or in a recession (e.g., McKeown, 1984; Henisz and Mansfield, 2006; Wren, 1996). The government is likely to have a more sympathetic ear when growth is weak. Similarly, when unemployment is high, workers are more likely to lobby for protection. The first variable measures real annual economic growth. The second indicator measures standardized rates on unemployment. Both sets of figures are taken from the OECD (2006a). However, none of them prove to be statistically significant in the majority of equations. Contrary to conventional wisdom, it appears that the disbursement of subsidies is generally unrelated to macroeconomic conditions. For this reason, I do not include the control variables in the reported equations.

I also considered the possibility of endogeneity. Subsidies at time *t* may theoretically affect exposure to economic forces at time *t+1*. Wooldridge (2002) recommends running a two-stage least squares regression with instruments for the globalization variables and their interaction. I did so, but the results came out substantively similar; all variables had the same sign except for FDI and portfolio investment in some equations, but the coefficients increased in most cases.

Analyzing the Disbursement of National Subsidies: A First Cut

I regress state subsidies on four main independent variables and their interactions: globalization, asset specificity, political power, and national institutions. Looking at the three equations that examine total subsidies (table 6.1), the model has moderate overall fit. The model explains overall about one-third of the variance in subsidies as a percent of GDP after taking into account the relevant variables. Because of multicollinearity among institutional variables, I estimate their effects separately and consequently report three equations per dependent variable.

There are several striking features about the table. Keeping in mind the general decrease in subsidies over time (figure 1.1), it is not surprising that the constant for this, and subsequent estimations, is negative. This means there is a general tendency toward fewer subsidies over time, but several factors arrest or accelerate the decline. The point is not that subsidies are multiplying, but rather that in the light of institutional and political commitment to free trade, why is there still so much protection?

Globalization has an important effect on subsidies. But not all globalization is created equal. Trade openness has a significant positive effect when accounting also for electoral system and veto points, but portfolio investment has a significant negative effect when also taking corporatism into account. Consistent with the hypotheses of the model, higher levels of openness lead to more subsidies. When exposure to global trade increases, demands for protection increase as well. Groups adversely affected by trade, organize and successfully lobby for more subsidies to ease the pain.

Portfolio investment has the hypothesized negative effect on subsidies. The threat of short-term capital flight is a powerful motivator against subsidy protection. A 1 percent increase in portfolio investment leads to a .005 percent decrease in subsidies. Although the effect appears to be small at present, as capital controls continue to fall and as the amount of portfolio investment increases (see figure 3.3),

Table 6.1 The determinants of total subsidies

	(1)	(2)	(3)
Labor specificity (LS)	.0176	.018	.162
	(.004)***	(.005)***	(.006)***
Capital specificity (CS)	.008	.001	.008
	(.005)	(.004)	(.006)
Political power	32.53	30.97	29.40
	(12.84)**	(11.78)***	(12.01)**
Foreign direct investment (FDI)	.0028	−.0028	−.012
	(.010)	(.010)	(.010)
Portfolio investment	−.005	.001	.004
	(.002)**	(.003)	(.003)
Trade openness	.014	.037	.049
	(.009)	(.014)***	(.011)***
Pluralism	−.686		
	(.274)**		
Electoral system		−.048	
		(.084)	
Collective veto points			.520
			(.222)**
Competitive veto points			.354
			(.21)*
LS*FDI	.0000	.0000	.000
	(.0001)	(.0001)	(.000)
LS*trade	−.0004	−.0005	−.0005
	(.0000)***	(.0001)***	(.0001)**
LS*portfolio	.00009	.0000	−.00004
	(00002)***	(.0000)	(8.16e−06)***
CS*FDI	.0000	.0000	.00009
	(.000)	(.0000)	(.00004)**
CS*trade	−.0003	4.18−e06	−.0001
	(.0001)**	(.0000)	(.0001)
CS*portfolio	.0000	−.0000	.000
	(0000)	(.0000)	(000)
Pluralism*trade	.0154		
	(.006)**		
Pluralism*FDI	−.004		
	(.003)		
Pluralism*portfolio	5.70e−07		
	(1.18e−06)		
Electoral system*trade		.000	
		(.002)	
Electoral system*FDI		.000	
		(.000)	
Electoral system*portfolio		−.0002	
		(.0002)	

(Continued)

Table 6.1 (*Continued*)

	(1)	(2)	(3)
Collective veto points*trade			.0099
			(.0038)**
Collective veto points*FDI			.002
			(.002)
Collective veto points*portfolio			.0008
			(.001)
Competitive veto points*trade			−.0098
			(.005)*
Competitive veto points*FDI			.0007
			(.0017)
Competitive veto points*portfolio			.001
			(.002)
Constant	−.403	−1.24	−1.87
	(.719)	(.634)*	(.76)**
Adjusted R-squared	.3248	.3103	.3483
Rho	.6452	.6799	.6265

Prais-Winsten estimates with robust standard errors in parentheses
N = 173; * .05 < p < .10; ** .01 < p < .05; *** p < .01; two-tailed

the magnitude of the impact is expected to grow over time (Drucker, 1997). Globalization affects the incentives of policymakers. As portfolio openness rises, policymakers become less sensitive to domestic political demands, that is, they give out fewer subsidies as they seek to balance the need to attract foreign investment against domestic constituent needs.

Labor specificity has a consistently positive effect on subsidies. As the coefficient of variation goes up by 1 percentage point, that is, moving labor assets across industries becomes costlier for various reasons, the amount of subsidies as a percent of annual economic output increases by .168 percent. Considering that the subsidy mean for all 14 countries in the sample for the period 1992–2004 was .85 percent of GDP, labor specificity has a sizable impact. Worker inability to move across industries effortlessly gives rise to demands for protection. Unions contribute to politicians' campaigns and politicians in turn reward these contributions with subsidy protection. Interestingly, capital specificity, that is, the ability of owners of capital to move assets across industries, does not have a statistically significant impact on the allocation of subsidies. It is possible that intranational movements of capital have indeed become less costly and the need for subsidies in favor of protecting profits in specific industries is subdued.

My findings contradict somewhat those of Hiscox (2002). Looking at the relationship between specificity and votes in the United States, the author finds that labor specificity has an overall positive effect and capital specificity has a negative effect on protection. However, a cross-national examination of a more direct relationship between specificity and protection fails to ascertain the impact of capital specificity. True, workers in the industrialized world make a difference. They demand and get protection when they feel threatened. However, capital owners do not appear equally capable or willing. It is not that they are opposed to protection, as Hiscox's results suggest. Capitalists in Europe are simply indifferent or at least eager to let workers do the talking. Perhaps they are content to let the workers expend the capital, both financial and political, to get protection that will ultimately serve industrialists as well. Or it could be that the benefits do not outweigh the costs. Although the maximum value of the coefficient of variation for capital specificity is higher than that of labor specificity, capital specificity has a lower mean. This means that profit differentials across industries are lower on average than labor differentials across industries. The implication is that owners of capital find it less costly than do workers to move assets in search of higher returns. They are experiencing lower opportunity costs and are consequently less motivated to act. This is a strong finding that applies similarly to all equations in this study.

Political considerations also have a strong impact. While globalization and asset specificity measure economic pressures and domestic group incentives for protection, domestic political considerations also affect the eventual outcome. Consistent with Grossman and Helpman's (1994) prediction, increases in group political power have a strong positive effect on the disbursement of subsidies. The result is not surprising, but it bears repeating. Groups with a stronger presence in domestic markets, that is, higher ratios of output over imports, are on average more successful in securing subsidy protection than others. Stated differently, in countries where imports have made significant inroads, protection is generally lower because the affected groups have grown politically weaker. The implication is that foreign competition eliminates over time domestic producers who will no longer lobby for protection. As a result, the overall trend of subsidies will decline. The data clearly bear out this prediction.

Institutional variables also exercise significant influence. The model predicts that national institutional configurations, both in socioeconomic and formal political terms, have a considerable influence on the ability to secure government subsidies. Confirming the model's prediction, as the degree of pluralism increases, the amount of subsidies goes down. Grossman and Helpman (1994) argue that greater levels of organization ought to lead to more protection. In highly organized national systems, such as those with corporatist arrangements, the level of subsidies on average is higher.

There are two reasons for this finding. First, pluralist systems are more susceptible to short-term demands for protection. Given the annual negotiations between workers and employers and the explicit need for stability and industrial peace, corporatist systems take a longer-term view of compensation from adverse effects from globalization. Long-term compensation measures are funded at higher rates, including welfare payments, unemployment insurance, and the like. Gains (losses) in pluralist systems loom large even in the short term, so there are likely to be higher fluctuations. The second reason is that in a highly organized system, disparities in organizational capacity will be minimal. Consequently, the marginal benefits of lobbying for protection are likely to be minimal. In the light of compensation schemes designed to minimize losses, the actual amounts of subsidies are likely to be higher.

The other institutional variables have variable effects. The disproportionality of the electoral system has the expected sign but it is not statistically significant. As the system moves away from PR, the amount of subsidies goes up. But this claim does not appear to hold on average. What is interesting is the effect of veto points on subsidy disbursements. Subsidies go up as the number of competitive veto points increases. Because they face a higher number of decisive no votes, policymakers have to bribe more groups to secure protection. As a result, the amount of subsidies increases. In addition, collective veto points also have a strong positive effect. As countries move closer to consensus democracy, that is, they become more inclusionary, their redistributive capacity increases. Institutions force more bargaining solutions, which lead to greater use of "logrolling," which ultimately expand the ability of the state to protect disaffected groups.

This argument partially confirms that of Crepaz (2001) and others who have explored the impact of institutions on welfare and trade policy. First, collective institutions do indeed lead to greater redistribution in the form of subsidy protection. Such institutions explain far more than inflation, which Lijphart (1999) originally reported. However, the findings here stand in sharp contrast to Crepaz (2001) and Crepaz and Moser (2004) who find that competitive veto points reduce redistribution and public expenditures. Government expenditures may be too broad of a measure to pinpoint the effects of institutions with mutually exclusive powers and the ability to veto each other's decisions. It may be that such institutions are in fact more susceptible to protectionist demands primarily because disaffected groups can block legislation and therefore call attention to their plight.

Somewhat similar and more directly relevant arguments are made by O'Reilly (2005) and Henisz and Mansfield (2006). O'Reilly finds that as the number of veto points goes up, the change in tariff levels is reduced. His argument is a bit more complicated because the author examines the absolute level of change, rather than decreases or increases in protection. Nevertheless, his finding is relevant because it implies that higher levels of institutional veto points are associated with smaller absolute changes in protection. Such systems are impervious to short-term demands by small, disaffected groups. Applying the insight to my equations, I expect to find lower rates of subsidization as the number of institutional veto points increases. Quite the contrary, I find that the rate of protection actually increases in such systems (within the context of an overall decline in subsidies as discussed above). Henisz and Mansfield (2006) test the impact of veto points on trade openness (but not protection *per se*). They find that in stable democracies, that is, the industrialized world, trade openness declines as the number of veto points increases. Using an indicator of veto points that corresponds somewhat to the indicator used here to measure competitive veto points, they find, with subsequent qualifications, that "changes in import penetration [their measure of commercial openness] are more likely to occur as the number of number of veto points declines" (Henisz and Mansfield, 2006, p. 209). In other words, greater openness is associated with fewer veto points. My study parallels their claim. Protection is more likely when veto points increase. Divided government, in other words, impedes rather than promotes free trade (Lohmann and O'Halloran, 1994). Institutions play a role as the literature contends, but not in directions that conventional wisdom expects.

The argument made here goes beyond the main effect. Globalization has a differential impact on subsidies depending on particular configurations in the domestic policy process. Societal demands and institutions have a conditional impact on protection (Henisz and Mansfield, 2006). As table 6.1 shows, many of the conditional relationships posited in earlier chapters hold true. Interestingly, the conditional hypotheses regarding trade and labor specificity are consistently in the same direction across the three equations and statistically significant, raising the confidence in the robustness of the relationship. The same is largely true regarding portfolio investment and labor specificity. Of the interactive variables pertaining to institutions, the degree of pluralism makes a big difference both independently and when it interacts with trade. The same holds in the case of collective veto points.

Counterfactuals were calculated on the basis of equation 1 in table 6.1. Low (high) trade refers to 20th (80th) percentile scores in the sample. Less (more) pluralism refers to the 20th (80th) percentile score on the pluralist index. Low (high) labor specificity refers to the 20th (80th) percentile score on the labor specificity coefficient of variation. All other variables are set at their means.

To get a better sense of the interactive relationships, I calculate the counterfactual simulations for two multiplicative terms that are statistically significant at the .05 level or better. I do so because the coefficient of the constitutive term X of each interaction accounts for the impact on Y when variable Z is held at 0 (Braumoeller, 2004). Consequently, the results as presented in each table do not reveal much. I want to show how the effects of some variables change conditional on the presence of specific levels of other variables to demonstrate the point that not only does globalization have important direct effects, but it also interacts with the domestic policy process to produce surprising and notable subsidy outcomes. The purpose of calculating counterfactuals for only two relationships, out of a potential universe of ten, is purely illustrative. The relationships reveal interesting patterns over and beyond the independent effects of each of the variables.

The data in figure 6.1 are calculated on the basis of table 6.1. All variables are set at their means, while trade and pluralism and trade

Pluralism

	Less	More
Trade Low	0.595	−0.057
Trade High	1.538	1.877

Labor specificity

	Low	High
Trade Low	1.008	1.152
Trade High	0.672	0.504

Figure 6.1   Counterfactual estimates of total subsidies (% GDP).

and labor specificity are allowed to vary respectively. I do not report the tail ends of the distributions in the sample; rather I rely on the 20th and 80th percentile figures in each variable. In this way, readers may gain better insight into what happens to particular relationships when variables acquire different values. For example, the 20th percentile in the pluralist index corresponds to Denmark, a relatively corporatist, but not the most corporatist, country in the sample, while the 80th percentile represents Spain, a country with a more pluralist organization of interest groups. Similarly, the 80th percentile in trade corresponds to Holland in 1995, while the 20th percentile is Italy in 1998; the 20th percentile in labor specificity is Finland in 2002, while the 80th percentile represents Greece in 2001.

The numbers inside the matrix cells represent state subsidy disbursements as a percent of GDP. Moving from left to right indicates whether more pluralism or higher labor specificity increased subsidies. Moving up or down suggests what happens to subsidies when trade exposure decreases or increases. Looking at the top box at the right corner, we see that the least amount of subsidies is disbursed in more pluralist countries at low levels of trade exposure. The simulated figure is negative, implying that in pluralist countries subsidies will fall. It validates G-H's prediction that there is "negative protection for those [groups] that have no political representation" (Grossman and Helpman, 2002, p. 12). Also more corporatist states give out more subsidies, validating the point that the likelihood of protection increases when the level of group organization goes up. At lower levels of trade of the interactive term this is true.

The amount of subsidies is supposed to be higher when the stakes are high, that is, at high exposure to trade. This is also borne out by the data. But the effects of pluralism reverse as trade exposure increases. At high levels of trade exposure, pluralism has a significantly positive effect on subsidies. The amount of subsidies increases dramatically and surpasses that of more corporatist countries. The implication is that the level of group organization has a significant effect, but the relationship, whether positive or negative, really depends on the level of trade exposure. In more pluralist systems, affected groups have disproportionately more power to get what they want in the short term. Political contributions make a big difference, as the model suggests, but only when the stakes are high, the losses are heavy, and policymakers are more accessible to a variety of groups. Protectionism is the outcome of a contingent relationship (Boix, 2004). Its effects truly depend on the level of exposure to world markets. Consequently, the compensation hypothesis posited by analysts (e.g., Katzenstein, 1985; Cameron,

1978; Rodrik, 1998) receives full support. Because countries with corporatist institutional arrangements aim to smoothen adjustment efforts, we expect them to experience less wild fluctuations than countries with pluralist arrangements. The implication is corporatist countries will subsidize more on average, but relatively less at extreme levels of trade. Indeed, the study uncovers a strong negative independent effect (more corporatist countries provide more subsidies), and a strong positive conditional effect (more corporatist countries provide fewer subsidies when trade exposure is high). In the light of the fact that more corporatist countries are also more exposed to world markets, the interactive term acquires greater theoretical significance. Whether or not policymakers adopt protectionism depends on independent and, perhaps more importantly, conditional relationships.

The situation is reversed when it comes to the effects of trade in the light of different levels of labor specificity. Labor specificity seems to be most effective at lower than higher levels of trade. As anticipated, higher specificity leads to more subsidies at low levels of trade, but the situation is surprisingly reversed at higher trade levels. This is an interesting puzzle. Labor specificity has independent positive effects on the disbursement of subsidies when taking into account the effects of trade, but when it interacts with different levels of trade, the situation is reversed. Acemoglu and Robinson (2001) posit a negative relationship between specificity and protection. Dubbing subsidies as a form of inefficient redistribution, the authors proceed to hypothesize that groups with less-specific assets will seek more subsidies because they want to encourage the entry of newcomers. They make a crucial assumption: the main form of a group's political pressure is size. All groups seek to increase their size to acquire more power. Groups with less-specific assets subsidize the entrance of newcomers, which dilutes to an extent an individual's benefits from subsidies but it also maintains them. This line of reasoning receives qualified empirical support here. At low levels of trade, groups with more-specific assets exert political pressure to demand subsidies because of the high cost of moving assets. At high levels of trade, however, it appears that different groups are activated: those with less-specific assets seek to increase subsidies to encourage potential switchers to that activity to stay. Under different conditions, asset specificity may have positive or negative effects.

Policy by Objective

Figures for total subsidies give a panoramic view of the puzzle, but they do not reveal all the wrinkles that may lie underneath. The second step is, therefore, to look at the objectives of subsidies. Not all subsidies have the same distortionary element. Some aid, such as that given to specific firms or that which aims to assist particular sectors, is far more distortionary than aid that applies to the entire economy. Attention now turns to address this issue.

There is considerable variation among subsidy objectives, but aid may be classified along two dimensions. Aid that affects specific firms or industries is more desirable from the point of view of individual firms for two reasons. First, different firms have different needs. Aid that is tailor-made for a specific firm obviously addresses company losses more directly and effectively. Second, sectoral aid is also distributionally sharper. Groups are more likely to put in more effort when they believe they will receive the lion's share of the spoils. This way, they may be assured of the efficiency of their allocation of resources. Costs are distributed widely and benefits are concentrated. Conversely, distributionally more blunt aid, such as horizontal subsidies, which apply economy-wide, are of less interest to specific firms. Costs are distributed widely but so are the benefits. Affected groups are less likely to lobby for this type of protection not simply because it may not address their present concerns but also because they may be able to free ride. When benefits are distributed among a large group of beneficiaries, such as the case of horizontal subsidies, groups have incentives to cheat (Olson, 1965). In true entrepreneurial politics fashion (Wilson, 1980), affected groups are less likely to devote substantial effort and money to lobby for horizontal subsidies because they expect others to do it for them. The efficiency of resource allocation is low, which implies that losses probably need to exceed a certain threshold before groups decide to devote money and time to organize lobbying activities. Examples of aid with horizontal objectives include worker training, environmental assistance, export aid, and aid to small and medium-sized enterprises (European Commission, 2006a; 2006c).

Horizontal Subsidies

Table 6.2 supplies the estimation results of horizontal subsidies. The adjusted R-squared coefficients are very high, which implies a good model fit. Note that this and subsequent equations involve a dependent variable that is logarithmically transformed. The control for economic size, GDP, is now placed on the right side of the equation. Not surprisingly, GDP has a consistently substantial and statistically significant positive effect on subsidies. It is self-evident that larger countries will disburse more subsidies. The constant is similarly negative, indicating that subsidies are going down over time.

Table 6.2   The determinants of horizontal subsidies

	(1)	(2)	(3)
GDP	1.09	1.16	1.11
	(.085)***	(.91)***	(.093)***
Labor specificity (LS)	.0205	.019	.020
	(.006)***	(.006)***	(.006)***
Capital specificity (CS)	.002	−.002	.002
	(.005)	(.004)	(.004)
Political power	12.39	12.27	14.97
	(11.18)	(12.34)	(11.51)
Foreign direct investment (FDI)	.008	.005	.001
	(.008)	(.007)	(.012)
Portfolio investment	.002	−.000	−.003
	(.003)	(.003)	(.003)
Trade openness	.019	.029	.047
	(.016)	(.016)*	(.014)***
Pluralism	−.586		
	(.0142)***		
Electoral system		−.085	
		(.037)**	
Collective veto points			.666
			(.122)
Competitive veto points			.038
			(.188)
LS*FDI	−.000	−.000	−.000
	(.000)	(.000)	(.000)
LS*trade	−.0005	−.0005	−.0005
	(.0002)***	(.0002)**	(.0004)**
LS*portfolio	−.000	.000	−.000
	(.000)	(.000)	(.000)
CS*FDI	.0002	.0001	.000
	(.00009)***	(.00002)***	(.000)
CS*trade	−.000	8.14e–06	−.000
	(.000)	(.000)	(.000)
CS*portfolio	.000	−.000	.000
	(.000)	(.000)	(.000)
Pluralism*trade	.010		
	(.003)***		
Pluralism*FDI	−.006		
	(.002)***		
Pluralism*portfolio	−2.04e–06		
	(1.25e–06)		
Electoral system*trade		.001	
		(.001)	
Electoral system*FDI		−.012	
		(.0005)***	
Electoral system*portfolio		.0002	
		(.0002)	

Table 6.2   (*Continued*)

	(1)	(2)	(3)
Collective veto points*trade			−.011
			(.004)**
Collective veto points*FDI			.002
			(.003)
Collective veto points*portfolio			.003
			(.002)*
Competitive veto points*trade			.000
			(.007)
Competitive veto points*FDI			−.002
			(.002)
Competitive veto points*portfolio			.002
			(.001)
Constant	−7.57	−8.36	−9.40
	(1.51)***	(1.64)***	(1.33)***
Adjusted R-squared	.9227	.9162	.9283
Rho	.8164	.8447	.7989

Prais-Winsten estimates with robust standard errors in parentheses
N = 173; * .05 < p < .10; ** .01 < p < .05; *** p < .01; two-tailed

Of the variables of interest in this study, labor specificity continues to have a strong independent positive effect on subsidies. As worker specificity increases by 1 percentage point, horizontal subsidies go up roughly by .02 percent in all equations.[5] Trade openness also continues to have strong positive effects. In contrast to Hathaway's (1998) argument and in agreement with Zahariadis (2001), as trade exposure increases, countries are likely to disburse more subsidies. Political power is in the hypothesized direction, but it is no longer significant. The institutional variables—pluralism and electoral system disproportionality—accelerate the decline of horizontal subsidies. Just as in the case of total subsidies, more pluralist countries give out on average fewer horizontal subsidies while countries with more electoral disproportionality, that is, majoritarian systems, similarly disburse fewer subsidies. Veto points are no longer statistically significant.[6]

Counterfactuals were calculated on the basis of equation 2 in table 6.2. Low (high) FDI refers to 20th (80th) percentile scores in the sample. Low (high) capital specificity refers to the 20th (80th) percentile score on the labor specificity coefficient of variation. Low electoral system refers to the 20th percentile on the index of disproportionality, which corresponds to a proportional representation system. High electoral system refers to the 80th percentile score on the index of disproportionality, which corresponds to a majoritarian system. All other variables are set at their means.

The interactive terms reveal very interesting patterns. I follow the same rationale as I explained above, calculating counterfactuals only in cases of statistical significance at the .05 level or above. I first estimate the logarithmic figures and then transform them back to constant million euros. The 20th percentile in FDI corresponds to Italy in 2000, while the 80th percentile refers to Holland in 2003. The 20th percentile in electoral disproportionality refers to Germany's level and the 80th percentile is Spain's. In terms of capital specificity, the 20th percentile is Belgium's level in 2003 while the 80th percentile is Ireland's level in 1991.

What is interesting about the interactive terms is that capital specificity may not have significant independent effects, but its impact varies conditional on different levels of FDI. The multiplicative term reveals an overall positive relationship, meaning that governments in countries with higher levels of FDI and higher levels of capital specificity will generally disburse more subsidies. Figure 6.2 bears out this fact. However, more subsidies are systematically doled out when FDI exposure is high at most levels of capital specificity. The situation is reversed in terms of

Capital specificity

		Low	High
FDI	Low	1,048.1	1,002.1
	High	1,133.6	1,120.5

Electoral system

		Low	High
FDI	Low	1,555.7	870.2
	High	1,609.2	830.3

Figure 6.2 Counterfactual estimates of horizontal subsidies (constant million €).

electoral disproportionality at different levels of FDI. The overall relationship is negative; at lower levels of FDI and in PR systems, governments disburse on average more subsidies. But figure 6.2 also shows that the relationship holds primarily for PR systems. The increase in horizontal subsidies in PR systems as opposed to majoritarian democracies is large, almost 2 to 1, and fairly stable at different FDI levels.

Sectoral Subsidies

Table 6.3 estimates the effects on aid with sectoral objectives. Political power is now very important, particularly when taking into account electoral disproportionality (equation 2). The coefficient is in the hypothesized direction, indicating that subsidies go up when the political power of affected groups increases. What is interesting is that labor specificity is no longer significant even though it is in the hypothesized direction. Unlike the study by Zahariadis (2001), the findings here indicate that specificity does not have a systematic independent impact on the disbursement of sectoral subsidies although it does have an overall negative effect when it interacts with different levels of trade exposure.

It is important to ponder for a moment what sectoral subsidies are. They refer to assistance to particular sectors as opposed to horizontal aid, which does not discriminate between sectors or firms. Usually this implies that funds are given to specific firms in pursuit of particular objectives. They may involve rescuing ailing firms or boosting the fortunes of select national champions (Busch, 1999). For example, in 1989 and 1991, the government in Portugal intervened three times to rescue state-owned enterprises, raising considerably the amount of subsidies to the manufacturing sector (OECD, 1998, p. 141). The implication is that a small number of industries got a disproportionate portion of the subsidies. It is plausible that such intervention would not have occurred had the enterprises not been state-owned. Under this scenario, the figure for labor specificity may be high, but the subsidies may not be forthcoming because the affected groups do not have access or are not the "right" kind. The situation is somewhat similar in Germany, where funding has been granted to the eastern *Länder* as a result of reunification. This support is geographic, not necessarily sectoral, in the sense that similar firms based in different regions may not be eligible for the same subsidies. Again the implication is that labor specificity and sectoral subsidies may not covary for the same reason.

Table 6.3 The determinants of sectoral subsidies

	(1)	(2)	(3)
GDP	1.39	1.35	1.10
	(.277)***	(.34)***	(.266)***
Labor specificity (LS)	.030	.046	.036
	(.030)	(.028)	(.023)
Capital specificity (CS)	.012	−.002	.004
	(.013)	(.012)	(.023)
Political power	62.11	88.70	39.38
	(33.35)*	(28.91)***	(26.68)
Foreign direct investment (FDI)	−.018	.002	−.062
	(.045)	(.041)	(.071)
Portfolio investment	−.005	−.027	.013
	(.011)	(.024)	(.016)
Trade openness	.005	.065	.088
	(.041)	(.063)	(.052)*
Pluralism	−1.86		
	(.95)**		
Electoral system		−.57	
		(.039)	
Collective veto points			.329
			(.756)
Competitive veto points			3.32
			(.73)***
LS*FDI	.000	.000	.000
	(.000)	(.000)	(.000)
LS*trade	−.001	−.001	−.0012
	(.0006)*	(.0005)**	(.0005)**
LS*portfolio	.000	.000	.000
	(.000)	(.000)	(.000)
CS*FDI	.000	−.000	.000
	(.000)	(.000)	(.000)
CS*trade	−.000	.000	.000
	(.000)	(.000)	(.000)
CS*portfolio	−.000	−.000	−.000
	(.000)	(.000)	(.000)
Pluralism*trade	.053		
	(.025)**		
Pluralism*FDI	−.014		
	(.023)		
Pluralism*portfolio	2.67e-06		
	(3.77e-06)		
Electoral system*trade		.017	
		(.012)	
Electoral system*FDI		−.010	
		(.005)**	
Electoral system*portfolio		.007	
		(.004)*	

Table 6.3 (*Continued*)

	(1)	(2)	(3)
Collective veto points*trade			−.003
			(.021)
Collective veto points*FDI			.007
			(.021)
Collective veto points*portfolio			−.013
			(.011)
Competitive veto points*trade			−.092
			(.022)***
Competitive veto points*FDI			.046
			(.020)**
Competitive veto points*portfolio			−.014
			(.013)
Constant	−13.93	−16.88	−12.82
	(4.88)***	(5.84)***	(5.70)**
Adjusted R-squared	.4777	.4495	.5511
Rho	.7420	.8472	.7183

Prais-Winsten estimates with robust standard errors in parentheses
N = 172; * .05 < p < .10; ** .01 < p < .05; *** p < .01; two-tailed

The European Commission has taken a hard line against aid to state-owned firms because of the special reporting requirements needed by states to convince the Commission that aid is legal and would be extended under normal commercial conditions. The fact that it is an impossible counterfactual, state-owned companies rarely operate under "normal" conditions, makes by definition suspect capital infusions or other funds given to them by the state. The fact that the Commission estimates the amount of non-notified aid to state-owned enterprises to be ten times that of private firms illustrates the point (Thomas, 2000, p. 126).

Counterfactuals were calculated on the basis of equation 3 in table 6.3. Low (high) trade refers to 20th (80th) percentile scores in the sample. Low (high) competitive veto points refers to the 20th (80th) percentile score on the competitive veto point index. Low (high) labor specificity refers to the 20th (80th) percentile scores on the labor specificity coefficient of variation. All other variables are set at their means.

The interactive terms for sectoral subsidies yield interesting findings. Figure 6.3 clarifies the relationship for two such terms: the impact of trade conditional on labor specificity and competitive veto points. The 80th percentile in trade corresponds to Holland in 1995, while the

Labor specificity

		Low	High
	Low	237.43	277.57
Trade			
	High	472.10	247.05

Competitive veto points

		Low	High
	Low	39.65	135.71
Trade			
	High	4,446.5	601.62

Figure 6.3   Counterfactual estimates of sectoral subsidies (constant million €).

20th percentile is Italy in 1998; the 20th percentile in labor specificity is Finland in 2002, while the 80th percentile represents Greece in 2001. The overall relationship is negative, indicating that subsidies will on average be inversely related to both trade and specificity.

But there are fascinating variations at different levels of trade and specificity. Note on the top left cell, when trade exposure is low and specificity is high, subsidies are also high. But the highest amount by far is disbursed when trade is high and specificity is low (bottom right cell). When holding specificity at low levels, increases in trade lead to a doubling of sectoral subsidies. Trade appears to be the defining factor. As levels of exposure to global economic forces increase, protection increases in volume. What is interesting is that increases in labor specificity, conditional on trade, do not seem to lead to corresponding increases in subsidies. Again it appears that Acemoglu and Robinson (2001) have a point. They argue that when there is less specificity, there need to be more subsidies to prevent marginal agents from leaving the sector as well as to encourage new entrants. In this way, the political power of affected groups is maintained if not increased. Just like in the case of total subsidies, sectoral subsidies seem to follow the same pattern. At high levels of trade, subsidies become a political power game more than a trade protection game.

Acemoglu and Robinson have a point but only at high levels of trade. Note that figure 6.3 also indicates that subsidies increase at low levels of trade when labor specificity moves from low to high.

The interactive term regarding competitive veto points and trade is perhaps the most interesting, largely because the increase in subsidies is dramatic. The 20th percentile in competitive veto points refers to Greece and the 80th percentile refers to Spain. Recall that competitive veto points measure the division of political power across separate institutions. Higher numbers indicate more veto points competing against one another. Lower numbers indicate more power concentration. As the number of veto points goes down, the amount of subsidies increases. But the effect is conditional on the level of trade exposure. At really low levels of trade, the stakes are low and the amount of sectoral subsidies is correspondingly low (top left cell). However, when the number of veto points increases and trade is low, the amount of subsidies witnesses more than a fourfold jump. This activity reinforces the independent effect of competitive veto points on subsidies (table 6.3) and the logic of logrolling. Groups have disproportionate political power in these settings because of logrolling dynamics. Notice what happens at high levels of trade. The situation is reversed and dramatically higher subsidies are associated with a low number of competitive veto points. Empirically it seems that in the case of high levels of trade, the fewer the number of potential opposition points, the higher the amount of subsidies will be. Interestingly, the absolute amounts are higher on average at high levels of trade exposure, suggesting that sectoral subsidies grow exponentially when groups stand to gain (or lose) a lot from trade. The costs are more concentrated under these conditions and so are the benefits.

Allocating Regional Subsidies

Regional subsidies involve geographically concentrated interests. Does the model explain the disbursement of such assistance as well? The issue of regional subsidies is very interesting because of the trend over time toward devolution of power to subnational units among members of the OECD in general, and the EU in particular (e.g., Hooghe and Marks, 2001). Whether this particular pattern has led to an increase in regional power or to a reorganization of the central state is a hotly contested issue (e.g., Le Galès and Lequesne, 1998; Ohmae, 1995).[7] What is not contested is that considerable amounts of assistance are channeled to subnational territories for regional development purposes. In this study I look only at funds distributed by the national treasury and do not take into consideration funds distributed by the EU.

Regional subsidies differ in terms of objectives from either horizontal or sectoral subsidies. Although the European Commission (2006c) classifies them as subsidies with horizontal objectives, that is, they are conceived as having economy-wide scope, the reality is that regional aid is territorially confined. It may apply to all enterprises in the region, but it does not apply to all regions. For example, quite often subsidy funds are given to promote energy efficiency and conservation. Some of them may be channeled *via* regional aid, while other programs may target the entire economy.

Regional aid similarly differs from but also overlaps with sectoral aid objectives. The bulk of regional aid is awarded to regions that face chronic unemployment or low economic development. In some cases, such as Germany, this may be constitutionally mandated, while in others, such as Greece, more ephemeral political considerations loom large (Le Galès and Lequesne, 1998; Zahariadis, 2006). Quite often, however, funds sent to a particular region in response to high unemployment carry disguised sectoral objectives if that region's unemployment is temporarily caused by the decline of a single major industry, such as steel or coal. In this case, regional aid ends up assisting specific industries although the ostensible intention is not so specific. In addition, much of this aid also ends up helping particular sectors, such as agriculture, primarily because less economically developed regions also tend to be more rural and agriculturally focused. A good example at the supranational level is the decline in the EU's agricultural subsidies and the subsequent increase of the EU's cohesion (regional) funds. Some funding that was previously given as agricultural assistance is now provided as regional aid. Germany, for example, has implemented the *Regionen Aktiv* initiative, which aims to reintegrate agriculture into regional economies. In 2002 the program spent €35 million for 200 programs in 18 regions (Dwyer, 2007, p. 87).

As table 6.4 shows, the determinants of regional subsidies are an eclectic mix of motives identified with both horizontal and sectoral subsidies. It is not surprising, therefore, to see that they follow somewhat the pattern of total subsidies identified in table 6.1. The overall explanatory capacity, measured by the adjusted R-squared, is high. The model explains more than 70 percent of the variance in regional subsidies for the period under investigation. This represents a higher capacity than that of sectoral subsidies but lower than that of horizontal subsidies. Just like in previous equations the negative constant

Table 6.4 The determinants of regional subsidies

	(1)	(2)	(3)
GDP	1.11	1.21	1.08
	(.276)***	(.25)***	(.281)***
Labor specificity (LS)	.030	.032	.032
	(.012)***	(.012)***	(.014)**
Capital specificity (CS)	.000	−.005	.000
	(.000)	(.007)	(.006)
Political power	28.41	50.31	41.60
	(23.36)	(24.14)**	(24.75)*
Foreign direct investment (FDI)	.037	.033	.028
	(.032)	(.032)	(.053)
Portfolio investment	.002	.001	−.008
	(.007)	(.007)	(.008)
Trade openness	.048	.041	.083
	(.038)	(.025)*	(.026)***
Pluralism	.007		
	(.604)		
Electoral system		−.020	
		(.096)**	
Collective veto points			.178
			(.670)
Competitive veto points			.279
			(.400)
LS*FDI	−.000	−.000	−.000
	(.000)	(.000)	(.000)
LS*trade	−.0007	−.0007	−.0008
	(.0003)**	(.0003)**	(.0003)**
LS*portfolio	.000	.000	−.000
	(.000)	(.000)	(.000)
CS*FDI	.000	−.000	−.000
	(.000)	(.000)	(.000)
CS*trade	−.000	.000	−.000
	(.000)	(.000)	(.000)
CS*portfolio	.000	−.000	.000
	(.000)	(.000)	(.000)
Pluralism*trade	.009		
	(.012)		
Pluralism*FDI	−.002		
	(.007)		
Pluralism*portfolio	−4.16e–06		
	(1.60e–06)***		
Electoral system*trade		.007	
		(.004)*	
Electoral system*FDI		−.000	
		(.002)	

(Continued)

Table 6.4   (*Continued*)

	(1)	(2)	(3)
Electoral system*portfolio		−.000	
		(.000)	
Collective veto points*trade			−.014
			(.016)
Collective veto points*FDI			−.000
			(.007)
Collective veto points*portfolio			.007
			(.003)***
Competitive veto points*trade			−.004
			(.013)
Competitive veto points*FDI			−.004
			(.004)
Competitive veto points*portfolio			.007
			(.003)**
Constant	−12.06	−13.43	−12.47
	(4.24)	(3.91)***	(4.34)***
Adjusted R-squared	.7050	.7103	.7136
Rho	.8805	.8723	.8752

Prais-Winsten estimates with robust standard errors in parentheses
* .05 < p < .10; ** .01 < p < .05; *** p < .01; two-tailed

term suggests a steep overall decline over time. The independent variables, therefore, arrest or facilitate the decline.

Labor specificity has a strong, positive, and consistently significant impact on subsidy disbursement. Higher specificity, that is, lower movement of workers across industries in search of higher wages, leads to more successful demands for a greater number of subsidies. Governments are politically sensitive to providing regional protection when workers face losses generated from greater exposure to global economic forces. This finding stands in agreement with the indicator's independent effects regarding horizontal subsidies and in contrast to sectoral ones.

Continuing in the vein of interpreting the disbursement of regional subsidies as the result of an eclectic mix of motives, political power has a strong positive effect. More politically powerful groups get more subsidies, in contrast this time to horizontal subsidies and in line with sectoral ones (compare the results with those in tables 6.2 and 6.3). The political power of regional groups helps explain economic nationalism and trade protection (Goff, 2005). For example, EU member states protect specific products from particular regions as trademarks—for example, the label feta cheese may only denote the feta produced in Greece, champagne may only be used in drinks coming from France's Champagne region, and so on. Trade openness has a positive effect, but the finding is not consistent across equations. Electoral disproportionality also has a negative impact on regional subsidies. Counter to the claim by Rogowski (1987), more majoritarian systems disburse on average less aid; conversely, PR systems are associated with more protectionism. The results are similar to those regarding horizontal subsidies. All these findings reinforce the point made earlier that regional subsidies share both horizontal and sectoral elements.

Counterfactuals were calculated on the basis of equation 3 in table 6.4. Low (high) portfolio investment refers to 20th (80th) percentile scores in the sample. Low (high) collective veto points refer to the 20th (80th) percentile score on the collective veto point index. Low (high) competitive veto points refer to the 20th (80th) percentile scores in the competitive veto point index. All other variables are set at their means.

Figure 6.4 offers an illustrative glimpse of interactive effects. I want to reinforce the point of conditional effects advanced earlier. While some variables may not have a statistically significant independent impact, they do affect the disbursement of subsidies depending on the levels of other key variables. Figure 6.4 explores the impact of three such variables: collective veto points, competitive veto points, and portfolio investment.

Collective veto points

		Low	High
Portfolio investment	Low	208.89	396.89
	High	212.84	407.18

Competitive veto points

		Low	High
Portfolio investment	Low	224.52	323.91
	High	190.87	304.16

Figure 6.4   Counterfactual estimates of regional subsidies (constant million €).

Although both interactive terms are positive on average, the actual trends in each term are quite different. What may be gleaned from both equations is that the amount of subsidies goes up in both cases when competitive and collective veto points increase, irrespective of the level of portfolio investment. The difference is quite dramatic in the case of a high number of collective veto points. The amount of subsidies nearly doubles when portfolio investment is high as well as when it is low (80th and 20th percentiles). It is important to recall what collective points represent. They are the number of veto points that operate within the same institution. Higher numbers indicate a system with greater shared responsibility and inclusiveness of different interests—that is, more coalition governments, more balance between executive and legislative branches, and a general tendency toward more consensus democracy (Lijphart, 1999). Because a greater number of interests need to be satisfied, logrolling tends to be more prevalent and the amount of regional subsidies is correspondingly higher. Competitive veto points constitute the dispersion of power across more or less equal institutions, each empowered with the ability to veto policy decisions. In this particular case, the data suggest that greater power among regional authorities (e.g., higher degree of federalism) leads to more subsidies at various levels of portfolio investment. There are, however, differences in patterns. As the number of collective points goes up, the amount of regional subsidies increases at high levels of short-term investment in contrast to the effect of competitive veto points.

All in all, the model proves useful in explaining the disbursement of regional subsidies. Actual levels follow a negative trend over time, with labor specificity, political power, trade openness, and PR arresting this decline. Veto points and portfolio investment do not have significant independent effects, but they have a strong impact on subsidies conditional on different levels. Regional aid appears to follow a mix of motives that apply to both horizontal and sectoral subsidies.

Conclusion

In this chapter I presented empirical evidence testing the hypotheses derived from the asset influence model. Drawing on data from the EU, I was able to demonstrate the significant independent and conditional effects of globalization, asset specificity, political power, and national institutions on the ability of governments to grant subsidy protection.

The data validate the argument in estimates of total subsidies. In the light of a negative overall trend, the findings confirm several hypotheses advanced earlier. Labor specificity, political power, veto points, and trade openness have a significant positive impact of the disbursement of subsidies. Pluralism affects them negatively. There are also major interactive relationships involving largely trade, labor specificity, pluralism, and portfolio investment. Interestingly, capital specificity does not exercise a significant independent effect on subsidies although it has a positive impact at different levels of FDI.

The variables also perform reasonably well in cases where objectives differ. Labor specificity has strong positive effects on subsidies with horizontal objectives, that is, economy-wide objectives, whereas pluralism and electoral disproportionality have strong negative effects in the same equations. Again, capital specificity does not exercise strong independent effects, but it shows positive significance at different levels of FDI. When it comes to sectoral subsidies, political institutions exercise the strongest independent effects. Political power and competitive veto points have positive effects, while pluralism has a strong negative impact. Globalization indicators explain surprisingly little by themselves regarding sectoral subsidies; their effects are greatest conditional on domestic institutional configurations.

Two conclusions emerge from the findings. First, the literature generally views horizontal subsidies to be the outcome of broad electoral contests (OECD, 2005a, p. 116). While the evidence here provides support for this conclusion, it also qualifies it. It is true, institutional constraints limit and shape access to policymakers (Zahariadis, 2002). Groups have to form broad coalitions to ensure greater levels of support, which has the effect of increasing overall subsidy levels. Nevertheless, specificity also plays a strong positive role. Confirming the evidence presented in earlier work with a broader panel of countries (Zahariadis, 2001), higher specificity leads to higher levels of subsidies. While labor specificity exercises independent effects, both capital and labor specificity affect subsidies conditional on different levels of trade and FDI. The implication is that although such logic appears to be more applicable to sectoral subsidies, where programs and benefits are more tailored to specific groups, it also has wider effects. Specificity is an important explanatory factor of protection, whose effects deserve more investigation.

Second, heavier exposure to globalization makes governments more susceptible to protectionist claims. Contrary to claims in the literature, increasing exposure to global economic forces puts the brakes on the decline in subsidy use. Globalization exercises powerful effects because it creates winners and losers, supplying actors with incentives to lobby for protection. Although subsidies appear to be on the decline over a long period of time, in the short term groups seek and receive more rents. But not all globalization is equal. While trade and FDI generally exercise strong positive effects, portfolio investment has the opposite impact. Ever-increasing amounts of short-term capital flowing in and out of the country accelerate the decline in subsidies. Protection is the outcome of domestic and international forces, whose effects must be disentangled and carefully circumscribed.

Chapter 7

Sectors and Instruments

It's a poor workman that blames his tools.

The empirical record has so far stopped with the various objectives of subsidies. That is not the only way subsidies may be differentiated. I extend the treatment of subsidies in two ways. First, there is good reason to suspect that subsidies to different sectors may be given for different reasons. The most significant differences are found in subsidies to manufacturing versus agriculture. Much of the stalemate in the Doha Round of world trade negotiations, and the rancor behind the Uruguay Round, is attributed to the problem of agricultural subsidies (Bagwell and Staiger, 2002, chapter 10). Is agriculture a special case? Second, I explore the calculus of instrument choice by looking at four policy tools: grants, tax incentives, soft loans, and capital guarantees. Different instruments have different rationales and expectations. To ascertain the robustness of the model, I examine the model's ability to explain the choice of policy tools. How well does the model fare?

Is Agriculture a Special Case?

There are many reasons why agriculture may be considered a special case when it comes to subsidies. For one, agricultural interests are well organized and very powerful on national and international, for example, European, levels (Keeler, 1996). Manufacturers are far less organized, with considerable variations across industries. In the light of the declining share of agriculture in the national economy, farmers organize to become disproportionately politically powerful.

Manufacturers do not have such incentives. One should, therefore, expect political power to be much more concentrated and more pronounced as an explanatory variable in agricultural as opposed to manufacturing subsidies.

Second, farmers normally have somewhat similar interests (low level of differentiation) and a vested interest in perpetuating the system. Manufacturers are not as homogeneous as a group in terms of economic interests. Their gains (and losses) are more differentiated than those of their agricultural counterparts, making factory workers and bosses much less inclined to coalesce in pursuit of common objectives. Because the cost of lobbying is high and strong incentives to coalesce are absent, the likelihood of subsidization is lower. Farmers in various developed countries seek to encourage, to an extent, the establishment of new farms by lowering barriers to entry (Coleman, Atkinson, and Montpetit, 1997; Hansen, 1991). Manufacturers generally tend to demand the opposite; they argue for higher barriers to ensure high profits. The politics of subsidy allocation should, therefore, differ.

Third, farm subsidies are an institutionalized form of welfare in ways that subsidies to manufacturing are not. For example, the Common Agricultural Policy (CAP) in Europe has long been considered to be a highly inefficient way of redistributing resources to farmers at the expense of taxpayers across Europe (e.g., Moyer and Josling, 1990; but see Gisser, 1993).[1] Originally, the CAP was conceived as a way of guaranteeing food production in the light of wartime experience. Article 39 of the European Economic Community Treaty calls for increasing agricultural production through the pooling of technical expertise, stabilizing markets, assuring adequacy of supplies, ensuring a fair standard of living for farmers, and ensuring that supplies reach consumers at adequate prices. A fair standard of living for farmers was achieved through guaranteed prices, import quotas and tariffs, and export subsidies. CAP over time acquired significant welfare functions (Zahariadis, 2003b; Rieger, 2005). Guaranteed prices and other similar measures were replaced in 1992 with direct income support measures. To avoid overproduction and storage costs caused by the CAP, it was decided that guaranteed prices in some products, for example, beef, would be lowered to levels closer to those of the world market while direct payments were introduced to farmers in certain sectors. All this meant that the objectives of the CAP shifted from encouraging production to protecting farmers' income. Following major reforms in 2003, member states were given options to decouple direct subsidies from production. Some states, such as the UK, opted for a system of flat rate compensation tied to an average level of historic receipts per hectare of eligible land for well-defined and specific regions of the country. The payment scheme began in 2005 at a 90 percent level, gradually decreasing payments over a transition period of seven years (Dwyer, 2007, p. 78). Although it is too early to judge the success of the reforms, EU farmers continue to oppose major shifts in subsidies, as the recent failure of the WTO's Doha Round clearly attests. The same story applies to the United States where the origins and rationale of many farm subsidies and other aid schemes go as far back as the Great Depression. Manufacturers cannot point to the same degree of policy continuity or welfare-enhancing experience.

The differences between manufacturing and agriculture provide an indirect test of *site* specificity. Recall from the discussion on asset specificity that site specificity refers to the value of immobile assets depending on location. In effect, the implication is that asset specificity in agriculture will be higher on average than in manufacturing. For one, value added is normally tied to the use of land, which is immobile. Farmers usually cannot just pack up and move the farm to a different location, especially when the main product comes from cultivating the land, such as cash crops or food crops. In those cases, losses simply mount until there is relief. If relief in the form of subsidy protection is not forthcoming, the farmer simply goes out of business. Factories may move; farms cannot. The higher the value of site specificity, the greater the amount of subsidies should be.

In essence, subsidies reinforce specificity because they bid up the value of land. Support schemes increase demand for land (among other factors of production). Because the amount of land is fixed, the price of land increases disproportionately. This helps current users because it increases the value of the landholdings they already possess, but it discourages new entrants because it raises land prices (Winters, 1987). This is the exact opposite of Acemoglu and Robinson's (2001) argument. Agricultural support schemes may actually discourage rather than encourage new entrants. Differences in the explanatory capacity of the independent variables between the two models may be attributed to site specificity.

I first look at subsidies to manufacturing to establish a base line. Because the asset influence model was developed with industrial subsidies in mind, the effects should be clear and illuminating. Then

I run the same set of equations examining agricultural subsidies to see whether there are differences. Is agriculture a special case?

Subsidies to Manufacturing

Subsidies to manufacturing are normally implemented under the old banner of industrial policy. All developed economies, including the United States, which is not commonly perceived as such, subsidize industry in the form of budget outlays, tax breaks, direct grants, or loans (Cooper, 1988). The overall objectives are to support ailing industries that suffer long-term decline or are in temporary crisis, such as shipbuilding or textiles; help nurture new or economically important industries, such as aircraft or communications; or encourage investments in equipment or regions where they would not have otherwise occurred (Lavdas and Mendrinou, 1999; Busch, 1999). Most aid to industry has a long-term horizon; studies have found that almost 60 percent of programs last five or more years (OECD, 1998, p. 28). This makes such assistance particularly interesting because of the attention it has traditionally received in the media and the fact that product life cycles have shrunk considerably, rendering questionable the policy rationale for long-term aid.

Just like in the majority of the models in chapter 6, the dependent variable, subsidies to manufacturing, is expressed in logarithmically transformed constant euros. For this reason, it is necessary to control for economic size by including the logarithmically transformed value (to the natural base) of annual economic output (GDP) on the right side of the equation. The coefficient of determination is close to .9, indicating a very good fit. This means that the model explains close to 90 percent of the variance in manufacturing subsidies after taking into account the variables in question.

Consistent with previous results, labor specificity makes a big difference. The slope is in the hypothesized direction and statistically significant. As the coefficient of variation goes up by 1 percent, the amount of subsidies to manufacturing increases by close to .4 percent. In other words, when workers find it difficult or costly to move across industries, they successfully lobby for more subsidies.

Of the three globalization indicators, trade openness has the most dramatic effect. The coefficient is consistently in the hypothesized direction and significant. As trade openness increases by 1 percent of GDP, subsidies rise by more than .5 percent in all cases. In terms of institutions, only competitive veto points make a difference. In systems with higher numbers of veto points, governments increase their subsidy protection by .48 percent.

In the light of the fact that subsidies are decreasing over time, the importance of trade openness points to some interesting implications. First, it provides evidence that the assumption of policymakers choosing between political contributions and voter welfare is reasonable. If we assume that the short- and long-term gains to society from free trade outweigh the short-term losses of affected groups, politicians are doing a marvelous job of lowering subsidies over time and still satisfying the needs of disaffected groups. Second, this argument provides indirect evidence supporting Feenstra and Bhagwati's (1982) claim that governments exercise a second-best policy of protecting disadvantaged groups by granting lower protection than otherwise would have been the case by compensating disaffected groups. Although the authors formulated their model in terms of tariff seeking, the idea seems to apply to protection in general, which includes subsidies. The essence of the argument is that targeted compensation works to reduce pressure for higher protection by using revenues to compensate groups adversely affected by free trade (Leipziger and Spence, 2007). Lobbying activity in favor of protection is lessened today and tomorrow because groups do not experience the same magnitude of losses over time. Domestic consumers also gain overall from less protection and do not rise in staunch opposition to the subsidies because the funds are miniscule per taxpayer although they may be significant per affected group.

Counterfactuals were calculated on the basis of equation 2 in table 7.1. Low (high) portfolio investment refers to 20th (80th) percentile scores in the sample. Low (high) capital specificity refers to the 20th (80th) percentile score on the labor specificity coefficient of variation. Low (high) trade refers to the 20th (80th) percentile scores in the sample. All other variables are set at their means.

The interactive terms reveal interesting patterns. I calculate the counterfactuals for two terms from equation 2 in table 7.1, which are statistically significant at the point of .05 or better. They are not the only interactive terms that are significant, but they raise important points. The data reported in figure 7.1 involve actual amounts in constant million euros. I calculate the data, varying the terms of interest—capital specificity, portfolio investment, labor specificity, and trade openness—while keeping all other variables at their means. Because the answer came out as a logarithm—recall the dependent variable is measured in such terms—I transformed the logarithm back to constant million euros by taking the exponential term of that number.

At first glance, figure 7.1 shows that although portfolio investment and capital specificity do not have significant independent effects,

Table 7.1 The determinants of subsidies to manufacturing

	(1)	(2)	(3)
GDP	1.204	1.23	1.07
	(.088)***	(.102)***	(.075)***
Labor specificity (LS)	.0375	.040	.040
	(.008)***	(.007)***	(.006)***
Capital specificity (CS)	−.006	−.006	−.008
	(.010)	(.006)	(.01)
Political power	22.48	16.46	18.03
	(12.63)*	(14.60)	(14.25)
Foreign direct investment (FDI)	−.006	−.007	−.023
	(.007)	(.015)	(.015)
Portfolio investment	.003	.002	.008
	(.004)	(.003)	(.003)
Trade openness	.050	.068	.051
	(.017)***	(.015)***	(.019)***
Pluralism	−.525		
	(.277)*		
Electoral system		−.044	
		(.069)	
Collective veto points		.215	
		(.163)	
Competitive veto points			.484
			(.202)**
LS*FDI	.000	.0001	−.000
	(.000)	(.0003)	(.000)
LS*trade	−.001	−.0011	−.001
	(.0002)***	(.0002)***	(.0002)***
LS*portfolio	.000	−7.48e−06	.000
	(.000)	(.00003)	(.000)
CS*FDI	.000	−.000	.000
	(.000)	(.000)	(.000)
CS*trade	−.000	.0002	.000
	(.000)	(.0001)*	(.000)
CS*portfolio	.00001	−.00009	−.0001
	(.000)**	(.00002)***	(.0001)
Pluralism*trade	.005		
	(.009)		
Pluralism*FDI	−.008		
	(.003)***		
Pluralism*portfolio	2.93e−06		
	(3.08e−06)		
Electoral system*trade		−.001	
		(.002)	
Electoral system*FDI		−.001	
		(.0006)**	
Electoral system*portfolio		.0007	
		(.0005)	

Table 7.1 (*Continued*)

	(1)	(2)	(3)
Collective veto points*trade			.005
			(.007)
Collective veto points*FDI			.004
			(.003)
Collective veto points*portfolio			−.000
			(.003)
Competitive veto points*trade			−.006
			(.007)
Competitive veto points*FDI			.000
			(.002)
Competitive veto points*portfolio			−.003
			(.004)
Constant	−10.27	−11.23	−9.38
	(1.64)***	(1.78)***	(1.45)***
Adjusted R-squared	.8802	.8799	.8965
Rho	.7499	.7427	.5866

Prais-Winsten estimates with robust standard errors in parentheses
N=173; * .05 < p < .10; ** .01 < p < .05; *** p < .01; two-tailed

they do exercise an impact on subsidies at different levels conditional on each other. The finding reinforces the argument made throughout this study that conditional relationships are an important component of subsidy disbursement. The term at the mean is negative (table 7.1), meaning that highest amounts should be found at the low ends of both variables. Capital specificity surprisingly seems to have the most impact when it is at lower levels, conditional on portfolio investment. But even more interestingly, the amount does not vary much when portfolio investment goes up. Notice the difference between the two left cells is a mere €4.3 million.

The effects of labor specificity and trade follow a somewhat similar pattern with that of total subsidies (figure 7.1). The strongest impact occurs at low levels of trade (top right cell) and high trade (bottom left cell). This means that as trade openness increases, the effects of specificity take a twist. At higher levels of openness (though still at the same level of specificity), subsidies go up significantly. However, as specificity now begins to increase, that is, workers do not move across industries, the level of subsidies drops by almost 40 percent. Trade plays a big role in providing incentives for subsidies, but only up to a point. The situation then is reversed. High levels of trade and specificity actually depress the disbursement

Capital specificity

		Low	High
Portfolio investment	Low	1,362.6	1,090.1
	High	1,358.3	1,047.5

Labor specificity

		Low	High
Trade	Low	1,164.9	1,506.9
	High	1,317.4	777.1

Figure 7.1   Counterfactual estimates of subsidies to manufacturing (constant million €)

of protection. At this point, the conditional expectations derived from the Ricardo-Viner model (chapter 4) should be amended. It posits that the effects of specificity increase as trade exposure goes up. Workers have more to lose from increased exposure. It appears that this happens but not at all levels of trade. It may be that the Stolper-Samuelson model is correct. Recall it expects coalitions to be formed under these conditions along class rather than sectoral lines, implying that protectionist coalitions will be weak at sectoral levels, which lead to fewer subsidies. Although the evidence here points to that direction, in the final analysis it does raise questions that merit further investigation. I note emphatically, however, that the debate should not be framed in its customary form, that is, which of the two models is correct. Rather the implication of the findings here suggests that a more fruitful research agenda should examine the conditions under which one model yields more accurate predictions than the other.

Subsidies to Agriculture

Table 7.2 presents the findings regarding agriculture. The model presented here represents an improvement on other models of agricultural subsidies that test specificity, for example, Thies and Porche

Table 7.2 The determinants of subsidies to agriculture

	(1)	(2)	(3)
GDP	.639	.55	.515
	(.152)***	(.19)***	(.215)**
Labor specificity (LS)	.016	.022	.020
	(.014)	(.015)	(.015)
Capital specificity (CS)	−.000	.000	.003
	(.005)	(.003)	(.006)
Political power	37.45	35.09	32.30
	(8.92)***	(7.49)***	(8.61)***
Foreign direct investment (FDI)	.001	−.000	.003
	(.010)	(.015)	(.016)
Portfolio investment	−.015	−.010	−.015
	(.003)***	(.005)*	(.004)***
Trade openness	.020	.040	.061
	(.030)	(.026)	(.023)**
Pluralism	−.719		
	(.367)**		
Electoral system		−.144	
		(.090)	
Collective veto points			.599
			(.475)
Competitive veto points			.323
			(.175)*
LS*FDI	.000	.000	−1.78e−06
	(.000)	(.000)	(.000)
LS*trade	−.000	−.000	−.000
	(.000)	(.000)	(.000)
LS*portfolio	.0002	.0002	.0002
	(.00005)***	(.00006)***	(.00006)***
CS*FDI	−.000	−.000	−.000
	(.000)	(.000)	(.000)
CS*trade	.000	.000	−.000
	(.000)	(.000)	(.000)
CS*portfolio	.0000	.000	.000
	(.000)	(.000)	(.000)
Pluralism*trade	.010		
	(.008)		
Pluralism*FDI	−.001		
	(.002)		
Pluralism*portfolio	2.19e−06		
	(1.13e−06)*		
Electoral system*trade		.004	
		(.002)*	
Electoral system*FDI		.000	
		(.000)	

(Continued)

Table 7.2   (*Continued*)

	(1)	(2)	(3)
Electoral system*portfolio		−.000	
		(.000)	
Collective veto points*trade			−.012
			(.011)
Collective veto points*FDI			.000
			(.000)
Collective veto points*portfolio			.001
			(.002)
Competitive veto points*trade			−.003
			(.007)
Competitive veto points*FDI			−.002
			(.002)
Competitive veto points*portfolio			.002
			(.003)
Constant	−2.39	−2.48	−2.70
	(2.02)	(2.40)	(1.20)
Adjusted R-squared	.8873	.8197	.8567
Rho	.9000	.9568	.9355

Prais-Winsten estimates with robust standard errors in parentheses
N=173; * .05 < p < .10; ** .01 < p < .05; *** p < .01; two-tailed

(2007), because it uses actual indicators of specificity rather than proxy ones. Just like in previous models outlined in this book, the constant is negative indicating an overall decline over time in agricultural subsidies. The independent variables, therefore, facilitate or arrest this trend. However, the amount of decline is lower than that of manufacturing, showing that agricultural subsidies tend to be "stickier" over time and less prone to large decreases.[2] Although the adjusted R-squared in all three equations is high, the number of statistically significant variables is low. One consolation is that the coefficients have the hypothesized direction, but in the absence of significance, one may conclude that the model does not have a good fit. There is something different about agriculture that renders the asset influence model less effective. Subsidization in that sector follows a different pattern than in manufacturing.

In terms of similarities, institutional effects follow the same broad patterns in both manufacturing and agricultural subsidies. Pluralism is significantly and inversely related to subsidies, meaning corporatist states allocate more agricultural subsidies. Veto points are in the same direction and somewhat similarly and positively strong: political systems with more competitive veto points tend to also disburse more subsidies. The findings are in broad agreement with those by Thies and Porche (2007). They find that institutional variables consistently exercise a significant effect on agricultural subsidies in the OECD. They do so in the EU as well.

The affected group's political power does play a big role. Just like in the case of manufacturing, the coefficients are big and positive, indicating that subsidies increase as the power of the group grows. Unlike manufacturing, however, all the coefficients are now strongly statistically significant. The implication is that political power is an essential ingredient of getting agricultural subsidies in a way that it is not in manufacturing. Farmers receive subsidies disproportionate to their size. It could be that political power plays a more important role in agriculture because of producer size. Most farms in the EU are small; they typically employ one to five persons (Dwyer, 2007, p. 74). This means that adaptability is low in the presence of lost revenues. If costs, in the form of lost revenues because of subsidy elimination, cannot be passed up and down the production or distribution chain, farms will go out of business. By implication, farmers stand to lose more if subsidies go down. They are, therefore, more eager to organize and more willing to sustain the high costs of lobbying despite the sector's small size. Policymakers may indeed respond to the higher stakes involved rather than the size of the group (Beghin and Kherallah, 1994, p. 485). More than manufacturers, farmers have to depend on politics and raw power for relief.

The finding complements arguments about agricultural reform. While economic analysis shows that intervention in favor of farmers in the form of subsidies is inefficient, it fails to account for why reforms often fail. Apart from the obvious role that path dependency, programmatic design, and implementation deficiencies play in derailing or reinforcing reforms (Harvey, 2004; Daugbjerg, 2003; Barg, Cosbey, and Steenblik, 2007), another factor must be added. Politically powerful farmers make reform difficult and frequently politically unacceptable. Agricultural reforms, and consequently schemes calling for greater efficiency and fewer subsidies, often fail because they are not politically acceptable to the majority of powerful, well-organized, and easily mobilized farmers.

Unlike manufacturing, globalization has a different effect on subsidies to agriculture. In contrast to the findings by Thies and Porche (2007), trade does not appear to exercise much influence other than in the case of the equation controlling for veto points. The coefficient is positive, meaning that when trade exposure increases by 1 percent, governments increase their absolute subsidy amounts by .06 percent. The more interesting finding refers to the impact of portfolio investment. Unlike the case of manufacturing, the coefficient is negative, as expected, and strongly significant. As portfolio investment decreases by 1 percent over GDP, subsidies go up on average by more than .01 percent. The overall coefficient is not as large as in the case of trade. Nevertheless, the consistent statistical significance suggests that international capital movements have an independent depressing effect on agricultural subsidies, just like they did in the case of total subsidies.

Why does portfolio investment matter more than trade? Agricultural trade tends to be relatively low in value and volume largely because domestic markets are heavily protected both at the border and inside the domestic economy, that is, they are protected by both tariffs and subsidies. In the light of relatively low volume of trade, losses or gains to farmers do not really come from trade but from other sources. Portfolio investment has a more general effect than trade in this case because the majority of capital coming in and going out of a country is not directly tied to agriculture. Nevertheless, portfolio investment provides powerful incentives for a more efficient allocation of resources in all sectors, including agriculture. As the amount of such "demanding" capital grows, governments find it more difficult to maintain high levels of inefficient subsidies. Because subsidization of agriculture normally comes from the government's budget and takes the form of direct assistance in the form of grants tied to farmer incomes, production, or price-support levels, there is pressure over time to reduce overall aid.

Counterfactuals were calculated on the basis of equation 1 in table 7.2. Low (high) portfolio investment refers to the 20th (80th) percentile scores in the sample. Less (more) labor specificity refers to the 20th (80th) percentile score on the labor specificity coefficient of variation. All other variables are set at their means.

Labor specificity does not have a significant independent effect on agricultural subsidies, but it does make a difference conditional on different levels of portfolio investment. The overall multiplicative term is positive, indicating that more subsidies are disbursed when both portfolio and labor specificity are high. Looking at the data in figure 7.2, the expectation is confirmed. At really high levels of specificity and portfolio (80th percentile in the sample), the amount of subsidies is almost 60 percent higher than it is when both portfolio and labor specificity are at low levels (the 20th percentile). Looking at both the left cells (low specificity) and contrasting them to the overall volume of aid on the right (high specificity) it becomes obvious

Labor specificity

		Low	High
Portfolio investment	Low	642.1	954.3
	High	637.5	1,019

Figure 7.2 Counterfactual estimates of subsidies to agriculture (constant million €)

that on average domestic considerations matter more. Note how the figures are higher under high labor specificity regardless of the level of portfolio investment. In contrast to Acemoglu and Robinson's (2001) claim, when farmers find it difficult to put assets to different uses, they demand and get on average higher levels of protection. Redistribution in this case may still be inefficient, but groups appear to get more subsidies as specificity grows.

Contrasting the results from tables 7.1 and 7.2, the general conclusion is that different factors drive the decision to disburse subsidies to manufacturing and agriculture. In manufacturing domestic variables—such as labor specificity and pluralism—and globalization factors—such as trade openness—have strong, independent effects, while labor and capital specificity have significant conditional effects. In agriculture, political power and portfolio investment make the biggest difference. Labor specificity has only conditional effects when it interacts with different levels of portfolio openness. Agriculture does indeed appear to be a special case.

THE CALCULUS OF INSTRUMENT CHOICE

Quite frequently, the question is not whether to subsidize a particular industry or industries, but how much and what instrument, or tool, to use. Economists have long struggled with the question of choice, but the literature remains primarily theoretical and limited. Political scientists have similarly treated the choice of subsidy instrument as exogenous (but see Zahariadis, 1997). A tool approach is significant because each subsidy instrument has its own distinct procedures, rationale, and network of organizational relationships (Verdier, 1995; Hood, 1986). It could be that choice is based primarily on "whether the instrument will be effective in addressing the problem" (Kraft and Furlong, 2004, p. 91). Nevertheless, "another possibility is that governments choose policy instruments that allow them to most effectively privilege those groups they care about" (McGillivray, 2004, p. 161). In this section, I tackle this question head on. Does the asset influence model explain the choice among instruments?

Little empirical attention has been paid to instrument choice in the case of protection. Of the few economists who have examined the issue, none has analyzed the issue of subsidies. In several instances, for example, Corden (1997) and Horvat (1999), analysts have examined the differences between subsidies and tariffs, focusing primarily on the differences between the two instruments. The implicit explanation is that governments choose between the two on the basis of welfare improvement, resource waste, and the like. As Corden suggests sometimes subsidies are to be preferred over tariffs. Bhagwati (1982) expands on this idea by considering various conditions of what he terms as directly-unproductive, profit-seeking activities (DUP). When the initial and final situations (after protection) are both distorted or the initial situation is distorted but the final is not, then DUP, for example, protection, may be indirectly productive or welfare improving. The problem with this reasoning is that it is not really an explanation. It does not take into account the budgetary politics that permeates this type of choice. While tariffs, quotas, or VERs may not result in equivalent resource allocation equilibria, considerations such as transparency have significant impact on the choice of instrument. However, just because subsidies are less transparent or take into account social costs as opposed to tariffs does not necessarily mean that they will be adopted. They may be preferred, but unless one examines politics, there is no clear indication to suggest they will actually be chosen.

Others examine the choice between tariffs and quotas. Cassing and Hillman (1985), for example, consider the calculus of choice between tariffs and quotas in the presence of a domestic monopoly. Using a political support function, they trace the trade-off between the benefits of protection to producers induced by increases in rents against the losses to consumers evidenced by increases in price. Depending on the equilibrium level under different scenarios and the revenue received, governments are likely to favor one or the other. Vousden (1990, pp. 195–198) goes beyond this argument to look at the level of risk aversion by both consumers and producers. Under certain conditions, and given a set amount of information, quotas are to be preferred to tariffs.

These types of arguments are limited in two respects. First, apart from not being empirically tested, the studies explain choice by appealing to the government's decision efficiency. In other words, analysis concentrates on the hypothetical consequences of adopting either instrument under similar conditions. Analysts then assume that governments will efficiently choose the instrument that maximizes net benefits (Rowley, Thorbecke, and Wagner, 1995, p. 77). Such logic is unrealistic because governments are assumed to be aware of intended effects, which is highly implausible. Second, the focus has been mostly on the choice between protections at the border. Given the prevalence of NTBs and the various treaties lowering tariffs, it is reasonable to conclude that such analyses are not very helpful. Quite often the question is not whether to impose distributionally blunt protection, such as tariffs, but whether to use more subtle and distributionally more precise forms of protection. Targeting benefits while spreading costs in politically inconspicuous ways goes a long way toward understanding why some instruments are likely to be chosen over others. Besides, "the actual aid element may differ from the nominal amount" in some instances, such as loans or guarantees (European Commission, 2006a, p. 26). Do soft (low-interest) loans or credit guarantees better prop up regional economies? Are grants the most effective way to support declining industries, or do tax incentives work just as well?

A First Look at the Numbers

I examine the allocation of four instruments employed by national governments: budget grants, tax incentives, soft loans, and capital guarantees.[3] Table 7.3 provides descriptive statistics regarding subsidy instruments. The figures are annual averages of consecutive three-year periods and are expressed as percentages of the total subsidy budget. They are taken from the European Commission's *State Aid Scoreboard* (2006c) and *Survey on State Aid in the European Union* (various years). As can be gleaned from the data, the instrument most

Table 7.3   Descriptive statistics of subsidy instruments*

Variable	Minimum	Maximum	Mean	Standard deviation
Grants	8.30	96.55	67.43	21.05
Tax incentives	0	83.3	21.29	19.59
Soft loans	0	23.47	6.76	5.80
Credit guarantees	0	18	3.17	4.18

* Percent of total subsidies
Source: European Commission (2006c) and European Commission, *Survey on State Aid in the European Union* (various years).

frequently used is outright grants from the government's budget. In the period 2003–2005, 50.49 percent of all aid was disbursed in the form of grants (European Commission, 2006a, p. 27). A little more than two-thirds of all subsidies in the EU have been disbursed in the form of grants since 1992. In contrast to the other instruments, every single government has used grants from its annual budget to subsidize sectors of its economy or some types of economic activities, with some governments, such as Greece in 1996–1998, providing almost 97 percent of all their aid in the form of grants. In addition, other countries, such as Denmark, Finland, and to a lesser extent Spain and the UK, have consistently disbursed on average more than 80 percent of their entire subsidy budgets in the form of grants.

The second most frequently used instrument is tax incentives (or tax expenditures). In the period 2003–2005, 39.53 percent of all aid was allocated using this instrument (European Commission, 2006a, p. 27). Tax incentives are deductions or credits to taxable income that would otherwise be owed under corporate taxes (Surrey and McDaniel, 1985). Unlike grants, tax incentives reduce the *future* revenue stream of government and the company's tax liability. Whereas subsidies in the form of grants are taxable, tax breaks are not. They do not involve any funding doled out by government, only funding saved that would have been paid otherwise. They are very prevalent in the United States and in many countries around the world. More than 21 percent of all subsidies for the period under investigation have been disbursed in the form of tax incentives. Only one country, Austria, did not give any money in the form of tax incentives. It was, therefore, dropped from consideration. The rest show affinity for this instrument, with some countries, such as Portugal, France, Ireland, and Sweden, disbursing at times more aid as tax incentives than any other instrument.

Soft loans and capital guarantees are the least frequently used subsidy instruments. Soft loans, which constitute loans under favorable terms leading to interest savings, take up 6.76 percent of the total 1992–2004 subsidy budget on average, while the percent portion of guarantees is even less, 3.17 percent. In the period 2003–2005, the numbers were even smaller. Only 3.49 percent of all aid was disbursed in the form of soft loans and an even smaller amount, 1.29 percent, was given out in the form of guarantees (European Commission, 2006a, p. 27). Germany and to a lesser extent Austria and Sweden show the greatest affinity for soft loans, with Germany providing as much as 23.47 percent of its total budget in 1996–1998 in loan subsidies. In contrast, France and to a lesser degree Greece and the Netherlands, offer systematically more capital guarantees than other EU members.

Capital guarantees are savings by recipients when loans are guaranteed explicitly or implicitly by the state. Such guarantees lead to lower premiums because of the lower risk associated with default. Greece provided the greatest amount, 18 percent, in 1994–1996.

The main conclusion that one draws from the data is that different countries prefer different instruments. But governments are not consistent in their preferences. In some countries, such as Portugal and Ireland, governments show consistently more preference for grants only to switch at some point to a consistent preference for tax incentives. Other countries, such as the Netherlands and the UK, systematically prefer grants over tax incentives. Italy and Belgium exhibit a decreasing preference for tax incentives over time, while Finland finds tax incentives increasingly a better option. Still a few, such as Denmark, show an increasing appetite for tax incentives only to see it dissipate in later years.

Choosing between Subsidy Instruments

Why do governments prefer on average to disburse subsidies in the form of grants and how well does the asset influence model explain this choice? The key assumption of my approach is that the essence of using diverse government programs may be captured by reference to a few instrument dimensions. Such dimensions allow classification of programmatic diversity into a manageable number of cases. The analyst may then explore the implications of these dimensions on broader models of policy choice.

Looking at the tools of government, Salamon and Lund (1989) distinguish between instruments along two key dimensions: the nature of the activity and the structure of the delivery system. The nature of the activity refers to the basic type of stimulus that the government uses to achieve its objectives. Two elements loom important. The first is the transparency of the instrument. As Hillman (1989) argues, governments seek to hide losses from the losers of protection, that is, the taxpayers, and highlight benefits to the winners, that is, the protected firms or industries. In this way they can maximize political support and minimize opposition. Magee, Brock, and Young (1989) formalize this idea into the principle of optimal obfuscation. Policymakers choose instruments on the basis of optimizing the trade-off between political costs and benefits. On the one hand, obfuscation leads to political gains because losers are not aware or sure of the magnitude of the income transfers from protection. On the other hand, less transparency leads to higher inefficiency, and consequently greater cost, because it incurs higher deadweight costs. Ono (2006) extends the argument by linking different protectionist instruments to democracy. He finds empirical support for the proposition that democracy encourages the use of less-transparent instruments by comparing the use of tariffs and NTBs in 75 countries in the 1990s.

Choice centers on the marginal costs and benefits of trade policy. How much additional cost will grants incur should they be chosen over tax incentives? Not only do grants incur a direct cost on the budget, but they are also highly visible to taxpayers and government-spending watchdogs. This means that they will likely raise far greater opposition than their cost would imply relative to tax incentives. The less transparent the activity, the more politically appealing it will be. Loans and credit guarantees are even more appealing because of their diffuse nature and because they do not appear in the budget. Governments can use them to satisfy a wide range of recipients with less visibility, and by consequence, less political cost. For example, portfolio investment constrains the ability of governments to increase budget items because of the ease of capital flight. Holders of such investment will likely move their money if they believe returns to their assets are threatened by inefficient government spending or inflation. In this case, as portfolio investment goes up, governments are more likely to shift their subsidy allocations from grants to less-transparent instruments, such as tax incentives or capital guarantees.

The second element is the time horizon of the instrument. How effective is the instrument in the short run versus the long run? Political demands for protection may require immediate relief or they may be of a longer nature. Consider the following situation. As long-term FDI goes up, demands for attracting newcomers and for temporary relief of domestic firms increase. In this case subsidies to attract and relief to retain industry are more likely to come in the form of tax incentives than they are in the form of capital guarantees. The case of Alabama illustrates the point. It attracted ThyssenKrupp in 2007 with a record of $350.3 million in tax incentives alone (Peacock, 2007). At the same time steel workers at Fairfield Works near Birmingham demanded similar treatment in fear of losing their jobs because of potential competition (Peacock, 2007; Lawrence, 2007). Guarantees are a short-term instrument that is highly effective for only the time needed to raise funds. Long-term issues created by FDI require that instruments have a longer time horizon, such as tax incentives, which may be carried over a period of 20 years or more.

The second dimension is the structure of the delivery system. What institutional arrangements are needed to carry out the government's objectives, and how strongly are the recipients likely to demand their use? Again, two elements are important. The first element refers to the degree of control that the government exercises on the activity. Money payments, such as grants, carry strings attached. Being political allocations, governments are eager to ensure that monies are spent in ways that benefit the program and whatever political objectives the policymakers intended it to have. The range of payable activities is controlled by the supplier. In contrast, loans are more flexible in that recipients have greater control over expenses. However, loans involve fiscal intermediaries, banks, which makes them a bit more expensive to administer relative to, say, tax incentives. There is no need to create new agencies to oversee the expenditure of tax incentives. Tax authorities are already equipped to deal with these issues. The net effect is that governments prefer to maximize their control, which means they have a marked preference for grants as opposed to tax incentives, loans, or capital guarantees. By implication, the political power of the affected groups should be inversely related to the degree of government control.

The second element of the delivery system, which is closely related to the first, refers to the directness of the instrument. The term "directness" "refers to the precision with which an instrument can be directed to a specific beneficiary or maleficiary" (Hood, 1986, p. 146). How directly does it affect the intended recipients? The answer provides a clue as to the preferences of the intended beneficiaries. While transparency may help explain the government's calculus of choice, directness offers a glimpse of the motives behind pressures by affected groups. Grants are distributionally more blunt instruments than, say, capital guarantees. Capital guarantees involve specific firms and aim to ease their cost of raising capital. Gains can be directed to a clear and specific target. Tax incentives also have clear and specific targets. They aim to improve the future profitability of business firms by reducing the future tax liabilities. Unlike grants, workers are less likely to expend political and personal capital to lobby in favor of instruments that may affect them only indirectly. They are far more likely to demand and prefer grants, which may target a variety of relevant activities, such as worker training.

Model Specification and Findings

Figures of aid instruments are expressed as percentages of total aid disbursed per year. Although the Competition DG included raw numbers in several earlier surveys of state aid, it stopped publishing them when it began to offer the *Scoreboard* beginning in 2000. Data are now found only as annual averages of a three-year period.

I am interested in exploring the potential of the asset influence model in explaining the choice of subsidy instruments. The independent variables are the same. However, because of the nonannual nature of the data in the dependent variable, the values of the independent variables have to be similarly transformed. To keep the budgetary logic outlined earlier intact, I take the average of the preceding two years in the independent variables, adding a weight of 1 to the *t-1* year and 0.5 to the *t-2* year. The net effect is that the weighted two-year annual average (*t-1, t-2*) of, say, portfolio investment is hypothesized to explain the three-year annual average (*t, t-1, t-2*) of grants.

Estimation issues remain the same in this set of equations as they were in previous ones. The independent variables show little problematic collinearity except for the institutional variables, whose effects are estimated separately.[4] In addition, in order to address serial correlation within units, I report the transformed OLS estimates *via* the Prais-Winsten technique with robust standard errors (cluster option in STATA). Because of the low number of degrees of freedom I do not explore the impact of any interactive terms.

Table 7.4 presents the findings regarding grants and tax incentives. The grant models have a relatively good fit. The coefficients of determination show that the models explain a little more than 43 percent of the variance in the dependent variable. The most striking feature of the table is the fact that two of the three indicators of globalization are consistently strongly significant in all equations. An increase of 1 percent in the amount of portfolio investment leads to a reduction of .21 percent in grant expenditures, when taking into account corporatist institutions (equation 1). The finding is consistent with the hypothesis advanced earlier. Governments prefer to hide losses from the losers. This preference includes a switch to less-transparent instruments when exposure to global economic forces increases. Greater amounts of short-term capital investment severely constrain the ability of governments to spend more money. Because grants are highly visible funds allocated in the annual budget, governments find it politically expedient to shift expenditures to less-visible instruments. This is where tax incentives become important. Although tax incentives are not universally favored by European governments, some governments find it important to shift allocations from grants to tax incentives. Note that the coefficients of portfolio investment in the tax-incentive models have now become positive and equally strongly significant. Greater exposure to portfolio investment leads to an increase in tax incentives.

Table 7.4 The choice between grants and tax incentives

	Grants			Tax incentives		
	(1)	(2)	(3)	(4)	(5)	(6)
LS[1]	.073	.074	.068	−.214	−.216	−.209
	(.136)	(.134)	(.136)	(.103)**	(.105)**	(.108)*
CS[2]	−.10	−.102	−.126	.077	.081	.086
	(.15)	(.140)	(.155)	(.138)	(.136)	(.144)
Political power	−214.2	−134.3	−219.6	−475.7	−537.0	−483.7
	(626.9)	(644.4)	(630.9)	(490.6)	(524.7)	(517.2)
FDI[3]	.381	.386	.372	−.355	−.359	−.353
	(.086)***	(.085)***	(.082)***	(.08)***	(.079)***	(.077)***
Portfolio investment	−.215	−.214	−.217	.251	.249	.251
	(.051)***	(.049)***	(.049)***	(.06)***	(.054)***	(.055)***
Trade openness	−.087	−.09	−.055	−.195	−.193	−.205
	(.367)	(.37)	.370)	(.302)	(.303)	(.309)
Pluralism	−.088			.320		
	(4.46)			(3.06)		
Electoral system		−.41			.335	
		(1.05)			(.673)	
Collective veto			−.91			−.232
			(4.82)			(3.68)

(*Continued*)

Table 7.4 (*Continued*)

	Grants			Tax incentives		
	(1)	(2)	(3)	(4)	(5)	(6)
Competitive veto			-3.37			1.14
			(3.93)			(1.98)
Constant	76.01	75.81	76.52	52.44	52.99	53.25
	(33.59)**	(32.34)**	(32.16)**	(25.26)**	(24.77)**	(24.15)**
Adjusted R-squared	.4311	.4321	.4351	.1754	.1791	.1764
Rho	.7087	.7028	.7027	.6345	.6257	.6339
N	81			75		

Prais-Winsten estimates with robust standard errors in parentheses

* $.05 < p < .10$; ** $.01 < p < .05$; *** $p < .01$; two-tailed

[1] Labor specificity

[2] Capital specificity

[3] Foreign direct investment

The same trade-off is visible when it comes to FDI. It was hypothesized that FDI has a positive impact on grants; that is, higher levels of FDI would lead to higher amounts of grant expenditures. The model confirms this hypothesis in all cases. A 1 percent increase in the amount of FDI correlates with a significant .38 percent increase in grants when taking into account the type of electoral system (equation 2). The opposite is true in the case of tax incentives. Confirming the trade-off identified earlier, the coefficient of FDI now becomes negative and still strongly significant. More FDI leads to fewer tax incentives, as in the cases of Finland and the Netherlands. Not all globalization is created equal! Complementing Bhagwati's (1998) argument, it makes a difference whether one trades in widgets or dollars. Short- and long-term investments have opposite effects on the choice of instrument. Perhaps Drucker (1997, p. 167) was right after all, at least in the case of instrument choice. Movements of capital rather than movements of goods are the engines of the global economy (and protection). The findings here support the claim that there is a marked shift in importance away from trade toward investment; but the argument holds only in the case of instrument choice.

Labor specificity has a moderately negative effect only on tax incentives. The coefficients are in the hypothesized direction and consistently significant. Higher levels of specificity lead to lower expenditures in tax incentives. Consistent with the differential pressure hypothesis, workers need direct and effective protection, which is not provided by tax incentives given the fact that they are disbursed to firms and not to individual workers. While not significant, the positive coefficients relating labor specificity to grants further reinforce the trade-off between instruments. Workers prefer grants because they affect them more directly and visibly. Although governments do not appear to respond to these demands when it comes to grants, they do appear to be more sensitive when it comes to the issue of tax incentives.

Table 7.5 describes the explanatory potential of the model regarding soft loans and capital guarantees. The model simply collapses when it comes to soft loans. Hardly any of the hypothesized relationships appear statistically significant. More pluralist countries appear to prefer spending relatively less on soft loans. Countries in which there are greater numbers of competitive veto points spend comparatively more on soft loans. But more interesting results may be found in the equations estimating the effects on capital guarantees.

The model's explanatory capability shines in the case of capital guarantees. The overall fit remains at similar levels to soft loans, but several variables are now statistically significant. Just like in the case of

Table 7.5   The choice between soft loans and capital guarantees

	Soft loans			Capital guarantees		
	(1)	(2)	(3)	(4)	(5)	(6)
LS[1]	−.249	.043	−.044	.067	.067	.078
	(.058)	(.058)	(.054)	(.037)*	(.038)*	(.026)***
CS[2]	.005	−.017	−.001	.028	.011	.045
	(.038)	(.037)	(.039)	(.029)	(.023)	(.029)
Political power	238.5	134.2	117.1	362.3	315.9	229.8
	(201.3)	(207.3)	(197.9)	(148.5)**	(166.7)*	(154.9)
FDI[3]	.005	.009	.015	−.052	−.049	−.027
	(.015)	(.017)	(.018)	(.01)***	(.015)***	(.022)
Portfolio investment	.009	.005	.003	.009	−.012	−.02
	(.009)	(.010)	(.010)	(.010)	(.011)	(.012)*
Trade openness	−.025	−.028	−.050	.205	−.198	.159
	(.108)	(.095)	(.096)	(.063)	(.070)***	(.068)**
Pluralism	−2.60			−1.18		
	(.963)***			(.805)		
Electoral system		−.203			−.075	
		(.241)			(.20)	
Collective veto	.		.386			−.48
			(1.21)			(.596)
Competitive veto			1.95			2.35
			(.785)**			(.49)***
Constant	8.89	7.15	7.94	−17.80	−17.53	−15.70
	(8.35)	(7.12)	(8.34)	(8.57)**	(8.69)**	(8.02)**
Adjusted R-squared	.2651	.2056	.2350	.2391	.2105	.3732
Rho	.6257	.6668	.6330	.4547	.4830	.2953
N	81			80		

Prais-Winsten estimates with robust standard errors in parentheses
*.05 < p < .10; ** .01 < p < .05; *** p < .01; two-tailed
[1] Labor specificity
[2] Capital specificity
[3] Foreign direct investment

tax incentives, higher levels of FDI lead to decreases in guarantees, as the cases of Denmark and the UK can attest. The finding is consistent with the time horizon argument advanced earlier. Capital guarantees are short-term instruments, affecting savings at the time of raising capital. FDI involves a long-term commitment, which diminishes the effectiveness of guarantees. Governments accordingly reduce their expenditures in capital guarantees to free up resources to be used in instruments with more long-term effects, such as grants. As the political power of groups increases, so does their ability to extract more guarantees. Nevertheless, one should not make much of this finding. Although the coefficient is comparatively large, the fact that guarantees represent a small portion of the budget, a little over 3 percent, implies that political power "in the grand scheme of things" plays a relatively minor role.

While it is important to highlight what the models explain, it is equally revealing to discuss what the models do not show. It seems that the choice of instrument is impervious to the effects of capital specificity and to a lesser extent national institutions. Consistent with the findings in previous sections of this chapter, capital specificity does not appear to affect the choice of subsidy instrument. Workers, and their lot, are a politically powerful motive to use one instrument over another. In addition, the structure of national institutions has little impact. In only three out of the twelve equations examining instrument choice did pluralism and competitive veto points make a difference.

CONCLUSION

In this chapter, I examined two questions. First, do agricultural subsidies follow a different pattern than those to manufacturing? Second, does the logic of the model explain not only levels of support but also the choice of instruments?

It was found that agriculture is a special case. The disbursement of agricultural subsidies differs significantly from that of subsidies to manufacturing. Agriculture tends to be the sector with the highest level of support, although figures for other sectors are likely underestimated (OECD, 2005a, p. 8). In terms of the model, political power makes a huge difference in the case of agriculture. This is hardly surprising given the strength of agricultural lobbies throughout the industrialized world and the ability of farmers to secure continued assistance for a host of different reasons. Unlike in the case of manufacturing, where trade seems to exercise consistently independent and conditional influence, portfolio investment plays this role in the case of agriculture. This is somewhat surprising because short-term investment does not directly affect agriculture. Nevertheless, the low levels of agricultural trade and the fact that portfolio investment generally directs capital, which farmers could use, to the most profitable uses suggest that different aspects of globalization affect are at work in different sectors. Drucker's (1997) claim that investment, rather than trade, is becoming the more important dimension of globalization does not hold in the case of protection in manufacturing.

With regard to instruments, the implications are clear. While national institutions have a significant impact on the level of subsidy protection, both independently and in interaction with globalization, they do not have a similarly strong effect on the choice of instrument. The latter appears to be far less resistant to external economic forces, especially FDI and portfolio investment. Bhagwati (1998) is right: trade in widgets is not only qualitatively different from trade in dollars, but it also leads to variable pressures in different sectors, for example, agriculture. In addition, instrument dimensions guide the choice between tools of protection. Under conditions of higher globalization and labor specificity, governments generally switch to more direct, more politically beneficial, and more temporally appropriate tools. The logic of the asset influence model appears to be illuminating not only at the level of subsidy protection, but also regarding the instrument of subsidization.

C H A P T E R   8

NATIONAL SUBSIDIES IN THE GLOBAL ECONOMY

There can't be one set of rules when your team plays away and a different set of rules when they play at home.

—Alan Johnson, UK Trade and Industry Minister[1]

Why is there still so much protectionism despite political rhetoric extolling the virtues of free trade, favorable economic theory and evidence, and legal pressure to dismantle protectionist measures? "Virtually every industrialized country and most of the developing world have utilized a variety of protectionist measures" (Lutz, 2000, p. 17). If this is an accurate description of reality, why do national governments still subsidize their industries with varying zeal?

The answer is based on a model of political economy that focuses on the domestic policy process and its interaction with external economic forces. Globalization motivates certain groups to demand protection. Increased mobility of capital coupled with rising volumes of international trade create winners and losers in the domestic economy. As former secretary of state H. Kissinger (2006, p. 6) says, "The success of globalization breeds a temptation for protectionism." Economic groups, particularly in import-competing industries, "feel the heat" and demand subsidies to alleviate the pain. Actors who find it less costly to redeploy assets to different activities are less likely to make demands. Those who stand to lose the most because their investments are more or less "stuck" in present activities are natu-rally going to be the most vocal proponents of subsidies. Lobbying demands take the form of campaign contributions. Elected officials have an appetite for contributions because they need to finance their political campaigns, but they must also balance it with consumer welfare. Unlike tariffs, where policymakers face a trade-off between higher domestic prices or marginally higher taxes, subsidies pose the almost opposite situation: lower domestic prices or marginally higher taxes. The argument rests on the intensity of four factors and the way they interact with one another: globalization, asset specificity, political power, and institutional access. Naturally, not all groups have equal access to politicians, and not all politicians are equally inclined to grant protection. A group's political power shapes policymakers' incentive to listen to protectionist demands, while national formal public institutions canalize the demands and shape the willingness or ability of elected officials to respond.

I divide the concluding chapter into three parts. I first summarize the major findings, amending models of subsidy protection and redistribution. Then I examine the political implications of my asset influence model by looking at the dynamics of coalition formation and international trade. Finally, I probe more deeply into the paradox of democracy and globalization. Is the state really impotent as some observers proclaim, or is the tide of globalization reversible in the face of political demands for more democratic governance?

SUBSIDIES AND REDISTRIBUTIVE POLITICS

Global markets affect the distribution of wealth in domestic economies as well as the ability and options of affected groups to take political action. Inevitably, domestic groups will form coalitions to demand policies that shield them from adverse economic consequences. Such redistributive activity is politically contentious and economically inefficient. To understand why, analysis must concentrate on the political and economic incentives of interest groups and the institutional context within which policy is made. Redistribution is a political game that is dependent on rent-seeking and rent-supplying capacity.

Politics and domestic institutions matter. But the results are not unambiguously conclusive as they vary across objectives, sectors, and instruments. Consistent with Grossman and Helpman's (1994) prediction, increases in group political power have a strong positive effect on the disbursement of subsidies. But the finding is validated only in the case of total subsidies, regional and sectoral subsidies, and especially agricultural subsidies. As the farmers' power increases, government's willingness to protect agriculture also rises. Evidently, farmers must rely on raw power more than factory workers do to get protection. But in the case of horizontal subsidies or manufacturing aid, political power does not appear to make a difference.

Access to policymakers as well as gains and losses are canalized and mediated by institutional configurations of policymaking. The findings support and expand the notion advanced in G-H that organization matters. For example, consider the principle of compensation. Side-payments in the form of adjustment assistance are expected on a continuous basis in the more organized corporatist system. The results support this contention on average. Conversely, more pluralist arrangements tend to lead to fewer subsidies. This is a consistently strong result applicable to the majority of cases examined. But again the findings are not as clear-cut. While pluralism restricts the use of subsidies, the final policy recommendation is not the destruction of corporatism. As the conditional relationship regarding total subsidies in figure 6.1 showed, the effects of pluralism reverse at higher levels of trade openness. More pluralist countries give out more subsidies at high levels of trade. If one considers the fact that countries may become more open over time, the message is that corporatism rather than pluralism is the preferred institution of choice in the long term.

The fragmentation of state power and the degree of electoral disproportionality also matter but in fewer cases. Fragmentation in the form of veto points reveals interesting patterns of subsidization. According to the literature, more collective veto points lead to more subsidies, just like they do in the case of government expenditures (Crepaz and Moser, 2004). However, counter to the literature, as the number of competitive veto points increases, the amount of subsidies also goes up. The likelihood of protection, in other words, increases as the number of institutions with veto power increases. Logrolling and the presence of multiple institutional venues from which one may derive (as well as oppose) protection lead to the need to satisfy the greatest number of interests. Broad coalitions reflect this need, with subsidies being a likely result. Although this finding appears consistent as an independent effect, it changes direction conditional mainly on different levels of trade and portfolio investment.

An interesting literature has developed around the effects of the electoral system on protection. Some analysts see PR as less conducive to more protection (Rogowski, 1987). Others find that the opposite holds (McGillivray, 2004). Still others maintain that the answer depends on the partisan composition of government (Milner and Judkins, 2004). The findings reinforce the conditionality proposed in Alt and Gilligan (1994) although they follow a different path when it comes to independent and some interactive effects. Greater PR necessitates the creation of bigger coalitions, and consequently, results in more, rather than fewer, subsidies. The effect holds in the cases of horizontal and regional subsidies. Above this impact, disproportionality has a general negative effect when it interacts with FDI. Fewer subsidies are disbursed on average at higher levels of FDI and in more majoritarian systems. Moreover, figure 6.2 clearly shows that more PR systematically yields more subsidies than greater or lower FDI. Domestic politics plainly creates risks and opportunities in the formulation of policy, which are sometimes reinforced and at other times negated by globalization. It is precisely the interactive nature of domestic politics with globalization that makes exploration of this and other relationships uncovered in this study a fruitful area of future research.

Protection and redistribution also imply a choice between different instruments. Rarely is the choice only between levels of protection; quite often policymakers must also choose the kind of protection. I explored the effects of the asset influence model on four subsidization tools: grants, tax incentives, soft loans, and capital guarantees. It was found that the model has the most explanatory power in the case of grants and the least in the case of tax incentives. Instrument characteristics, such as transparency, control, time horizon, and directedness, appear to play a role in the preference of one instrument over the other. For example, exposure to capital investment appears to exercise the greatest influence on choice. Whereas more FDI leads to a disbursement of higher amounts of grants, it appears to dim the prospects of disbursing more tax incentives. Conversely, more portfolio investment leads to fewer grants but more tax incentives. Politicians appear on average to substitute one tool for the other, showing a preference for less-transparent tools as globalization intensifies, although there is no consistency among countries. More research is clearly needed to specify the precise conditions that facilitate trading off one instrument for the other.

Beyond Models of Coalition Formation and International Trade

Since the publication of Rogowski's (1989) book on trade and coalitions, a lively academic debate has ensued regarding the ability of groups to form protectionist coalitions and the conditions under which this is feasible. The argument here amends this debate in two ways. First, it qualifies the enabling conditions by finding that trade and capital flows have significant but often contradictory effects on coalition formation. Protectionism is not simply the result of trade effects. Second, my argument shifts the terms of the debate away from its current dichotomous form toward a more nuanced answer. The problem is not whether the Stolper-Samuelson or the Ricardo-Viner models are right, as the literature asks. They are both right under different conditions. The key is to specify those conditions and add nuance to substance.

It Is More than Just Trade

Exposure to the global economic environment affects the formation of coalitions. Globalization, as the literature predicts, creates winners and losers who seek to be compensated by the state. But not all globalization is created equal. Coalitions are not formed simply in response to increasing trade as Rogowski and much of the coalition formation literature conceptualize (e.g., McGillivray, 2004; Hiscox, 2002). Trade is important, but increasing exposure to capital movements qualifies the dynamics of coalition formation in domestic economies. Bhagwati (1998) argues forcefully that analysis must differentiate between globalization in trade and capital. Frieden (1991) extends this argument by showing that increasing exposure to capital investment from abroad alters the dynamics of coalition formation, enabling some and discouraging others.

What I have presented here is systematic evidence that buttresses and extends these arguments. Counter to Bhagwati's (1988) claim, increasing exposure to global market forces may in many instances increase rather than decrease the likelihood of protection. Trade has a positive impact. Losers coalesce and contribute to policymakers' political campaigns. Their coalitions overcome the trade-off between contributions and consumer welfare, and ultimately get subsidized. The same goes for long-term investment, or FDI. The presence of foreign manufacturers in developed democratic economies increases the likelihood of subsidization. Contrary to expectations, FDI does not appear to buy goodwill. It merely stirs the pot of economic nationalism and protectionism. But not all is doom and gloom. What analysts have failed to show, and what clearly emerges from this study, is that short-term investment matters. As exposure to portfolio investment increases, the pressures for protection decrease. Not only does analysis have to differentiate between the various dimensions of globalization, but careful specification also provides valuable insight. Globalization does not lead to more or less protectionism. The answer is more complicated than that. And there is more. If one accepts Drucker's (1997) assertion that capital movements in the future will matter more than trade, claims about globalization must be further qualified. Whereas globalization supplied incentives that generally encouraged the formation of protectionist coalitions in the past, it may not do so in the future.

Beyond the Impact of Traditional Models of Trade

Although the expansion of trade in recent decades has generated political conflict by creating both winners and losers, the character of conflict and the societal cleavages that it represents have changed over the years. The literature does not agree on what groups will be able to coalesce as a result of greater exposure to international trade to demand protection. On the one hand, Rogowski (1989) extols the wisdom of Stolper and Samuelson (1941), suggesting that protectionist coalitions will form along class lines, that is, workers against employers, when countries are forced by trade to utilize more intensively their abundant factor of production. Thus in countries with more abundant capital, that is, today's developed democracies, labor is likely to lose from increased exposure to trade. Consequently, it will coalesce to demand more protection. On the other hand, analysts have questioned the model's assumption of perfect factor mobility, suggesting that the crucial determinant of coalitions is asset specificity (Hiscox, 2001). According to the Ricardo-Viner model, owners of more specific assets are likely to coalesce along sectoral lines to fight for protection because the dividing line will be asset mobility rather than factor abundance. If owners can move their assets to more productive uses in the domestic economy, their losses will be small and their demands muted, whether the factor is abundant or not.

The evidence presented here suggests that the answer is not as clear-cut. The question is not whether one model is correct and the other is not. Rather the answer is both are right under certain conditions. The problem is in specifying and empirically validating the conditions under which one model yields more accurate predictions than the other. Following the logic of the Ricardo-Viner model, the expectation is created that governments are more likely to disburse sectoral subsidies when asset specificity is high. The data do not unambiguously confirm this conclusion. The null hypothesis of no relationship cannot be rejected. In addition, labor specificity has a negative effect on sectoral subsidies conditional on different levels of trade openness. Quite contrary to expectations, low specificity leads to dramatic increases in subsidies but only at high levels of trade. As Acemoglu and Robinson (2001) maintain, low specificity may increase rather than decrease demands for protection because groups want to encourage the entry of more actors in the same activity for fear of losing political power and ultimately subsidies over time.

Does this mean that the model's predictions are empirically invalid? Not really. The cases of horizontal subsidies, total subsidies, and subsidies to manufacturing point to the importance of high specificity in generating subsidy protection. Stolper and Samuelson (1941) argue that higher levels of exposure will increase the scope of losses along factoral lines. By implication, one expects more horizontal subsidies to be disbursed. Because horizontal subsidies apply to the entire economy and do not discriminate between sectors or firms, it is reasonable to expect they are the result of broad factoral coalitions. The fact that labor specificity is a major determinant of these subsidies reflects the wisdom of expecting labor to lose the most in developed economies, and therefore, to demand protection. The positive effect of trade openness further validates Rogowski's (1989) claim. However, the fact that more labor specificity leads to more subsidies muddies the waters. The implications of the Stolper-Samuelson model cannot be unambiguously validated because the evidence shows that higher, rather than lower, specificity produces the expected results. Groups which stand to lose the most because they cannot (or find it very costly to) move their assets to more productive uses in the domestic economy can successfully demand more protection.

The main conclusion to emerge is a complex picture of numerous interactions among explanatory variables. The dividing line is asset specificity, as the Ricardo-Viner model predicts. But the effects of specificity are different from those expected in the crucial case of sectoral subsidies. Moreover, the expectations do not hold in all cases. Predictions generated by the Stolper-Samuelson model are empirically validated in some instances. Sweeping generalizations about the accuracy of independent effects are misplaced. Both models generate empirically valid predictions under different circumstances and conditional on varying levels of exposure to global economic forces.[2]

An Impotent Democratic State?

The globalists have it wrong. The politicians are not powerless, as the economist Jean-Paul Fitoussi categorically asserts (quoted in Hollinger et al., 2006a, p. 13). But they face an uncomfortable dilemma. Greater exposure to global economic forces produces significant benefits, but it also carries significant costs. Full global market integration and democratic governance are engaged in a zero-sum confrontation (Rodrik, 2005). The more policymakers push for one, the more they undermine the other.

Globalization is intimately tied to MNCs. More than any other organization, MNCs are the players propelling globalization forward. Although the number of MNCs is estimated to be in the thousands, the sales of their subsidiaries exceed the world's exports by more than 50 percent (Vernon, 1998, pp. 9–10, 12). In Japan, a handful of MNCs account for all of the country's foreign trade. In the light of the findings of this study one may conclude that they are responsible for the rise in protectionist sentiment. To be sure, not all of the subsidies generated in response to external "foes" go to domestic producers. Some, in the form of tax expenditures, grants, and other incentives, are used to lure MNCs to relocate (Thomas, 2000).

The expanded presence of MNCs has given rise to a major dilemma. Governments need to balance the benefits from attracting MNCs with the costs of maintaining an open economy. This is not an easy task. Increases in exposure to trade and long-term capital create social dislocations and costs that government compensates by raising production subsidies. The social costs of exposure are channeled and mitigated through domestic institutions. Such configurations have served government in developed countries reasonably well so far. Greater pressure for protectionism places strains on democratic institutions to deliver outstanding performance in the face of a rapidly changing and challenging external economic environment. However, increased fiscal profligacy in the face of severe pressure toward greater efficiency emanating from globalization is not really an option. The new institutions that have been created as a response aim to insulate economic policymaking bodies from democratic politics to reduce the likelihood of economic inefficiency because of political interference (Rodrik, 2005, p. 205). This is precisely the motive behind attempts in the past decade or so to create strong, national, independent central banks in Europe and elsewhere. In this sense, globalization undermines democratic accountability.

However, the relationship goes the other way as well. The present study demonstrates that governments cannot resist adjustment assistance in the form of producer subsidies. As Leipziger and Spence (2007, p. 11) note: "As you would expect in a healthy democracy, there are internal voices that are opposed [to globalization] on the grounds of equity." Under certain conditions groups successfully get the protection they want. Politics tames the market, producing economic inefficiency and seeking to control the effects of globalization. In this sense, democratic discourse undermines global economic markets. More globalization sometimes leads to higher social costs, which in turn create the requisite conditions for more protection. The problem becomes that the more globalization undermines democratic politics, the more democratic politics will strive to tame globalization.

To the extent that protectionist demands go unheeded, government grows unresponsive, increasing the chances of political turmoil, social unrest, and policy instability. What good is a democratic state if it cannot provide for its citizens' welfare, however contentious and inefficient such redistribution may be? The stronger the government's response, however, the more production is skewed toward economic inefficiency and away from the supposed benefits of globalization. What good is globalization if does not deliver all the economic benefits while it retains all the social costs?

In this context, the current political sentiment makes sense: liberalization attack abroad and protection practice at home (O'Brien, 1997). This policy is of course unsustainable in the long term. Many years ago, Polanyi (1957) persuasively demonstrated the catastrophic effects of this contradiction. Analyzing the political economy of the nineteenth century, he wrote that "inevitably, society took measures to protect itself [from adverse market effects], but whatever measures it took impaired the self-regulation of the market, disorganized industrial life, and thus endangered society in yet another way" (pp. 3–4). It is unlikely that the twenty-first century is heading for a similar catastrophe. Affected groups do not seek unilateral nationalist measures against globalization, especially dislocations caused by international capital flows (Helleiner, 2001). Subsidies (as well as tariffs) are on the decline.

But there are indications of a significant rise in protectionist sentiment around the world. As business executives of some of the biggest European and U.S. companies warned recently in a letter to members of the U.S. Congress, "Those promoting economic nationalism abroad . . . [which increasingly finds] support in Europe and elsewhere . . . would surely find comfort from restrictions imposed by the US" (Kirchgaessner, 2006, p. 3). Betts (2006, p. 18) further informs that "the French concept of 'economic patriotism' appears to be gaining converts across Europe." Protectionism is partly rationalized on the basis of security concerns. For example, Washington recently abandoned the sale of several ports to a Dubai-owned company on the rationale that it might somehow compromise national security. In 2005, French policymakers ascertained their right to block acquisitions of French firms in areas they consider strategic. The problem is not new. Technology has long been used as a commercial and military weapon where policymakers seek to both curb its use and sell it as widely as possible at the same time.[3] But the main "threat" comes from destabilizing forces owing to increasing openness to the world economy (Vernon, 1998, p. 172). Greater openness exposes both domestic labor and capital to greater external risk, against which they seek social insurance and other compensation. The domestic social contract between owners of productive assets has generated significant demands for adjustment assistance to compensate for the losses and dislocations caused by globalization (Bhagwati, 1988; Moran, 1999). My study empirically validates the way this normative request has turned into public policy.

Germany epitomizes the conundrum facing many countries. Globalization has been great for German companies but terrible to the German economy. "Germany is now more integrated in the international division of labour [*sic*] than any other comparable economy," boasts improbably a senior trade expert at the German economics ministry (Benoit and Milne, 2006, p. 11). The latest data show that Germany retained the title of *Exportweltmeister* in 2004, surpassing exports of the United States despite a slowdown in the last few months (Atkins, 2006, p. 3). German companies are seeing their profits soar to new heights. At $1.5 billion, sales of their foreign affiliates now exceed national exports. To appreciate the magnitude of this figure, consider the fact that German exports are valued at roughly the same amount as the exports of the UK, France, and Holland combined (Benoit and Milne, 2006, p. 11)! At the same time, the domestic economy has tanked. Unemployment remains stubbornly high, and economic growth is still low by U.S. or British standards. Consumer demand is very low because Germans are complaining the factories are not hiring. Demands for retraining, social insurance, and other subsidies continue to be forcefully made. As a result, the federal budget continues to be unacceptably high by historical and European standards, making a mockery of the EU's stability pact. The success of increasing globalization has come at a tremendous social cost. There is widespread resentment at the fact that wages have stagnated since 2000 yet corporate profits have since increased dramatically. Despite repeated efforts, successive governments have so far proved unable to resolve the dilemma. At the same time, "the pool of the anti-globalization discontent is large and growing" (Benoit and Milne, 2006, p. 11).

More democracy is desirable. Citizens naturally expect government to respond to their needs as much as possible. More globalization is also desirable because it creates wealth and generally lowers economic costs. Unfortunately, having our cake and eating it too does not appear to be an option. One risks undermining the other. Contrary to political rhetoric and academic expectations, full global market integration and a strong democracy may indeed prove to be incompatible.

Notes

Chapter 1

1. Comment made on the occasion of President Bush's visit to India in March 2006 (Kissinger, 2006, p. 6).
2. Comment made in support of Spain's decision to fight against unwanted foreign takeover of Endesa, its largest power company, despite the European Commission's pressure to open up the Spanish energy market (Rix and Leaniz, 2006).
3. In addition to subsidies, NTBs include a very long list of instruments, such as labeling, quality assurance requirements, unusual certification or approval procedures, public procurement practices, and food safety and health requirements. For insight into the range of NTBs gathered from various business surveys, see Fliess (2005).
4. The downward slope of total subsidies masks differences across sectors as well. For example, "energy subsidies continue to grow in part due to rapidly rising energy prices and heightened concerns over the security of supply" (Koplow, 2007, p. 95). While the author argues the U.S. federal government subsidizes energy producers every year with funds worth an estimated $49–100 billion (p. 106), it is not unrealistic to assume the trend is similar in other OECD countries. For example, subsidies for biofuels such as ethanol have increased in recent years, covering support for the construction of plants, aid for production of biofuels, or support for the production of feedstock that is used to produce biofuels. Without the aid of the public purse, it would have been unrealistic, perhaps impossible, for the EU to set a target of biofuels supplying 5.75 percent of all motor fuel needs by 2010 (Barg, Cosbey, and Steenblik, 2007, p. 48).
5. The concept of state aid (and its objectives) in the EU differs from the concept of direct industrial support used by the OECD. The main difference exists in categories. The OECD lumps together sectoral aid with aid to employee training and research and development as specific aid. It differentiates these objectives from nonspecific aid, such as environmental or energy efficiency assistance (Pretchker, 1998a, p. 108). In contrast, the EU considers environmental aid and employee training as part of aid serving nonspecific horizontal objectives.
6. The countries include Austria, Belgium, Denmark, Finland, France, Germany, Greece, Ireland, Italy, the Netherlands, Portugal, Spain,

Sweden, and the United Kingdom. Luxembourg was excluded because of its unusually small size.

7. Despite considerable political upheaval in Europe's capitals and one counteroffer from Russia's Severstal, Arcelor was eventually sold to Mittal Steel in June 2006 for $33.9 billion (Marsh, 2006).

CHAPTER 2

1. The quote is taken from Benn Steil (2006, p. 13), director of international economics at the Council on Foreign Relations.

CHAPTER 3

1. The remark was made on the occasion of a two-day business conference in Brussels in March 2006, which called on European political leaders to reform their economies or face obsolescence (Bounds and Smyth, 2006, p. 2).
2. Comment made in response to the proposed removal of U.S. limits on air service between Europe and the U.S (Adams, 2006, p. 1B).
3. Leipziger and Spence (2007) in an editorial essay that appeared in the *Financial Times*.
4. Simmons (1999, p. 44) points out that at the height of the gold standard in the nineteenth century, Britain and France invested overseas 153 and 97 percent of their annual economic output respectively. Most of the money was in the form of debt securities going increasingly to private rather than government users (Davis and Gallman, 2001). The numbers of course reflect the size of the empires of both countries, but they serve to remind us that global capital integration still remains lower in some respects than in years past.

CHAPTER 4

1. Comments made by Lou Dobbs in his book *Exporting America,* lamenting the fact that outsourcing and globalization in general are having on balance significant negative effects on the U.S. economy because they lead to job losses even when they yield higher corporate profits. The quote is taken from Steil (2006, p. 13).
2. The lack of economic growth in closed, e.g., Communist, economies and its presence in others, such as Asian economies, according to some analysts, may be attributed to gains from total factor productivity (Krugman, 1994).
3. The other two types described by Joskow are site specificity, that is, the value of immobile assets depending on location, and dedicated asset specificity, that is, the ability to continue sales to particular customers. I deal with site specificity in chapter 7. Dedicated assets are irrelevant for my purposes as they focus on a single firm.

4. Data on wage costs for Ireland represent labor compensation of employees.

Chapter 5

1. Comments made by O'Brien (2006, p. 11) in defense of taking uneven but definite steps toward greater European integration in the aftermath of the rejection of the European constitution by French and Dutch voters.
2. The Dutch MEP spoke on behalf of the Socialist group, the second largest group in the European Parliament, in response to Competition Commissioner Neelie Kroes's comments on fighting member states over undue national economic intervention (Minder, 2006, p. 2).

Chapter 6

1. The quote is taken from Steil (2006, p. 13).
2. However, the variance inflation factors linking trade openness and political power (inverse of import penetration) approach the problematic level of 9.64. I ran the equations omitting political power, but the results were identical. The coefficients of trade openness were in the same direction and statistically significant (or not) in the same equations. For this reason and because each indicator measures a different concept, I chose to include and report both variables.
3. The coefficients were calculated using the cluster option in STATA 9.0 Special Edition, which treats observations across units, but not within each unit, as independent. I also ran the analyses calculating panel-corrected standard errors, and got essentially the same results.
4. The same thing happened with Belgium in 2000 and Greece in 1998. Belgium received by far the highest amount of FDI of those in the sample, and Greece received the least amount, making them possible outliers. I ran the equation deleting those observations, but the results remained unchanged.
5. I follow Tufte's (1974, p. 125) claim that when the predictor variable is not logarithmically transformed, but the dependent variable is, and when the unstandardized coefficient is small, the results can be interpreted as quasi-elasticities. A unit change in X leads to a percent change in Y; in this case X is measured in percentages.
6. One of the more interesting findings is that despite high correlation between pluralism, electoral disproportionality, and collective veto points, the results differ in terms of instances of significance occasionally within the same equation and frequently across equations. This point implies that the indicators measure conceptually and empirically distinct phenomena.

7. Ohmae (1995, p. 143) anticipates the end of the nation-state and foresees the development of what he calls the "region-state," which refers to "an area (often cross-border) developed around a regional economic center with a population of a few million to 10–20 million."

Chapter 7

1. Bagwell and Staiger (2002, p. 179) conclude that on a general level agricultural export subsidies may not be beneficial to importing countries because agreements at the WTO to limit them restrict trade and increase prices. They do, however, benefit exporting countries.
2. The constant terms in both sets of equations (manufacturing and agriculture) are comparable in the sense they are measured in constant million euros. Although their interpretation is difficult because the numbers are logarithmically transformed, the point that needs to be emphasized is that the slope is considerably lower in the equations measuring agriculture.
3. The Commission also publishes figures for subsidies in the form of equity participation and tax deferments. The problem with these numbers is that they constitute a small part of the overall budget, 1.94 and 1.2 percent respectively. In addition, seven governments did not disburse aid in either or both forms, rendering the importance of any estimation effects rather trivial.
4. I ran into the same problem of collinearity as I did in previous equations. I dealt with it the same way I did before. See note 2 in chapter 6.

Chapter 8

1. Comments made by the British minister in response to the tightening of the rules for foreign investment in the United States. He charged that inconsistent scrutinizing standards proposed by members of the U.S. Senate's Banking Committee would invite criticism of hypocrisy. The quote is taken from an editorial in the *Financial Times* ("Capitol Hill Plays at Economic Patriotism," 2006, p. 10).
2. Alt and Gilligan (1994) also specify conditional effects with a similar set of variables. However, they emphasize the importance of only domestic variables while I stress the significance of interactions between the domestic process and globalization.
3. Witness the current imbroglio over nuclear technology with Iran and the sale of similar technology to India at roughly the same time.

References

Acemoglu, D., and J. A. Robinson (2001). Inefficient redistribution. *American Political Science Review* 95:649–661.

Acs, Z., and S. Isberg (1991). Innovation, firm size, and corporate finance. *Economic Letters* 35:323–326.

Adams, M. (2006). Door threatens to slam on open skies. *USA Today,* March 3, pp. 1B–2B.

Adserà, A., and C. Boix (2002). Trade, democracy, and the size of the public sector: The political underpinnings of openness. *International Organization* 56:229–262.

Allesina, A., V. Grilli, and G. M. Milesi-Ferretti (1994). The political economy of capital controls. In *Capital mobility: The impact on consumption, investment and growth,* ed. L. Leiderman and A. Razin, pp. 289–321. Cambridge, UK, and New York: Cambridge University Press.

Alt, J., F. Carlsen, P. Heum, and K. Johansen (1999). Asset specificity and the political behavior of firms: Lobbying for subsidies in Norway. *International Organization* 53:99–116.

Alt, J., J. A. Frieden, M. J. Gilligan, D. Rodrik, and R. Rogowski (1996). The political economy of international trade: Enduring puzzles and an agenda for inquiry. *Comparative Political Studies* 29:689–717.

Alt, J., and M. J. Gilligan (1994). The political economy of trading states: Factor specificity, collective action problems, and political institutions. *Journal of Political Philosophy* 2:165–192.

Arnold, M. (2005). French farmers dig in against subsidy reform. *Financial Times,* December 8, p. 7.

Atkins, R. (2006). Germany's weaker trade data point to slower growth. *Financial Times,* February 9, p. 3.

Bagwell, K., and R. W. Staiger (2002). *The economics of the world trading system.* Cambridge, MA: MIT Press.

Baldwin, R. E. (1985). *The political economy of US import policy.* Cambridge, MA: MIT Press.

——— (1989). The political economy of trade policy. *Journal of Economic Perspectives* 3:119–135.

——— (1994). *Towards an integrated Europe.* London: Centre for Economic Policy Research.

Barg, S., A. Cosbey, and R. Steenblik (2007). A sustainable development framework for assessing the benefits of subsidy reform. In OECD, *Subsidy*

174   REFERENCES

reform and sustainable development: Political economy aspects, pp. 31–60. Paris: OECD.

Basinger, S. J., and M. Hallerberg (2004). Remodeling the competition for capital: How domestic politics erases the race to the bottom. *American Political Science Review* 98:261–276.

Beamer, G. (1999). *Creative politics: Taxes and public goods in a federal system*. Ann Arbor, MI: University of Michigan Press.

Beck, N., and J. Katz (1995). What to do (and not to do) with time-series-cross-section data in comparative politics. *American Political Science Review* 89:634–647.

Beck, N., J. Katz, R. M. Alvarez, G. Garrett, and P. Lange (1993). Government partisanship, labor organization, and macroeconomic performance: A corrigendum. *American Political Science Review* 87:945–948.

Becker, G. S. (1986). The public interest hypothesis revisited: A new test of Peltzman's theory of regulation. *Public Choice* 49(3): 223–234.

Beghin, J. C., and M. Kherallah (1994). Political institutions and international patterns of agricultural protection. *Review of Economics and Statistics* 76:482–489.

Benoit, B., and R. Milne (2006,). Germany's best-kept secret: How its exporters are beating the world. *Financial Times*, May 19, p. 11.

Berger, S. (and the MIT Industrial Performance Center) (2005). *How we compete: What companies around the world are doing to make it in today's global economy*. New York: Currency Doubleday.

Betts, P. (2006). Economic nationalism gains pace. *Financial Times*, February 23, p. 18.

Bhagwati, J. N. (1982). Directly-unproductive, profit-seeking (DUP) activities. *Journal of Political Economy* 90:988–1002.

——— (1988). *Protectionism*. Cambridge, MA: MIT Press.

——— (1998). The capital myth: The difference between trade in widgets and dollars. *Foreign Affairs* 77(3): 7–12.

——— (2004). *In defense of globalization*. New York: Oxford University Press.

Birchfield, V., and Crepaz, M. (1998). The impact of constitutional structures and collective and competitive veto points on income inequality in industrialized democracies. *European Journal of Political Research* 34:175–200.

Blais, A. (1986). *A political sociology of public aid to industry*. Toronto: University of Toronto Press.

Blyth, M. (2003). The political power of financial ideas: Transparency, risk, and distribution in global finance. In *Monetary orders: Ambiguous economics, ubiquitous politics*, ed. J. Kirshner, pp. 239–259. Ithaca, NY: Cornell University Press.

Boix, C. (1997). *Political parties, growth and equality*. Cambridge: Cambridge University Press.

——— (2004). *Between redistribution and trade: The political economy of protectionism and domestic compensation*. University of Chicago, mimeo.

Boulding, K. E. (1989). *Three faces of power.* Newbury Park, CA: Sage.

Bounds, A., and C. Smyth (2006). Call for EU economic reforms. *Financial Times,* March 17, p. 2.

Braumoeller, B. F. (2004) Hypothesis testing and multiplicative interaction terms. *International Organization* 58:807–820.

Brawley, M. R. (1997). Factoral or sectoral conflict? Partially mobile factors and the politics of trade in imperial Germany. *International Studies Quarterly* 41:633–653.

Buck, T., and P. Hollinger (2006). Brussels plans action against France on takeover rule. *Financial Times,* March 31, p. 2.

Busch, M. L. (1999) *Trade warriors: States, firms, and strategic trade policy in high-technology competition.* Cambridge: Cambridge University Press.

Busch, M. L., and E. Reinhardt (1999). Industrial location and protection: The political and economic geography of U.S. non-tariff barriers. *American Journal of Political Science* 43:1028–1050.

Calomiris, C. W. (2005). Capital flows, financial crises, and public policy. In *Globalization: What's new?* ed. M. M. Weinstein, pp. 36–76. New York: Columbia University Press.

Cameron, D. R. (1978). The expansion of the public economy: A comparative analysis. *American Political Science Review* 72:1243–1261.

——— (1988). Distributional coalitions and other sources of economic stagnation: On Olson's *Rise and decline of nations. International Organization* 42:561–603.

Cassing, J. H., and A. L. Hillman (1985) Political influence motives and the choice between tariffs and quotas. *Journal of International Economics* 19:279–290.

Cerny, P. G. (1994). The dynamics of financial globalization. *Policy Sciences* 27: 319–342.

——— (1995). Globalization and collective action. *International Organization* 49:595–626.

Chatterjee, S., A. Hadi, and B. Price (2000). *Regression analysis by example.* 3rd ed. New York: Wiley.

Clark, W. R. (2003). *Capitalism, not globalism: Capital mobility, central bank independence, and the political control of the economy.* Ann Arbor: University of Michigan Press.

Coleman, W. D., Atkinson, M. M., and Montpetit, E. (1997). Against the odds: Retrenchment in agriculture in France and the US. *World Politics* 49:453–481.

Cooper, R. N. (1988). Industrial policy and trade distortion: A policy perspective. In *International Competitiveness,* ed. A.M. Spence and H. A. Hazard, pp. 115–147. Cambridge, MA: Ballinger.

Corden, W. M. (1997). *Trade policy and economic welfare.* Oxford: Clarendon Press.

Cox, A. (2007). Easing subsidy reform for producers, consumers, and communities. In OECD, *Subsidy reform and sustainable development: Political economy aspects,* pp. 61–68. Paris: OECD.

Crawford, S. E. S., and E. Ostrom (1995). A grammar of institutions. *American Political Science Review* 89:582–600.

Crepaz, M. (2001). Veto players, globalization and the redistributive capacity of the state: A panel study of 15 OECD countries. *Journal of Public Policy* 21:1–22.

Crepaz, M., and A. W. Moser (2004). The impact of collective and competitive veto points on public expenditures in the global age. *Comparative Political Studies* 37:259–285.

Damania, R. (2005). The political economy of environmentally harmful subsidies. In OECD, *Environmentally harmful subsidies: Challenges for Reform,* pp. 111–125. Paris: OECD.

Daniel, C. (2006). Bush loyalist takes international economics to the political stage. *Financial Times,* January 3, p. 4.

Daugbjerg, C. (2003). Policy feedback and paradigm shift in EU agricultural policy: The effects of the MacSharry reform on future reforms. *Journal of European Public Policy* 10:421–437.

Davis, L. E., and R. Gallman (2001). *Evolving financial markets and international capital flows: Britain, the Americas, and Australia, 1865–1914.* Cambridge: Cambridge University Press.

Davis, S. J., and J. Haltiwanger (1992). Gross job creation, gross job destruction, and employment reallocation. *Quarterly Journal of Economics* 107:819–863.

Dean, C. J. (2007). Riley says two major industries target the city. *The Birmingham News,* May 31, pp. 1B, 6B.

Destler, I. M. (1992). *American Trade Politics.* 2nd ed. Washington, D.C.: Institute for International Economics.

Dixit, A. K. (1996). *The making of economic policy.* Cambridge, MA: MIT Press.

Dixit, A., G. M. Grossman, and E. Helpman (1997). Common agency and coordination: General theory and application to government policy making. *Journal of Political Economy* 105:752–769.

Dixit, A. K., and J. Londregan (1995). Redistributive politics and economic efficiency. *American Political Science Review* 89:856–866.

Drucker, P. F. (1997). The global economy and the nation-state. *Foreign Affairs* 76(5): 159–171.

Dwyer, J. (2007). Agriculture. In OECD, *Subsidy reform and sustainable development: Political economy aspects,* pp. 71–91. Paris: OECD.

Echenique, F., and J. X. Eguia (2005). An explanation of inefficient redistribution: Transfers insure cohesive groups. California Institute of Technology, mimeo.

Economist (2005). Boeing vs Airbus: Nose to Nose. June 25, pp. 67–69.

Eggertsson, T. (1990). *Economic behavior and institutions.* Cambridge: Cambridge University Press.

Ekdahl, H. (2006). WTO should focus on non-tariff issues (letter to the editor). *Financial Times,* April 5, p. 12.

Eriksen, T. H. (2007). *Globalization: The key concepts.* Oxford, UK, and New York: Berg.

European Commission (Various years). Competition Directorate, *Survey on state aid in the European Union.* http://ec.europa.eu/comm/ competition/state_aid/studies_reports/archive/scoreboard_arch.html (accessed February 8, 2006).

———— (2006a). Competition Directorate, *Report: State aid score-board.* http://ec.europa.eu/comm/competition/state_aid/studies_ reports/2006_autumn_en.pdf (accessed May 22, 2007).

———— (2006b). Competition Directorate, *State aid overview.* http:// europa.eu.int/comm/competition/state_aid/overview (accessed January 25, 2006).

———— (2006c). Competition Directorate, *State aid scoreboard.* http:// europa.eu.int/comm/competition/state_aid/scoreboard (accessed January 28, 2006).

Feenstra, R. C., and J. N. Bhagwati (1982). Tariff seeking and the efficient tariff. In *Import competition and response,* ed. J. N. Bhagwati, pp. 245–261. Chicago: University of Chicago Press.

Feldstein, M., and C. Horioka (1980). Domestic savings and international capital flows. *Economic Journal* 90:314–329.

Financial Times (2006). Capitol Hill plays at economic patriotism. March 31, p. 10.

Findlay, R., and S. Wellisz (1982). Endogenous tariffs, the political economy of trade restrictions, and welfare. In *Import competition and response,* ed. J. N. Bhagwati, pp. 223–243. Chicago: University of Chicago Press.

Fliess, B. (2005). Overview of non-tariff barriers: Findings from existing business surveys. In OECD, *Looking beyond tariffs: The role of non-tariff barriers in world trade,* pp. 19–57. Paris: OECD.

Fox, J. (1991). *Regression diagnostics.* Newbury Park, CA: Sage.

Frankel, J. A. (1992). Measuring international capital mobility: A review. *American Economic Review, Papers and Proceedings* 82:197–202.

Frieden, J. A. (1991). Invested interests: The politics of national economic policies in a world of global finance. *International Organization* 45:425–451.

Frieden, J. A., and R. Rogowski (1996). The impact of the international economy on national policies: An analytical overview. In *Internationalization and domestic politics,* ed. R. O. Keohane and H. V. Milner, pp. 25–47. Cambridge: Cambridge University Press.

Garrett, G. (1998). *Partisan politics in the global economy.* Cambridge: Cambridge University Press.

Garrett, G., and P. Lange (1996). Internationalization, institutions, and political change. In *Internationalization and domestic politics,* ed. R. O. Keohane and H. V. Milner, pp. 48–75. Cambridge: Cambridge University Press.

Gawande, K., and U. Bandyopadhyay (2000). Is protection for sale? A test of the Grossman-Helpman theory of endogenous protection. *Review of Economics and Statistics* 82:139–152.

Gilligan, M. J. (1997). *Empowering exporters: Reciprocity and collective action in twentieth century American trade policy.* Ann Arbor: University of Michigan Press.

Gisser, M. (1993). Price support, acreage controls, and efficient redistribution. *Journal of Political Economy* 101:584–611.

Goff, P. M. (2005). It's got to be sheep's milk or nothing! Geography, identity and economic nationalism. In *Economic nationalism in a globalizing World,* ed. E. Heleiner and A. Pickel, pp. 183–201. Ithaca, NY: Cornell University Press.

Goldberg, P. K., and G. Maggi (1999). Protection for sale: An empirical investigation. *American Economic Review* 89:1135–1155.

Goodin, R. E. (1996). Institutionalizing the public interest: The defense of deadlock and beyond. American Political Science Review 90:331–343.

Goodman, J. B., and L. W. Pauly (1993). The obsolescence of capital controls? Economic management in an age of global markets. *World Politics* 46:50–82.

Gordon, A. (1998). *The wages of affluence: Labor and management in postwar Japan.* Cambridge, MA: Harvard University Press.

Grant, J. (2006). US farmers' resistance to overhaul of subsidies threatens to land Bush in mire. *Financial Times,* January 19, p. 6.

Green, D. P., S. Y. Kim, and D. H. Yoon (2001). Dirty pool. *International Organization* 55:441–468.

Greenspan, A. (1998) The globalization of finance. *Cato Journal* 17: 243–250.

Grimwade, N. (1989). *International trade: New patterns of trade, production and investment.* London: Routledge.

Grossman, G. M. (1983). Partially mobile capital: A general approach to two-sector trade theory. *Journal of International Economics* 15:1–17.

Grossman, G. M., and E. Helpman (1994). Protection for sale. *American Economic Review* 84:833–850.

——— (1995). Trade wars and trade talks. *Journal of Political Economy* 103:675–708.

——— (2002). *Interest groups and trade policy.* Princeton, NJ: Princeton University Press.

Guerrera, F., and A. Yeh (2005). S&P study reveals $500 bn spent in government support for Asian banks. *Financial Times,* September 29, p. 7.

Hall, P. A. (1999). The political economy of Europe in an era of interdependence. In *Continuity and change in contemporary capitalism,* ed. H. Kitschelt, P. Lange, G. Marks, and J. D. Stephens, pp. 101–134. New York and Cambridge: Cambridge University Press.

Hall, P. A., and D. Soskice, eds. (2001). *Varieties of capitalism: The institutional foundations of comparative advantage.* Oxford: Oxford University Press.

Hall, P. A., and R. Taylor (1996). Political science and the three new institutionalisms. *Political Studies* 44:936–957.

Hansen, J. M. (1991). *Gaining access: Congress and the farm lobby, 1919–1981.* Chicago: University of Chicago Press.

Harvey, D. R. (2004). Policy dependency and reform: Economic gains versus political pains. *Agricultural Economics* 31:265–275.

Hathaway, O. (1998). Positive feedback: The impact of trade liberalization on industry demands for protection. *International Organization* 52:575–612.

Helleiner, E. (2001). Financial globalization and social response? A Polanyian view. In *Structure and Agency in International Capital Mobility,* ed. T. J. Sinclair and K. P. Thomas, pp. 168–205. New York: Palgrave Macmillan.

Helliwell, J. F., and L. L. Schembri (2005). Borders, common currencies, trade, and welfare: What can we learn from the evidence? *Bank of Canada Review* (Spring):19–33.

Helpman, E. (2002). Politics and trade policy. In *Interest groups and trade policy,* G. M. Grossman and E. Helpman, pp. 173–198. Princeton, NJ: Princeton University Press.

Henisz, W. J., and E. D. Mansfield (2006). Votes and vetoes: The political determinants of commercial openness. *International Studies Quarterly* 50:189–211.

Hill, J., and J. Mendez (1983). Factor mobility and the general equilibrium model of production. *Journal of International Economics* 15:19–25.

Hillman, A. L. (1982). Declining industries and political-support protectionist motives. *American Economic Review* 72:1180–1187.

——— (1989). *The political economy of protection.* New York: Harwood.

Hirschman, A. O. (1970). *Exit, voice and loyalty.* Cambridge, MA: Harvard University Press.

Hiscox, M. J. (2001). Class versus industry cleavages: Inter-industry factor mobility and the politics of trade. *International Organization* 55:1–46.

——— (2002). *International trade and political conflict: Commerce, coalitions, and mobility.* Princeton, NJ: Princeton University Press.

Hoekman, B. M., and M. M. Kostecki (2001). *The political economy of the world trading system.* 2nd ed. Oxford: Oxford University Press.

Hollinger, P., P. Jenkins, and L. Saigol (2006a). A bid for strength: Why corporate Europe is smashing through the merger barriers. *Financial Times,* February 24, p. 13.

Hollinger, P., P. Marsh, C. Adams, and S. Laitner (2006b). UK minister attacks French protectionism over Arcelor. *Financial Times,* February 2, p. 15.

Hood, C. C. (1986). *The tools of government.* Chatham, NJ: Chatham House.

Hooghe, L., and G. Marks (2001). *Multi-level governance and European integration.* Lanham, MD: Rowman and Littlefield.

Hooper, P., K. Johnson, and J. Marquez (2000). *Trade elasticities for the G-7 countries* (Princeton Studies in International Economics No. 87). Princeton, NJ: Department of Economics, International Economics Section.

Horvat, B. (1999). *The theory of international trade: An alternative approach.* New York: St. Martin's.

Hrebenar, R. J. (1997). *Interest group politics in America.* 3rd ed. Armonk, NY: M. E. Sharpe.

Huber, J. D., and B. G. Powell (1994). Congruence between citizens and policymakers in two visions of liberal democracy. *World Politics* 46:291–326.

Hummels, D., J. Ishii, and K. M. Yi (2001). The nature and growth of vertical specialization in world trade. *Journal of International Economics* 54:75–96.

International Monetary Fund (IMF) (Various years). *International financial statistics yearbook.* Washington, D.C.: IMF.

Irwin, D. A. (1996). *Against the tide: An intellectual history of free trade.* Princeton: Princeton University Press.

———— (2005). Trade and globalization. In *Globalization: What's new?* ed. M. M. Weinstein, pp. 19–35. New York: Columbia University Press.

Iversen, T. (1999). *Contested economic institutions: The politics of macroeconomics and wage bargaining in advanced democracies.* Cambridge: Cambridge University Press.

Iversen, T., and D. Soskice (2001). An asset theory of social policy preferences. *American Political Science Review* 95:875–893.

Jaccard, J., R. Turrisi, and C. K. Wan (1990). *Interaction effects in multiple regression.* Newbury Park, CA: Sage.

Jensen, J. B., and K. R. Troske (1999). Increasing wage dispersion in U.S. manufacturing: Plant-level evidence on the role of trade and technology. In *Growing apart: The causes and consequences of global wage inequality,* ed. A. Fishlow and K. Parker, pp. 118–148. New York: Council on Foreign Relations.

Jones, B. D., and F. Baumgartner (2005). *The politics of attention: How government prioritizes problems.* Chicago: University of Chicago Press.

Jones, R. W. (1971). A three-factor model in theory, trade, and history. In *Trade, balance of payments and growth,* ed. J. N. Bhagwati, R. N. Jones, R. A. Mundell, and J. Vanek, pp. 3–21. Amsterdam: North Holland.

Joskow, P. (1988). Asset specificity and the structure of vertical relationships: Empirical evidence. *Journal of Law, Economics, and Organization* 4:95–117.

Kapstein, E. B. (2000). Winners and losers in the global economy. *International Organization* 54:359–384.

Katzenstein, P. J. (1985). *Small states in world markets.* Ithaca, NY: Cornell University Press.

Kauppinen, V. (1998). Downsizing subsidies: The Finnish example. *Science, Technology, Industry Review* 21:75–89.

Keeler, J. T. S. (1996). Agricultural power in the European Community: Explaining the fate of CAP and GATT negotiations. *Comparative Politics* 28:127–149.

Keohane, R. O., and H. V. Milner, eds. (1996). *Internationalization and domestic politics.* Cambridge: Cambridge University Press.

Kindleberger, C. P. (1951). Group behavior and international trade. *Journal of Political Economy* 59:30–46.

Kirchgaessner, S. (2006). Business chiefs attack US moves to toughen law on foreign deals. *Financial Times,* May 13–14, p. 3.

Kissinger, H. A. (2006). Anatomy of a partnership. *International Herald Tribune,* March 11–12, p. 6.

Koplow, D. (2007). Energy. In OECD, *Subsidy reform and sustainable development: Political economy aspects,* pp. 93–110. Paris: OECD.

Koremenos, B., C. Lipson, and D. Snidal (2001). The rational design of international institutions. *International Organization* 55:761–799.

Kraft, M. E., and S. R. Furlong (2004). *Public policy: Politics, analysis and alternatives.* Washington, D.C.: Congressional Quarterly Press.

Krasner, S. D. (1978). *Defending the national interest.* Princeton, NJ: Princeton University Press.

Krugman, P. R. (1994). The myth of Asia's miracle. *Foreign Affairs* 73 (6):62–78.

Kume, I. (1998). *Disparaged success: Labor politics in postwar Japan.* Ithaca, NY: Cornell University Press.

Kurzer, P. (1993). *Business and banking: Political change and economic integration in Western Europe.* Ithaca, NY: Cornell University Press.

Ladewig, J. W. (2006). Domestic influences on international trade policy: Factor mobility in the United States, 1963–1992. *International Organization* 60:69–103.

Lake, D. A. (1988). *Power, protection and free trade: International sources of U.S. commercial strategy: 1887–1939.* Ithaca, NY: Cornell University Press.

Lane, J.-E., and S. Ersson (1997) The institutions of Konkordanz and corporatism: How closely are they connected? *Swiss Political Science Review* 3(1): 5–29.

Lavdas, K. A., and M. M. Mendrinou (1999). *Politics, subsidies and competition: The new politics of state intervention in the European Union.* Cheltenham, UK: Edward Elgar.

Lawrence, E. (2007). Will corporate subsidy really help the state? *The Birmingham News,* May 27, p. 3C.

Le Galès, P., and C. Lequesne, eds. (1998). *Regions in Europe.* London and New York: Routledge.

Leipziger, D., and M. Spence (2007). Globalisation's losers need support. *Financial Times,* May 15, p. 11.

Levy, J. S. (1997). Prospect theory, rational choice, and international relations. *International Studies Quarterly* 41:87–112.

Lijphart, A. (1999). *Patterns of democracy.* New Haven, CT: Yale University Press.

Lijphart, A., and M. Crepaz (1991). Corporatism and consensus democracy in eighteen countries: Conceptual and empirical linkages. *British Journal of Political Science* 21:235–246.

Lohmann, S. (1998). An informational rationale for the power of special interests. *American Political Science Review* 92:809–828.

Lohmann, S., and S. O'Halloran (1994). Divided government and U.S. trade policy: Theory and evidence. *International Organization* 48:595–632.

Lusztig, M. (2004). *The limits of protectionism: Building coalitions for free trade.* Pittsburgh: University of Pittsburgh Press.

Lutz, J. M. (2000). *Import propensities of industrialized countries: Protectionism revealed.* New York: Palgrave Macmillan.

Magee, S. P., W. A. Brock, and L. Young (1989). *Black hole tariffs and endogenous policy theory.* Cambridge, UK: Cambridge University Press.

Mansfield, E. D., and M. L. Busch (1995). The political economy of non-tariff barriers: A cross-national analysis. *International Organization* 49:723–749.

Marsh, P. (2006). Deal finalised in a palace, but sealed in an airport. *Financial Times,* June 27, p. 18.

Mathieson, D. J., and L. Rojas-Suarez (1994). Capital controls and capital account liberalization in industrial countries. In *Capital mobility: The impact on consumption, investment and growth,* ed. L. Leiderman and A. Razin, pp. 329–347. Cambridge, UK, and New York: Cambridge University Press.

Mayer, W. (1984). Endogenous tariff formation. *American Economic Review* 74: 970–985.

McCallum, J. (1995). National borders matter: Canada-U.S. regional trade patterns. *American Economic Review* 85:615–23.

McGillivray, F. (2004). *Privileging industry: The comparative politics of trade and industrial policy.* Princeton, NJ: Princeton University Press.

McKeown, T. J. (1984). Firms and tariff change: Explaining the demand for protection. *World Politics* 36:215–233.

——— (1999). The global economy, post-Fordism, and trade policy in advanced capitalist countries. In *Continuity and change in contemporary capitalism,* ed. H. Kitschelt, P. Lange, G. Marks, and J. D. Stephens, pp. 11–35. New York and Cambridge: Cambridge University Press.

Mendoza, E. G. (1994). The robustness of macroeconomic indicators of capital mobility. In *Capital mobility: The impact on consumption, investment and growth,* ed. L. Leiderman and A. Razin, pp. 83–111. Cambridge, UK, and New York: Cambridge University Press.

Milner, H. V. (1988). *Resisting protectionism: Global industries and the politics of international trade.* Princeton, NJ: Princeton University Press.

Milner, H. V., and B. Judkins (2004). Partisanship, trade policy, and globalization: Is there a left-right divide on trade policy? *International Studies Quarterly* 48: 95–119.

Milner, H. V., and D. B. Yoffie (1989). Between free trade and protectionism: Strategic trade policy and a theory of corporate trade demands. *International Organization* 43:239–272.

Minder, R. (2006). Backing of national champions seen as outdated. *Financial Times,* March 16, p. 2.

Mitra, D. (1999). Endogenous lobby formation and endogenous protection: A long-run model of trade policy determination. *American Economic Review* 89:1116–1134.

Mitra, D., D. D. Thomakos, and M. Ulubaşoğlu (2002). Protection for sale in a developing country: Democracy versus dictatorship. *Review of Economics and Statistics* 84:497–508.

Moran, T. H. (1999). Foreign direct investment and good jobs/bad jobs: The impact of outward investment and inward investment of jobs and wages. In *Growing apart: The causes and consequences of global wage inequality,* ed. A. Fishlow and K. Parker, pp. 95–117. New York: Council on Foreign Relations.

Moyer, H. W., and T. E. Josling (1990). *Agricultural policy reform: Politics and process in the EC and the USA.* Ames: Iowa State University Press.

Murphy, D. D. (2004). *The structure of regulatory competition: Corporations and public policies in a global economy.* Oxford: Oxford University Press.

Mussa, M. (1974). Tariffs and the distribution of income: The importance of factor specificity, substitutability and intensity in the short and long run. *Journal of Political Economy* 82:1191–1203.

Neary, J. P. (1978). Short-run capital specificity and the pure theory of international trade. *Economic Journal* 88:488–510.

——— (1982). Intersectoral capital mobility, wage stickiness, and the case for adjustment assistance. In *Import competition and response,* ed. J. N. Bhagwati, pp. 39–67. Chicago and London: University of Chicago Press.

Neyer, J., and D. Wolf (2003). Horizontal enforcement in the EU: The BSE case and the case of state aid control. In *Linking EU and national governance,* ed. B. Kohler-Koch, pp. 201–224. Oxford: Oxford University Press.

Nezu, R. (1998). Trends and patterns of public support to industry in the OECD area. *Science, Technology, Industry Review* 21:13–24.

O'Brien, D. (2006). Europe is winning the war for economic freedoms. *Financial Times,* March 31, p. 11.

O'Brien, R. (1997). *Subsidy regulation and state transformation in North America, the GATT and the EU.* New York: St. Martin's.

Obstfeld, M., and A. M. Taylor (2003). *Global capital markets: Integration, crisis, and growth.* Cambridge and New York: Cambridge University Press.

Odell, J. S. (1990). Understanding international trade policies. *World Politics* 43:139–167.

Ohmae, K. (1991). *The borderless world.* New York: Harper Perennial.

——— (1995). *The end of the nation-state: The rise of regional economies.* New York: Free Press.

Olson, M. (1965). *The logic of collective action.* Cambridge, MA: Harvard University Press.

——— (1982). *The rise and decline of nations.* New Haven, CT: Yale University Press.

Ono, D. (2006). Optimal obfuscation: Democracy and trade policy transparency. *American Political Science Review* 100:369–384.

Organisation of Economic Cooperation and Development (OECD) (Various years). *Labour force statistics.* Paris: OECD.

——— (Various years). *National accounts.* Paris: OECD.

——— (1998). *Spotlight on public support to industry.* Paris: OECD.

——— (2004). *Structural analysis (STAN) Database.* Paris: OECD.

———— (2005a). *Environmentally harmful subsidies: Challenges for Reform.* Paris: OECD.

———— (2005b). *International investment perspectives.* Paris: OECD.

———— (2006a). *OECD factbook 2006.* Paris: OECD.

———— (2006b). *OECD trade statistics database.* Paris: OECD.

O'Reilly, R. F. (2005). Veto points, veto players, and international trade policy. *Comparative Political Studies* 38:652–675.

Ostrom, E. (2007). Institutional rational choice: An assessment of the institutional analysis and development framework. In *Theories of the policy process,* ed. P. A. Sabatier, 2nd ed., pp. 21–64. Boulder, CO: Westview.

Pareto, V. (1927). *Manual of political economy.* New York: A. M. Kelley.

Parker, G., and C. Smyth (2006). Mandelson warns on EU protectionism. *Financial Times,* March 8, p. 2.

Peacock, R. A. (2007). Record incentives to German steelmaker will cost taxpayers, current steelworkers (letter to the editor). *The Birmingham News,* June 3, p. 3B.

Persson, T., and G. Tabellini (2000). *Political economics.* Cambridge, MA: MIT Press.

Peters, B. G. (2005). *Institutional theory in political science: The new institutionalism.* 2nd ed., New York: Continuum.

Polanyi, K. (1957). *The great transformation.* Boston: Beacon Press.

Pontusson, J., and P. Swenson, (1996). Labor markets, production strategies and wage-bargaining institutions: The Swedish employer offensive in comparative perspective. *Comparative Political Studies* 29:223–250.

Popper, H. A. (1997). *Issues in international capital mobility.* New York: Garland.

Pretchker, U. (1998a). Defining subsidies for R&D and industrial innovation. *Science, Technology, Industry Review* 21:105–141.

———— (1998b). Introduction: The OECD's mission in the field of public support to industry. *Science, Technology, Industry Review* 21:7–11.

Rieger, E. (2005). Agricultural policy: Constrained reforms. In *Policy-making in the European Union,* ed. H. Wallace, W. Wallace, and M. A. Pollack, 5th ed., pp. 161–190. Oxford: Oxford University Press.

Riezman, R., and J. D. Wilson (1995). Politics and trade policy. In *Modern political economy: Old topics, new directions,* ed. J. S. Banks and E. A. Hanushek, pp. 108–144. Cambridge and New York: Cambridge University Press.

Rix, K., and M. Leaniz (2006) Spain vows to fight EU on utility. *International Herald Tribune,* March 8, p. 15.

Rodrik, D. (1986). Tariffs, subsidies, and welfare with endogenous policy. *Journal of International Economics* 21:285–299.

———— (1997). *Has globalization gone too far?* Washington, D.C.: Institute for International Economics.

———— (1998). Why do more open economies have bigger governments? *Journal of Political Economy* 106:997–1032.

———— (2005). Feasible globalizations. In *Globalization: What's new?* ed. M. M. Weinstein, pp. 196–213. New York: Columbia University Press.

Rogowski, R. (1987). Trade and the variety of democratic institutions. *International Organization* 41:203–233.

——— (1989). *Commerce and coalitions: How trade affects domestic political alignments.* Princeton, NJ: Princeton University Press.

Rose, R., and P. L. Davies (1994). *Inheritance in public policy: Change without choice in Britain.* New Haven, CT: Yale University Press.

Rothstein, B. (1998). *Just institutions matter: The moral and political logic of the universal welfare state.* Cambridge: Cambridge University Press.

Rowley, C. K., W. Thorbecke, and R. E. Wagner (1995). *Trade protection in the United States.* Aldershot, UK: Edward Elgar.

Sabatier, P. A., and C. M. Weible (2007). The advocacy coalition framework: Innovations and clarifications. In *Theories of the policy Process,* ed. P. A. Sabatier, 2nd ed., pp. 189–220. Boulder, CO: Westview.

Salamon, L. S., and M. S. Lund (1989). The tools approach: Basic analytics. In *Beyond privatization: The tools of government action,* ed. L. S. Salamon, pp. 23–50. Washington, D.C.: Urban Institute Press.

Santarelli, E. (1991). Asset specificity, R & D financing, and the signaling properties of the firm's financial structure. *Economics of Innovation and New Technology* 1:279–294.

Sayre, A. (2007). Louisiana cuts teeth in bid for steel mill. *The Birmingham News,* May 22, p. 2D.

Scharpf, F. W. (1997). *Games real actors play: Actor-centered institutionalism in policy research.* Boulder, CO: Westview.

Schattschneider, E. E. (1935). *Politics, pressures and the tariff.* New York: Prentice-Hall.

Scheve, K. F., and M. J. Slaughter (2001). What determines individual trade-policy preferences? *Journal of International Economics* 54:267–292.

Schmidt, M. (1996). When parties matter: A review of the possibilities and limits of partisan influence on public policy. *European Journal of Political Research* 30:155–183.

Schmidt, V. A. (2002). *The futures of European capitalism.* Oxford: Oxford University Press.

Scholte, J. A. (2005). *Globalization: A critical introduction.* 2nd ed. New York: Palgrave Macmillan.

Schwartz, G., and B. Clements (1999). Government subsidies. *Journal of Economic Surveys* 13(2): 119–147.

Schwartz, H. M. (2000). States versus markets: The emergence of a global economy. New York: St. Martin's.

Siaroff, A. (1999). Corporatism in 24 industrial democracies: Meaning and measurement. *European Journal of Political Research* 36:175–205.

Simmons, B. A. (1999). The internationalization of capital. In *Continuity and change in contemporary capitalism,* ed. H. Kitschelt, P. Lange, G. Marks, and J. D. Stephens, pp. 36–69. New York and Cambridge: Cambridge University Press.

Sinclair, T. J. (2001). International capital mobility: An endogenous approach. In *Structure and Agency in International Capital Mobility,* ed. T. J. Sinclair and K. P. Thomas, pp. 193–110. New York: Palgrave Macmillan.

Sloof, R. (1998). *Game-theoretic models of the political influence of interest groups.* Boston: Kluwer Academic.

Smith, M. P. (1996). Integration in small steps: The European Commission and member-state aid to industry. *West European Politics* 19:563–582.

Smith, P. (2006). Private equity begins to fear for its freedom. *Financial Times,* February 24, p. 13.

Snape, R. H. (1991). International regulation of subsidies. *The World Economy* 14:139–164.

Sobel, A. C. (1999). *State institutions, private incentives, global capital.* Ann Arbor: University of Michigan Press.

Soskice, D. (1999). Divergent production regimes: Coordinated and unco-ordinated market economies in the 1980s and 1990s. In *Continuity and change in contemporary capitalism,* ed. H. Kitschelt, P. Lange, G. Marks, and J. D. Stephens, pp. 101–134. New York and Cambridge: Cambridge University Press.

Steil, B. (2006). Dobbsism, unintelligently designed for our times. *Financial Times,* March 27, p. 13.

Steger, M. B. (2003). *Globalization: A very short introduction.* Oxford and New York: Oxford University Press.

Stephens, P. (2005). Leaders sink or swim with the irresistible tide of globali-sation. *Financial Times,* September 30, p. 17.

Stigler, G. (1975). *The citizen and the state.* Chicago: University of Chicago Press.

Stiglitz, J. E. (2003). *Globalization and its discontents.* New York: W. W. Norton.

Stimson, J. (1985). Regression in time and space: A statistical essay. *American Journal of Political Science* 29:914–947.

Stolper, W. F., and P. A. Samuelson (1941). Protection and real wages. *Review of Economic Studies* 9:58–73.

Strange, S. (1996). *The retreat of the state: The diffusion of power in the world economy.* Cambridge and New York: Cambridge University Press.

Surrey, S. R., and P. R. McDaniel (1985). *Tax expenditures.* Cambridge, MA: Harvard University Press.

Swank, D. (2002). *Global capital, political institutions, and policy change in developed welfare states.* Cambridge and New York: Cambridge University Press.

Thelen, K. (2004). *How institutions evolve.* Cambridge and New York: Cambridge University Press.

Thies, C. G., and S. Porche (2007). The political economy of agricultural protection. *Journal of Politics* 69:116–127.

Thomas, K. P. (1997). *Capital beyond borders: States and firms in the auto industry, 1960–94.* New York: St. Martin's.

———(2000). *Competing for capital: Europe and North America in a global era.* Washington, D.C.: Georgetown University Press.

Thornhill, J. (2006). Forget the bogeyman, Arcelor's owners must decide. *Financial Times,* February 2, p. 13.

Tracy, M. (1989). *Government and agriculture in Western Europe: 1880–1988.* New York: New York University Press.

Tsebelis, G. (2000). Veto players and institutional analysis. *Governance* 13:441–474.

——— (2002). *Veto players: How political institutions work.* Princeton, NJ: Princeton University Press.

Tufte, E. R. (1974). *Data analysis for politics and policy.* Englewood Cliffs, NJ: Prentice-Hall.

Tullock, G. (2005). *The rent-seeking society,* ed. C. Rowley. Indianapolis, IN: Liberty Fund.

Verdier, D. (1994). *Democracy and international trade.* Princeton, NJ: Princeton University Press.

——— (1995). The politics of public aid to private industry: The role of policy networks. *Comparative Political Studies* 28:3–42.

Vernon, R. (1998). *In the hurricane's eye: The troubled prospects of multinational enterprises.* Cambridge, MA: Harvard University Press.

Vousden, N. (1990). *The economics of trade protection.* Cambridge: Cambridge University Press.

Wartenberg, T. E., ed. (1992). *Rethinking power.* Albany, NY: State University of New York Press.

Weimer, D. L., and A. R. Vining (2005). *Policy analysis: Concepts and practice.* Upper Saddle River, NJ: Pearson Prentice Hall.

Weinstein, M. M. (2005). Introduction. In *Globalization: What's new?* ed. M. M. Weinstein, pp. 1–18. New York: Columbia University Press.

Williams, F. (2007). World trade grows 8% but WTO warns over market jitters. *Financial Times,* April 13, p. 5.

Williamson, O. (1985). *The economic institutions of capitalism.* New York: Free Press.

Wilson, J. Q., ed. (1980). *The politics of regulation.* New York: Basic Books.

Winters, L. A. (1987). The economic consequences of agricultural support: A survey. *OECD Economic Studies* 9(Autumn): 7–54.

Wolf, M. (2006). Integration marches onward despite growth in imbalances. *Financial Times (Special Report, The World: 2006),* January 25, p. 1.

Wooldridge, J. M. (2002) *Econometric analysis of cross sectional and panel data.* Cambridge, MA: MIT Press.

World Trade Organization (WTO) (2007a). *Agreement on subsidies and countervailing measures.* http://www.wto.org/english/thewto_e/whatis_e/tif_e/agrm8_e.htm#subsidies (accessed May 22, 2007).

——— (2007b). *Trade topics: Goods-tariffs.* http://www.wto.org/english/tratop_e/tariffs_e/tariffs_e.htm (accessed May 22, 2007).

Wren, C. (1996). *Industrial subsidies: The UK experience.* New York: St. Martin's.

Wriston, W. B. (1998). Dumb networks and smart capital. *Cato Journal* 17:333–344.

Zahariadis, N. (1997). Why state subsidies? Evidence from European Community countries, 1981–86. *International Studies Quarterly* 41:341–354.

———— (2001). Asset specificity and state subsidies in industrialized countries. *International Studies Quarterly* 45:603–616.

———— (2002). The political economy of state subsidies in Europe. *Policy Studies Journal* 30:285–298.

———— (2003a). *Ambiguity and choice in public policy: Political decision-making in modern democracies.* Washington, D.C.: Georgetown University Press.

———— (2003b). Complexity, coupling, and the future of European integration. *Review of Policy Research* 20:285–310.

———— (2005). Policy networks, elections, and state subsidies. *Review of Policy Research* 22:115–131.

———— (2006). Greece: A most enthusiastic, reluctant European. In *The European Union and the member states,* ed. E. E. Zeff and E. B. Pirro, 2nd ed. Boulder, CO: Lynne Rienner.

Zahariadis, N., and L. Morgan. (2005). Local government and the implementation of Alabama's economic development policy. *Public Administration Quarterly* 29:1–31.

INDEX